D1571494

Blessings in Disguise; or, The Morality of Evil

BLESSINGS IN
DISGUISE; OR,
THE MORALITY
OF EVIL

Jean Starobinski

Translated by Arthur Goldhammer

HARVARD UNIVERSITY PRESS
CAMBRIDGE, MASSACHUSETTS
1993

ı

Originally published as Le Remède dans le mal: Critique et légitimation de
l'artifice à l'âge des Lumières. Copyright © Editions Gallimard, 1989.

This book is printed on acid-free paper, and its binding materials
have been chosen for strength and durability.

Translation of this volume has been aided by a grant from the French Ministry of Culture.

Library of Congress Cataloging-in-Publication Data
Starobinski, Jean.
[Remède dans le mal. English]
Blessings in disguise; or, The morality of evil / Jean Starobinski;
translated by Arthur Goldhammer.
p. cm.
Translation of: Le remède dans le mal.
Includes bibliographical references and index.
ISBN 0-674-07647-8 (alk. paper)
1. French literature—18th century—History and criticism.
2. French literature—Greek influences. 3. Mythology in literature.
4. Ethics in literature. 5. Evil in literature. I. Title.
II. Title: Blessings in disguise. III. Title: Morality of Evil.
PQ265.S7313 1993
840.9'353—dc20
92-17519
CIP

CONTENTS

Blessings in Disguise; or, The Morality of Evil

1

THE WORD
CIVILIZATION

I

The major milestones in the history of the word *civilization* are today more or less satisfactorily understood.[1] The French words *civil* (thirteenth century) and *civilité* (fourteenth century) readily reveal their Latin antecedents. The verb *civiliser* is not attested until somewhat later. One finds it used in the sixteenth century with two different meanings:

> 1. To bring to civility, to make manners civil and mild. For example, Montaigne: "Ceux du Royaume de Mexico estoient aucunement plus *civilisez* et plus artistes ques les autres nations de là" (The people of the Kingdom of Mexico were in some ways more civilized or more artistic than the other nations of that part of the world).

> 2. In jurisprudence, *civiliser* meant to change a criminal case into a civil one.[2]

The second meaning would survive until at least the end of the eighteenth century (Littré, in his dictionary, indicates that the word was used this way "in the past"). This sense was the basis for the noun *civilisation,* which the *Dictionnaire universel* (Trévoux) defined as follows in 1743: "Term of jurisprudence. An act of justice or judgment that renders a criminal trial civil. *Civilisation* is accomplished by converting informations *(informations)* into inquests *(enquêtes)* or by other means." The neological formation of the signifier is an important moment. The somewhat later appearance of the same word in the *modern* sense was not so much a lexical neologism as the emergence of a rival "signified" of the same signifier, a rival that would soon win out. The juridical meaning of *civilisation* is no longer mentioned in the *Dictionnaire de l'Académie* of 1798.[3]

The first dictionary to mention the word *civilisation* in the "modern" sense is the *Dictionnaire universel* (Trévoux) of 1771. Here is the entry:

> 1. Term of jurisprudence. [The 1743 definition was then repeated.]

> 2. The *ami des hommes*[4] *used this word for sociabilité.* See that word. Religion is undeniably the first and most useful brake on humanity; it is the first source of civilization. It preaches to us and continually recalls us to confraternity, to soften our hearts.

In 1798 the *Dictionnaire de l'Académie* (fifth edition) gave a more precise definition: "Action of civilizing or state of that which is civilized." But as early as 1795 L. Snetlage's *Nouveau Dictionnaire français contenant de nouvelles créations du peuple français* (Göttingen, 1795) gave this definition:

> This word, which was used only in a technical sense to say that a criminal case was made civil, is used to express the action of civilizing or the tendency of a people to polish or rather to correct its mores and customs by bringing into civil society a luminous, active, loving morality abounding in good works. (Every Citizen of Europe is today embarked upon this last combat of civilization. Civilization of mores.)

As Moras has pointed out, the word *civilisation* flourished to such an extent during the Revolution that it was easy to attribute to the revolutionary spirit a neologism that in fact belonged to an earlier period.[5] Yet as Frey observes, *civilization* caught on during the Revolution all the more easily because the period was one in which any number of nouns ending in *-ation* were formed from verbs ending in *-iser: centralisation, démocratisation, fédéralisation, francisation, fraternisation, municipalisation, nationalisation, panthéonisation, utilisation.*[6] *Civilization* was so well accepted that by 1801 Sébastien Mercier did not count it as a neologism.[7] Thus the word quickly ceased to be seen as new.

II

To this day there is no reason to doubt what was first proposed by Moras and later by Benveniste: Mirabeau, in his 1756 text *L'Ami des hommes* (pp. 136, 176, 237), was the first person in France to use the word *civilisation* in the soon widely accepted nonjuridical sense.[8] Littré had ascribed paternity to Turgot, who allegedly used the word in a fragment of his *Discours sur l'histoire universelle* in 1751, but he was misled by Dupont de Nemours, the editor and annotator of Turgot's *Oeuvres* (1811), who often took liberties with the original.[9]

The Trévoux authors did not choose their example at random. In it they found a welcome argument in their battle against the philosophy of the Enlightenment and the Encylopedists. Mirabeau, far from asserting that "social virtues" and "natural morality" had supplanted religion, argued that religion was "the principal source" of civilization, which was taken as synonymous with *sociabilité*. Thus the word civilization first appeared in a eulogy of religion, which was praised not only as a repressive force (a "brake") but also as unifying and moderating influence ("confraternity").

Around 1775 Diderot contributed to the abbé Raynal's *Histoire des deux Indes* an essay on Russia in which the word *civilization* appears several times: "Emancipation, or what is the same thing by another name, civilization, is a long and difficult work."[10]

Thus already there were abundant signs that civilization might well become a secularized substitute for religion, an apotheosis of reason.

III

The word *civilization* thus gained rapid acceptance because it drew together the diverse expressions of a preexisting concept. That concept included such notions as improvements in comfort, advances in education, politer manners, cultivation of the arts and sciences, growth of commerce and industry, and acquisition of material goods and luxuries. The word referred first to the process that made individuals, nations, and all mankind *civilized* (a preexisting term) and later to the cumulative result of that process. It served as a unifying concept.

Not surprisingly, as the term gained currency thanks to its synthetic powers, it, too, became a subject of theoretical reflection. From the end of the eighteenth century on, countless writers would attempt to identify the prerequisites of civilization as well as its material and moral components. Among the most important was Guizot (1828). "Included under this one paramount fact," he said, "are two other facts. [Civilization] subsists on two conditions and is revealed by two symptoms: the development of social activity and of individual activity, the progress of society and the progress of humanity. Wherever man's external condition is gaining, thriving, improving; wherever man's inner nature is revealing itself more splendidly and imposingly—by these two signs, and often despite the profound imperfection of the social state, the human race applauds and proclaims civilization."[11]

The word *civilization*, which denotes a process, entered the history of ideas at the same time as the modern sense of the word *progress*. The two words were destined to maintain a most intimate relationship. Although both could be used in a vague, sweeping manner, they were soon eliciting reflections of a genetic order aimed at discerning successive periods: it became essential to determine the precise phases of the civilizing process, the stages of social progress. History, both speculative and empirical, set out to sketch a "*Tableau historique des progrès de l'esprit humain*" (or historical synopsis of the advances of the human spirit, to borrow a phrase from Condorcet)—in other words, a representation of the march of civilization through stages of gradually increasing perfection.

In his study of the subject the great linguist Emile Benveniste says it well: "From primitive barbarism to the present condition of man in society, people discovered a universal gradation, a slow process of education and refinement, in short a constant progress in an area that the static term *civility* no longer adequately conveyed and that, in order to capture its sense and continuity, had to be called *civilization*. This was not simply a historical view of society; it was also an optimistic, resolutely nontheological, and sometimes unwitting interpretation of its evolution."[12]

Ferguson, influenced by lectures given by Adam Smith in 1752, seems to have been the first to use the word *civilization* in English. He also gave the clearest statement of the theory according to which there are four stages of human social organization as defined by economic activity and mode of subsistence: savage (hunter-gatherer) society, nomadic pastoral, sedentary agricultural, and industrial-commercial. Millar followed his lead.[13] Without using the word *civilization* Rousseau and Goguet proposed a similar evolutionary model, which enabled them to establish correlations between the mode of subsistence and the power structure. Diderot, as we saw earlier, envisioned the history of civilization as the history of liberty on the march. Later, Condorcet distinguished nine periods from the earliest tribes to the French Republic, with a tenth era reserved for the "future progress of the human spirit." Still later, Comte proposed his "law of three states."[14]

But these theories or philosophies of history are not the important thing. The crucial point is that the use of the same term, *civilization*, to describe both the fundamental process of history and the end result of that process established an antithesis between civilization and a hypothetical primordial state (whether it be called nature, savagery, or barbarism). Minds were thus spurred to imagine the avenues, the causes, the mechanisms of the journey taken through the ages. The action suffix *-ation* forces us to think of an agent. If that agent is confounded with the action itself, it becomes autonomous. Or it may refer to some determining factor (which Mirabeau calls religion; Rousseau, perfectibility; and others, Enlightenment). Or it may be pluralized or distributed among multiple factors, each acting at a different point in time. For Ferguson and Rousseau, for example, the civilizing process is not based on a consistent, conscious design but constructed by way of unforeseen consequences of various conflicts, projects, and innovations as modified by "circumstances" only partially under man's control. What happens in history, Ferguson tells us, is "the result of human action but not the execution of any human design."[15]

IV

Is civilization an uninterrupted collective process in which all mankind has been engaged from its inception? Has it varied only in proceeding more slowly in some times and places, more rapidly in others? The marquis de Mirabeau's abundant writings fail to ascribe a single clear meaning to the term. In *L'Ami des hommes* (1756–1757, p. 176), he implies that because civilization is not a universal or linear process, it constitutes only a brief apogee in the cycle of social existence, in the "*natural circle* from barbary to decadence by way of civilization and wealth." History would thus consist of cycles, and presumably certain nations, having been through all phases of the cycle, had simultaneously achieved a pinnacle of perfection. Addressing the king at the beginning of his *Théorie de l'impôt* (1760, p. 99) Mirabeau makes the same point when he invokes the "example of all the empires that have preceded yours and traversed the *circle of civilization.*"

Elsewhere, Mirabeau uses the word *civilization* to refer not to a process but to a state of culture and material abundance: "The movable wealth of a nation depends . . . not only on its civilization but also on that of its neighbors" (*Ephémérides du citoyen,* 1767, V, p. 112).

Thus even in the writings of the first man to use the word, *civilization* was apt to take on plural meanings. When it referred to a process, it was a process that had occurred several times in history only to give way, each time, to ineluctable decadence. When it referred to a more or less stable state, that state was one that might take different forms in different nations. Civilization was not one but many.

Here, of course, ancient history was a tacit source of models. Rome was the great example of an empire that had traversed the "circle of civilization." From Herodotus, from Polybius, Plutarch, Tacitus, and Ammianus Marcellinus, modern writers had learned to compare the Greeks and the Persians, the Greeks and the Romans, the Romans and the barbarians.

From the outset, then, it was clear that the word could take on a pluralist, ethnological, relativistic meaning yet retain certain implications of the most general sort, implications that made "civilization" a unitary imperative and determined the unique direction of "march" of all humankind.

V

Before the word *civilization* was coined or disseminated, an extensive critique of luxury, refined manners, hypocritical politeness, and the corruption due to the cultivation of the arts and sciences was already in place. From Montaigne to Rousseau by way of La Hontan and many other travelers to the New World, moreover, the comparison of the civilized man with the savage (and even the cannibal) did not favor the former. Accordingly, the marquis de Mirabeau sought to distinguish true from false civilization in the realm of *fact* as well as *value*. In a manuscript entitled "L'Ami des femmes, ou Traité de la civilisation" (The Friend of Women, or Treatise on Civilization; probably from 1768) Mirabeau insisted on the moral criterion that authenticates civilization and without which the whole code of manners and and the sum total of learning are mere masks:

> I am astonished, when it comes to civilization, at how distorted our thinking is. Ask most people what their idea of civilization is and they would answer that it is perfection of manners, urbanity, and politeness and diffusion of knowledge such that the proprieties are observed in the absence of detailed regulations—all of which to me is but the mask of virtue and not its true face, and civilization does nothing for society if it does not establish the foundations and form of virtue. It is in societies made soft by the aforementioned factors that the corruption of humanity begins.[16]

No sooner was the word *civilization* written down, in other words, than it was found to contain a possible source of misunderstanding. In another text Mirabeau speaks of "false civilization."[17] In still another he goes so far as to obliterate the distinction between barbarian and civilized by denouncing "the barbarity of our *civilizations*."[18] Note, in this last example, that the dynamic value of the suffix *-ation* has disappeared. The word no longer refers to a process but to a state—and it is a state that does not deserve its name. The plural implies that each of the nations of contemporary Europe has its own civilization, but that instead of getting rid of the violence of "primitive" societies these civilizations perpetuate the brutality beneath deceptive exteriors. Instead of open barbarity contemporary civilizations practice a dissimulated violence.

Clearly, the word *civilization*, as used by its French "inventor," did not possess a single, unequivocal meaning. The concept was novel in its very form, but it was not initially considered to be incompatible with the traditional spiritual authority (religion). On the contrary, it was a product of that authority. It referred to a process of perfecting social relations and material resources, and as such it stated a "value" and defined what might be called an "ideal." It was coupled with the imperatives of virtue and reason. Yet the same writer also used the term in a purely descriptive and neutral sense to denote the range of institutions and technologies that all the great empires possessed at their peak and lost when they fell into decadence. Societies, it was conceded, could differ in structure without forfeiting the right to be embraced within the general concept of civilization. Finally, the term applied to the contemporary situation with all its irregularities and injustices. Civilization in the latter sense was the object of critical reflection, whereas civilization in the ideal sense described above was a normative concept on the basis of which it was possible to discriminate the civilized from the uncivilized, the barbarian, and the incompletely civilized. The critique thus took two forms: a critique of civilization and a critique formulated in the name of civilization.

VI

Civilization belongs to the family of concepts that either define an opposite or are formulated in order to permit the definition of an opposite. "Greek" and "barbarian" are linked notions. "Without the Greek," François Hartog reminds us, "there is no barbarian."[19] Communities of people who speak the *true* language must exist in order for others to be considered "mute," incapable of speech (which is the root meaning of "barbarian").

Before *rusticus* and *rusticitas* can be defined as antonyms of *urbanus* and *urbanitas,* there must be cities and people who live in cities. And only a person who lives in a city can boast of superior *civility* or regret, in melodious and exquisitely studied verse, the loss of pastoral happiness or Arcadian tranquillity.

The manners of the peasant *(villanus)* are defined as *vilenie* in opposition to the manners of the court *(courtoisie).* Disapproval of rural society is clearly evident in definitions of civility found in dictionaries of the classical period. For example, Furetière's *Dictionnaire* (1694) gives:

> Civility: decent, mild, and polite way of acting and conversing. One should treat everybody with civility. Children are given instruction in civility for the young *(civilité puérile).* Only peasants, people of crude upbringing, lack civility.

Civilize: to render civil and polite, amenable and courteous. The preaching of the Gospel civilized the most savage barbarian peoples. Unlike the bourgeois, peasants are not civilized.

The eclogues of the classical age elegantly denounced rustic crudeness. Listen to Fontenelle:

> Pastoral poetry has no great charms if it is as crude as the natural or if it deals in detail only with rural matters. There is nothing pleasing in talk about sheep and goats or about the care that must be taken of such animals. What is pleasing is the idea of tranquillity connected with the lives of those who care for sheep and goats . . .
>
> Because the pastoral life is the most idle of all, it is also most apt to serve as a basis for such pleasant representations. Plowmen, harvesters, vineyard workers, and hunters are far less suitable for eclogues than shepherds. Therein lies further proof that the beauty of the eclogue is connected not with rustic things but with the tranquillity of rural life.[20]

Here, the term to which positive value is attached, "tranquil pleasure," is associated with art, artifice, and effort. "Adornments" are products of what Fontenelle calls a "cultivated mind." They "require spirits that are in a position to rise above life's pressing needs, spirits polished by lengthy habituation to society."[21] As such they involve an element of fiction, and critics would later contrast such "artificial" adornments unfavorably with truth or nature. This in turn would lead to rehabilitation of the antonym, *primitive,* which came to stand for the contrary of duplicitous, that is, for *wholeness.* By the end of the century "rustic crudeness" was again respectable, and the jejune adornments admired by Fontenelle had become objects of derision. Diderot went so far as to declare that "poetry wants something enormous, barbarous, and savage."[22]

Another strategy was to take a term like *civility,* initially highly valued but later taken to connote complicity in deception, and introduce alongside it a second term cleansed of all suspicion. The second term then became a substitute for the first, which subsequently lost all value. Thus *politeness,* which was at first virtually a synonym for *civility,* gained preference among lexicographers and moralists until it too became tainted by suspicion.

The article "*civilité*" in the 1752 Trévoux dictionary cites numerous contradictory examples, many of which attach pejorative attributes to the word:

> Civility is a certain jargon that men have established for hiding the hostile feelings they have toward one another (Saint-Evremond).

> Civility is nothing other than continual commerce in ingenious lies to deceive one another (Fléchier).

> Civility is a desire to be treated with civility, and to be esteemed polite in certain circumstances (La Rochefoucauld).

> Civility is often only a desire to pass for polite, and a fear of being seen as savage and crude (M. Esprit).

The discrediting of civility created a need for another concept of sounder alloy. While civility and politeness might seem synonymous, the specialist finds that allowance must be made for a separation of values, for a moral distinction. Beauzée states that "to be polite says more than to be civil. The polite man is necessarily civil, but the merely civil man is not yet polite: politeness implies civility but adds something to it."[23]

The relation of civility to politeness became analogous to that of outside to inside, of appearance to reality.

> Civility stands to men as public worship does to God, an external and perceptible indication of hidden inward feelings. For that reason it is precious, for to affect a benevolent exterior is to confess that benevolence ought to exist within.

> Politeness adds to civility what devoutness adds to the practice of public worship, namely, the marks of a more affectionate humanity, more concerned with others, more refined.[24]

Despite this shift, the opposition is maintained between civilized and rustic or crude. Individuals of the latter sort may possess civility but are denied politeness:

> A man of the people, even a simple peasant, can be civil, but only a man of the world can be polite.

> Civility is not incompatible with a bad education; politeness, by contrast, requires an excellent education, at least in certain respects.

Overly ceremonious civility is both tiring and pointless. Affectation arouses suspicion of falseness, and enlightened people have banished it entirely. Politeness is exempt from this excess. The more polite one is, the more amiable.[25]

Despite the insistence on the moral superiority of politeness over civility, even politeness is susceptible to being used as a mask. Often it is found to be suspect. Beauzée continues: "But it can also happen, and all too often does happen, that this most amiable politeness is but a means of doing without the other social virtues, which it falsely affects to imitate."[26]

If civility is simply the external expression or artificial imitation of politeness, politeness can be seen as a deceptive art, a way of imitating absent virtues. It can be attacked in the very same terms as civility. Already at the end of the seventeenth century La Bruyère could write: "Politeness does not always inspire goodness, equity, toleration, gratitude; it gives at least the appearance of those things and makes man appear outwardly as he ought to be inwardly" (*De la société*, 32). There is no need to multiply examples. The pattern is always the same: an ostensible virtue is discredited by reducing it to a mere outward appearance, a sham, instead of something truly inherent in an individual, group, or society. Reduced to mere appearances, politeness and civility give free rein, inwardly, in depth, to their opposites, malevolence and wickedness—in short, to violence, which was never truly forsaken. Or so it appears by the light of the critical torch, which has been raised to bare the contradiction between appearance and reality, between the flattering mask and the true face, wherever it can. Accusatory thought finds inauthenticity wherever it looks. Thus in terms of moral substance, rigorous scrutiny generally inverts the meaning of "civilized" and "savage." This reversal is best expressed by Voltaire, who, when his Huron is locked up in the Bastille, has him say: "My compatriots in America would never have treated me so barbarously; they cannot even imagine it. People call them savages. They are good people but crude. And the men of this country are refined scoundrels" (*L'Ingénu*, chap. 10). The adjectives "crude" and "refined," which express the accidental, the apparent, are linked to nouns that capture the—radically different—underlying reality: good people, scoundrels.

VII

Poli (polite), *policé* (orderly): phonetically the two words are quite similar. French writers of the seventeenth and eighteenth centuries played on this similarity and sometimes used the two words interchangeably. Yet few of them were unaware of the difference in etymology: *poli* comes from the Latin *polire*, to polish, whereas *policé* is derived from the Greek *polis, politeia* by way of the French *politie, police*. But the affinity between the two words is not merely phonetic; it is also semantic. Consider Richelet's *Dictionnaire* (1680). What is the meaning of *polir*? Six uses are offered:

1. To clean. To make more beautiful, clearer and more polished. *Aequarre, adaequare.* To polish a marble . . .

2. Term of polisher. To give more luster to the glass of a mirror, to make it brighter . . . *Polire.*

3. Term of cutler and grinder. To hone on a polishing stone. To polish a razor. To polish a knife.

4. Figuratively: to civilize, to make more civil, more gallant, more decent. *Ad urbanitatem informare.*

5. Figuratively: this word is used in speaking of oratory and style. *Limare, politius ornare, excolere.* (To polish a speech. To polish one's style . . . That is, to make one's style more correct and more disciplined.)

6. Figuratively: to polish oneself is to make oneself more perfect.

Owing to the association of the "literal" image of brightness and smoothness with the idea of perfection, the manual act of polishing *(expolitio, exornatio)* establishes a figurative equivalence between "to polish" and "to civilize." To civilize, whether men or things, is thus to flatten all rough edges and "crude" unevenness, to eliminate all harshness, to exclude all possible sources of friction, to make sure that all contacts are easy and smooth. The file and polishing stone are the instruments that make possible the figurative transformation of crudeness and rusticity into civility, urbanity, and culture. (It is no accident that I bring the word *culture* into the discussion. The notion of cultivation was closely associated with that of polishing. For example, the *Dictionnaire de l'Académie* for 1694 defines *polir* as follows: "Figuratively said of all that serves to *cultivate*, to adorn, to soften the spirit and mores and render more suitable for the ordinary commerce of society.") Polishing is the work of the sculptor (who puts "finish" on his shapes and volumes), of the cutler (who whets and hones his blade), and of the mirror-maker (who seeks reflective clarity in his glass). Other dictionaries, more accurate than Richelet as to the literal meaning, define *polish* as "unifying the surface of an object, removing all its irregularities, removing the small protuberances that make the surface rough; to make clear and shiny by rubbing . . . Said particularly of hard things" (Trévoux). In the figurative sense, therefore, *polish* was close to *enlighten* in the sense of "Enlightenment philosophy." The treatment that removed the roughness from things and individuals was not exempt from a certain violence of its own. To polish one's style, Richelet has told us, was to "discipline" *(châtier)* it. It sometimes took effort: as an example of the use of the word *polisseur* (polisher), Richelet gives "the polisher is painstaking." The expenditure of energy necessary to produce polish and politeness was amply compensated, however, by the savings made possible by the amelioration of mores and manners. Human relations were now governed by a symbolic code in which signs had the value of acts.

As complex and demanding as the obligations of politeness might be, those obligations engaged individual interests at the level of word-play rather than swordplay, unless it happened that a word caused offense that led to a renewal of violence, in which, despite the codification of combat itself, one of the participants in the duel might lose his life. A contradiction could lead to a duel, but at least civilized combat (harking back to the era when *civilité* was also known as *courtoisie*) took place, after the usual polite exchanges, "on the field of honor." It was not a brawl or melee. Nevertheless, the reality of violent death pointed up the hypocrisy of a politeness that required insults to be washed away with blood. There was no shortage of seventeenth- and eighteenth-century protests against the "barbarity" of dueling.

In eighteenth-century dictionaries (which continue to define the verb *to polish* as *to civilize*) examples of figurative uses of the term alternate between the idea that polishing is difficult and the idea that it is a *gentle* process, an effect obtained by means of *gentleness*. Note, in particular, the kinds of agents deemed capable of polishing individuals:

> It is not easy to polish barbarians and give them a proper place in a civil and humane form of society. The peoples of the North used to be fierce; *time* and *letters* have polished them and made them learned. It is also said that the *Court* does a good job of polishing people from the provinces . . .

> "It is the job of *art* to polish what is too crude in nature." The *conversation of ladies* does a good job of polishing a young man, of making him more gallant and tactful. (Trévoux)

Along with the list of civilizing agencies (time, letters, the court, art, the conversation of ladies), this article provides a list of candidates in need of polishing: barbarians, provincials, youths—in a word, "fierce" and "crude" nature as it exists before art begins the process of perfection, the effort to transform nature by smoothing, adornment, and education. This assertion of the equality of all who stand in need of polish (and *police,* discipline) is not without importance: barbarians, savages, provincials (and a fortiori, peasants), youths (and a fortiori, children) are offered as interchangeable paradigms. Compared with the perfection of the *polished,* the barbarian is a sort of child, the child a sort of barbarian. Those concerned about the peril of barbarism could all too easily make out its presence in their own midst: in the populace of remote provinces, in children left to their own devices, and indeed wherever educational polishing had been unable to penetrate. Conversely, those confident in the powers of education could easily look upon savages as children, ready to be made more like themselves by benevolent and patient polishing. Similarly, those who railed against the blandness and hypocrisy of polite conventions could avail themselves of "primitivist" rhetoric to celebrate simultaneously the "noble savage," the rural populace, and the spontaneous genius of childhood. Because the verb *to polish* implied a process, a progressive action, it could easily be equated with *to civilize*. But *polish* lacked a correlative noun of action (*politesse* being the term for a quality and not an action and *polissage* being limited to the literal sense), whereas *civilization* could refer to the transformative process.

To polish was to civilize individuals, to polish their manners and language. Both the literal and the figurative senses evoked ideas of collective order, laws, and institutions as elements of a smoothly functioning society. The intermediate link in this chain of associations was provided by the verb *policer,* which applied to groups of individuals or to nations: "*Policer:* to make laws and regulations *(règlements de police)* for preserving the public tranquillity. *Legibus informare, instituere*" (Trévoux). Through the influence of the common antonym *(barbarity),* the word *police* assumed a place alongside civility, politeness, and civilization:

> *Police:* Laws, order, and conduct to be observed for the subsistence and maintenance of states and societies.

> *Politia:* In general, the opposite of *barbarity.* The savages of America had neither laws nor order *(police)* when they were discovered. (Trévoux)

Linked by a common antonym, phonetically similar, but different in etymology, *poli* and *policé* could be paired in dictionaries of synonyms and thus give rise to fine semantic discriminations. The same considerations that served to distinguish the respective merits of civility and politeness thus cropped up again in discriminating between *poli* and *policé.* A difference in values emerged. In contrasting civility with politeness Beauzée had attached suspicions of inauthenticity to civility. In the opposition between *poli* and *policé* the suspicion, the imputation of falseness and externality, was attached to *poli,* which lacked the institutional solidity of *policé:*

> *Poli, policé:* these two terms, both of which concern the reciprocal duties of individuals in society, are synonyms through this common idea, but the ideas associated with each establish a significant difference between them.

> *Poli* attaches only to external signs of benevolence. Such signs are always equivocal and, unfortunately, often at odds with actions. *Policé* presupposes laws to determine the reciprocal duties of common benevolence and a power authorized to enforce those laws.[27]

When politeness becomes unreliable because "refinement" suggests a possibility of corruption and loss of primitive veracity, one must rely instead on laws and social and political institutions as the basis of order *(police)*.

Of course a perfect match between laws and mores is the best guarantee of prosperity and stability. But if the mores of a polite people are already corrupt, is there still time to secure social order by strengthening laws? Duclos warns of the dangers that threaten social cohesion, which is to say, *police*:

> The most polite peoples are not the most virtuous. Simple and severe mores are found only in peoples among whom reason and equity have established order *(ont policés)* and who have not yet corrupted that order through misuse of their intelligence. Disciplined *(policés)* peoples are better than polite peoples. Among barbarians laws must shape mores; among disciplined peoples, mores perfect laws and sometimes supplant them. A false politeness causes the laws to be forgotten.[28]

In another chapter Duclos (who does not use the word *civilization*) treats politeness, which he defines as pleasantness in commerce between individuals, as indubitably subordinate to the social virtues, which attach paramount importance to the general interest. True politeness, he says, can be reduced to other sentiments. In itself it is only an art of imitation; it is the *aesthetic* parody of reason's *ethical* demands. Under certain conditions politeness becomes superfluous. It can be replaced by self-interest properly understood and simple humanity:

> One must not . . . regret those crude times when man, impressed solely by his own interest, pursued it with ferocious instinct to the detriment of others. Grossness and crudeness do not exclude deception or artifice, for these things can be seen in the least disciplinable of animals.
>
> Only through disciplining *(poliçant)* themselves did men learn to reconcile their particular interests with the common interest; only in that way did they understand that, through this agreement, each derives more from society than he puts into it.
>
> Men therefore owe one another respect because they owe one another a debt of gratitude. They owe one another a politeness worthy of them, made for thinking beings, and varied by the different sentiments that ought to inspire it . . .

The most unfortunate effect of the customary politeness is to teach art to do without the virtues it imitates. Let education inspire humanity and beneficence in us and we will either have politeness or no longer need it.

If we do not have that which is manifested by the graces, we shall have that which heralds the honest man and citizen; we will not need to resort to counterfeit.[29]

Rejecting both savage nature and "customary politeness," Duclos emphasizes those qualities that were destined to enjoy growing success with prerevolutionary elites: humanity, beneficence, civic spirit.

These were precisely the values that were associated with the word *civilization* in the revolutionary period. Indeed, they were among its inescapable connotations, at least in the works of theorists of progress such as Volney and Condorcet. Moras is correct to say that the word *civilization* almost never appears in the political texts of the younger Mirabeau, Danton, Robespierre, Marat, Desmoulins, or Saint-Just, who prefer the words *patrie* (fatherland) and *peuple* (people) and who invoke the great civic values—liberty, equality, virtue—and celebrate decisive revolutionary progress in metaphors based on light.

It is particularly important to note that, because of these associated values, because of the connection with the ideas of perfectibility and progress, the word *civilization* denoted more than just a complex process of refinement of mores, social organization, technical progress, and advancing knowledge; it took on a sacred aura, owing to which it could sometimes reinforce traditional religious values and at other times supplant them. The history of the word *civilization* thus leads to this crucial observation: once a notion takes on a *sacred* authority and thereby acquires the power to mobilize, it quickly stirs up conflict between political groups or rival schools of thought claiming to be its champions and defenders and as such insisting on the exclusive right to propagate the new idea.

A term fraught with sacred content demonizes its antonym. Once the word *civilization* ceases to denote a fact subject to judgment and becomes an incontestable value, it enters the verbal arsenal of praise and blame. Evaluating the defects and merits of the civilization is no longer the issue. Civilization itself becomes the crucial criterion: judgment is now made in the name of civilization. One has to take its side, adopt its cause. For those who answer its call it becomes grounds for praise. Or, conversely, it can serve as a basis for denunciation: all that is not civilization, all that resists or threatens civilization, is monstrous, absolute evil. As rhetoric heats up it becomes legitimate to ask for the supreme sacrifice in the name of civilization. This means that the service or defense of civilization can in certain circumstances justify the recourse to violence. Civilization's enemies, the barbarians, if they cannot be educated or converted, must be prevented from doing harm.

Here I shall cite only one particularly illustrative example. It concerns the justification for colonization. Enlightenment philosophy, as epitomized for example in Condorcet's *Esquisse* (1794), condemned colonial conquest and especially Christian proselytism in foreign lands. Epithets traditionally reserved for barbarians ("bloody, tyrannical, stupid") were applied to colonizers and missionaries as well as to those in the Old World who clung to ancient "superstitions." But a new task appeared on the scene: to educate, to emancipate, to civilize. The sacred value of civilization supplanted that of religion. Yet Condorcet's text shows quite clearly that the ultimate objective remained the same: the assimilation of other cultures into the catholicity of the Enlightenment supplanted the missionary enterprise, whose goal had been to rally all humankind beneath the banner of Christ. It is worth citing at some length from the original:

> Survey the history of our ventures and settlements in Africa or Asia and you will see our commercial monopolies, our betrayals, our bloody contempt for men of another color or creed, our insolent usurpations, and the extravagant proselytism and intrigues of our priests destroy those feelings of respect and good will that the superiority of our enlightenment and the advantages of our commerce had initially obtained.
>
> But surely the time is fast approaching when, ceasing to show them only our corrupters and tyrants, we will become for them useful instruments and generous liberators.
>
> Europeans, then, limiting themselves to free commerce and too enlightened about their own rights to circumvent those of others, will respect the independence that they have hitherto so audaciously violated . . . The monks who brought these people only shameful superstitions and who provoked rebellion by threatening a new

domination will give way to men whose business it is to spread among these nations truths useful to their prosperity and to enlighten them as to their interests as well as their rights. Zeal for the truth is also a passion, and when it has no more rough prejudices to combat at home, no more shameful errors to dispel, it ought to carry its efforts into far-off lands.

Some of these vast countries hold numerous peoples who, in order to civilize themselves, seem to be awaiting only our resources and who want to look on Europeans as brothers in order to become their friends and disciples. Others, populated by nations oppressed by sacred despots or stupid conquerors, have for centuries been awaiting their liberators. Elsewhere one finds almost savage tribes deprived by their harsh climate of the benefits of a perfected civilization, while that same harshness repels those who would like to teach them its advantages; or conquering hordes, who know no law but force and no trade but plunder. The progress of the latter two classes of people will be slow and stormy. Perhaps, their number diminished *as they find themselves repelled by the civilized nations, they will eventually disappear or be absorbed.*

. . . Thus there will come a time when the sun will no longer shine on men who are not free on this earth, on men who recognize any master other than their reason; when tyrants and slaves, priests and their stupid or hypocritical instruments will exist only in history books and theaters.[30]

Condorcet thus turns Gibbon's argument for a more temperate theory of progress on its head. For Gibbon, if the barbarian peoples of Asia wished to regain superiority over the Europeans, they would have to adopt European military arts and industry and thus join civilization.[31] Condorcet, as this passage shows, found it easier to imagine civilization *repelling* the savage and nomadic peoples until they became physically or culturally extinct. For him, the image of *spreading* enlightenment remained a dynamic model even after his condemnation of territorial conquest.

Since civilization is both a process and a sacred value, since it is spreading enlightenment, it is important to know the extent of its influence and the source of its radiance. Postrevolutionary language naturally identified the sacred values of the Revolution with those of civilization and therefore claimed for France, the fatherland of revolution, the privilege of leading civilization's advance guard, of serving as its beacon.

Condorcet had already claimed this role for the nation. To an even greater extent it became a theme of Napoleonic rhetoric: "Soldiers! You are about to embark on a conquest whose effects on the world's civilization and commerce are incalculable."[32] The history of this nationalist-cum-revolutionary theme can be traced right through the nineteenth century. The substitution of civilization for religion, of France and its people for the Church, can be seen clearly in a long series of texts. In 1830 Laurent de l'Ardèche wrote: "Noble people of France, thou art still, of all nations, the chosen and cherished of God; for if thy kings are no longer eldest sons of the Church, . . . thou art still the eldest son of civilization."[33] In 1831 Michelet claimed for France "the pontificate of the new civilization."[34] Victor Hugo contributed more than any other writer to the sacralization of the word *civilization* while attributing to France the supreme sacerdotal role: "The French people have been the missionary of civilization in Europe."[35] The fullest statement of the nationalist monopolization of civilization, an epiphany of the sacred in the modern age, can be found in one of Hugo's post-exile speeches:

> One can say that in our century there are two schools. These two schools condense and epitomize the two contrary currents that carry civilization in opposite directions, one toward the future, the other toward the past: the first of these two schools is called Paris, the second, Rome.
>
> Each of these two schools has its book; the book of Paris is the Declaration of the Rights of Man; the Book of Rome is the Syllabus. These two books answer Progress. The first says yes; the second says no.
>
> Progress is God's footstep.[36]

Traditionally the contrary of civilization was barbarity. Nations not as directly identifiable as France with the spirit of civilization were accordingly not exempt—particularly in times of international crisis— from suspicion of barbarity. On March 1, 1871, following the German victory in the Franco-Prussian War, Hugo spoke to the National Assembly, then meeting in Bordeaux:

And while the victorious nation, Germany, the slave horde, will bend its brow beneath its heavy helmet, France, the sublime vanquished nation, will wear the crown of a sovereign people.

And civilization, once again set face to face with barbarism, will seek its way between these two nations, one of which has been the light of Europe, and the other of which will be the night.

. . . In Strasbourg, Gentlemen, there are two statues, of Gutenberg and Kléber. Within us a voice is welling up, a voice that swears to Gutenberg not to let civilization suffocate, and that swears to Kléber not to let the Republic suffocate.[37]

This sense of the word *civilization*—patriotic, republican, and fraught with sacred intensity—would continue to be used against the German enemy[38] in the twentieth century until it found in Hitlerism a barbarity unquestionably hideous enough to embody its opposite.

VIII

Given the postrevolutionary appropriation of the word *civilization* and its sacred connotations, it will come as no surprise that the adversaries of the Revolution also appropriated the term for purposes of their own. Edmund Burke set the tone as early as the end of 1790. For him, civilization was identified with the traditional values of religion and chivalry—precisely those values that revolutionary thought condemned as crude and barbarous: "Nothing is more certain, than that our manners, our civilization, and all the good things which are connected with manners, and with civilization, have, in this European world of ours, depended for ages on two principles; and were indeed the result of both combined; I mean the spirit of a gentleman, and the spirit of religion."[39]

Writing to his French correspondent, Burke envisioned the worst eventualities: economic collapse compounding the destruction of social and religious institutions.

If commerce and the arts should be lost in an experiment to try how well a state may stand without these old fundamental principles, what sort of a thing must be a nation of gross, stupid, ferocious, and at the same time, poor and sordid barbarians, destitute of religion, honor, or manly pride, possessing nothing at present, and hoping for nothing hereafter?

I wish you may not be going fast, and by the shortest cut, to that horrible and disgustful situation. Already there appears a poverty of conception, a coarseness and vulgarity in all the proceedings of the assembly and of all their instructors. Their liberty is not liberal. Their science is presumptuous ignorance. Their humanity is savage and brutal.[40]

This inversion of terms is fraught with consequences. The sacred character of civilization is held to be in *peril*. The danger comes from within. Barbarity lies in the equality advocated by demagogues, in the rebellion of the "crude multitude." Savagery no longer lies outside the nation, on foreign shores or in the distant past. It is hidden among the people, waiting to burst forth from society's shadowy depths. Mallet du Pan would echo the same idea: "The Huns and the Heruli, the Vandals and the Goths, will not come from the North or the Black Sea; they are among us."[41] Chateaubriand, at the end of *Mémoires d'outre-tombe* (book 44, chap. 2), shifts the location of the danger within to the realm of the spirit: "The invasion of ideas has succeeded the invasion of the barbarians. Today's decomposed civilization is lost. The liquid from the vessel that contains it has not been poured into another vessel; the vessel itself has broken."

Sometimes the danger within assumed a social aspect: the threat was seen as coming from the "dangerous classes," from the proletariat, from the so-called Apaches and Mohicans of the industrial cities. At other times it was perceived as a consequence of an unshackling of instincts brought about by intellectual movements of emancipation and revolt ("religious indifference," for example). Individualism, or the ascribing of paramount importance to self-interest, was said to justify crime, to sanction a resumption of the war of all against all: sophisticated swindling was no better than ordinary murder.[42] The lower classes were not the only source of savagery, which was supposed to lurk in the hearts of all men but hidden beneath a reassuring exterior.[43]

Once recognized, this danger within called for a response, which naturally took a variety of forms, the simplest of which was "reaction." To react was to protect the sacred values of Christian civilization by all available means: repression, discipline, education, and propaganda.[44] Bear in mind, moreover, that the word *reaction* had a physical meaning before it took on a pejorative political one. For Joseph de Maistre, for example, *reaction* was still a neutral, mechanical notion.

IX

As intense and persistent as the sacralization of the term *civilization* was, it was difficult for the men of the French Restoration not to see the danger within as either the product of civilization itself or an irreducible residue of savage nature. It was therefore difficult to refrain from turning against aspects of civilization itself an accusation that its sacred value justified making against those who denied or compromised it. Something in civilization worked against civilization. In the preface to *De la religion* (1827) Benjamin Constant cleverly combines two seemingly contradictory attitudes: a belief in the almost unlimited perfectibility of the human race[45] and a self-accusatory, despondent sense of a collapse of conviction and moral strength, said to be an ineluctable consequence of the sophistication and softness of advanced civilizations. The crucial paradigm here was the fall of the Roman Empire, which was blamed on Roman opulence. While adopting many of Gibbon's views, Constant also argued against him on the matter of religion (or, more precisely, religious sentiment):

> Contemplate man, governed by his senses, beset by his needs, softened by civilization, and all the more enslaved to his pleasures because civilization makes them so easy to obtain. See how many holds he offers to corruption. Think of that suppleness of language that surrounds him with excuses and hides his selfishness . . . In the end there are only two systems. One assigns us interest for our guide and well-being for our goal. The other proposes perfection as our goal and, for our guide, an inward feeling *(le sentiment intime),* self-abnegation, and a spirit of sacrifice.[46]

If we adopt the "system" of interest and well-being, it will make no difference that we consider man to be "the most skillful, adroit, and sagacious of animals" and rank him "uppermost in the material hierarchy; he will still fall below the lowest echelon of any moral hierarchy." It is therefore pointless to appeal to *humanity:* "Your institutions, your efforts, your exhortations will be useless; though you may triumph over all your external enemies, the *enemy within* will remain invincible." An account of Roman decadence, said to be caused by the reign of selfish interest, follows: "Once before the human race seemed to fall into the abyss. Then, too, a lengthy civilization had sapped its strength." But Christianity had provided the antidote: "The world was filled with slaves, exploiting servitude or enduring it. The Christians appeared: they laid their foundations outside of egoism. They did not vie for material interest, which material force held in chains. They did not kill, they died, and in dying they triumphed."[47] This argument seems to favor religion over civilization, but the counterargument is given in a note, which reaffirms faith in progress and restores validity to the idea of civilization:

> The effects of civilization are of two kinds. First, civilization leads to discovery, and every discovery is a source of power. Thus it adds to the stock of resources by means of which the human race perfects itself. Second, civilization makes pleasure easier to obtain and increases its variety, and habituation to pleasure creates a need in man that turns him away from elevated and noble thoughts. Hence each time the human race achieves an exclusive civilization, it seems to be degraded for several generations. Eventually it recovers from this temporary degradation and sets to work again and with the new discoveries it has added to its store attains a still higher degree of perfection. Thus we are, proportionately speaking, perhaps as corrupt as the Romans in the time of Diocletian. But our corruption is less revolting, our manners are milder, our vices more veiled because we are not burdened with polytheism become licentious and with the inevitable horrors of slavery. We have also made immense discoveries. Generations more fortunate than our own will profit from the destruction of abuses from which we are delivered and will also profit from the advantages we have obtained. But if those generations are to advance along the trail that has been blazed for them, they will need what we lack, what we must lack, namely, conviction, enthusiasm, and the ability to sacrifice interest to opinion.
>
> It follows that civilization ought not to be proscribed and that one neither can nor should do anything to stop it. To do so would be to stop a child from growing because what causes it to grow also causes it to grow old. But one must appreciate the times, divine what it is possible, and, while supporting what partial good can still be achieved, work above all to lay the foundations for a future good, for the better the groundwork that is laid, the fewer the obstacles that

will have to be overcome and the lower the cost that will have to be paid.[48]

Constant is implicitly calling for new Christians capable of sacrifice and "enthusiasm."[49] By contrast, others, long before Rimbaud, had called for new barbarians. Jacobi in 1779 did not yet ask them, as Rimbaud would, to bring "new blood . . . pagan blood." He merely looked forward to the benefits of their torrential energy: "The present state of society looks to me like a dead and stagnant sea, and that is why I hope for some kind of inundation, even by Barbarians, to get rid of these stinking marshes and discover virgin land."[50] The counterpart and corollary of Constant's desire for re-Christianization was thus a wish for rebarbarization—it, too, justified by feelings of lassitude and diminished vitality and inspired by interpretive myths projected onto the end of the ancient world and the dawn of the Christian era.

Constant and some of his contemporaries clearly could not refrain from criticizing civilization as a current *fact* in order to preserve the long-term principle of civilization as a *value* associated with religious epiphany. Progress as he envisions it is intermittent, interrupted by long phases of moral weakness and political servitude. As distressing as the present might be, comparison with the ancient past justified belief in progress, which could be seen with all the clarity of a verifiable fact. Constant's contemporary Saint-Simon saw the progress of history as an alternating series of "organic" and "critical" periods.

Nevertheless, the concept of civilization was leaking badly by the early nineteenth century. It could no longer hold its sacred content. Malaise, irony, and dissatisfaction could not be held indefinitely in check. Official rhetoric quickly turned the concept of civilization into a cliché. (In *Madame Bovary* civilization would come in for its share of mockery along with other platitudes on the great day of the county fair.) To establish a social order it was therefore necessary to drum up enthusiasm for a whole set of complementary, mutually reinforcing values, yet even then authority would not rest totally secure. As Claude Lefort rightly points out:

> In the early days of democracy the discourse that can be imputed to bourgeois ideology evolved under the threat of social decomposition. Such institutions and values as Property, Family, State, Authority, Fatherland, and Culture were presented as ramparts against barba-

rism, against unknown outside forces that threatened to destroy Society and Civilization. The attempt to sacralize institutions through rhetoric was tailored to match society's loss of substance, to the defeat of the body politic. The bourgeois cult of order, which thrived on the assertion of authority in its various guises, on the formulation of rules, and on the fixing of appropriate distances between those who filled the role of master, property owner, culti- vated man, civilized man, normal man, and adult vis-à-vis the *other*—that cult attests to the bewilderment of those who faced the void of a formless society.[51]

X

In Constant's writing, then, the word *civilization* has multiple mean- ings: it suggests growing resources, security, pleasures, and the like (things reflecting, in the realm of *fact*, the style of life of the more prosperous classes in modern industrial society), but it also implies the inward perfection of individuals, a flourishing of emotional and intel- lectual qualities, and a healthy broadening and deepening of interper- sonal relations—things without which it would be impossible to look upon civilization as a *value*. As in the case of civility and politeness, we thus have both an inner and an outer face of civilization, and, while ideally these were of course supposed to coincide, in fact they would remain contradictory and incompatible as long as justice, liberty, and morality did not go hand in hand with the accumulation of wealth and the complex evolution of laws and public institutions. As we saw earlier, Guizot insisted on the dual aspect of civilization: to fully satisfy the demands of civilized life it was not enough simply to *instruct* men, to develop their instrumental aptitudes; it was also necessary to *educate* them, that is, to teach them to act as free and rational human beings capable of resisting the pervasive demands of material production. But industrial society aggravates the disparity between the two components of the ideal civilization. It becomes increasingly difficult to hold on to the notion of a civilization without internal conflict. Critics seeking to discredit industrial and democratic society would attack what they called "civilization" by portraying it as, in Baudelaire's words, a "great barbarity illuminated by gas."[52] At the same time Baudelaire praised the American savage by endowing him with all the spiritual qualities that civilization-as-value ought to have promoted:

> By nature, by necessity even, [the savage] is encyclopedic, whereas the civilized man is confined to infinitesimal areas of specialization. The civilized man invents the philosophy of progress in order to console himself for his abdication and downfall, whereas the savage man, a feared and respected husband, a warrior obliged to display personal bravery, a poet in the melancholy hours when the setting sun encourages him to sing of the past and of his ancestors, sticks close to the contours of the ideal. What shortcomings can we find? He has his priest, his witch doctor, and his physician. And, yes, he has his dandy, the supreme incarnation of the idea of the beautiful transported into the material realm.[53]

The moral strength and aesthetic sophistication that were supposed to cap material civilization had to be sought outside Europe, among the savages. But the values enumerated by Baudelaire so strongly imply an idea of civilization (that is, both a civilized man's ideal and an ideal civilization) that he is able to use the word without pejorative connotations: "Perhaps Civilization has taken refuge in some tiny, as yet undiscovered, tribe." He has already denounced France for being, like Belgium, a "truly barbarous country."[54]

Thus the word *civilization* cannot easily sustain a dualizing of its implications and presuppositions: when these do not coincide, they lead to contradictory uses of the term. When fact contradicts value, *civilization* is used to denote the fact and other terms are sought for the value (just as, in the previous century, *politeness* was substituted for the unsatisfactory *civility*). Of course one solution to the dilemma is to add an epithet connoting authenticity: "true civilization." But more systematic thinkers are likely to opt for firmer lexical ground. Charles Fourier, for example, used the word *harmony* to denote the perfected social state. The task of the utopian dreamer was then to detail the functioning of this harmony, which would ultimately triumph over the miseries and injustices of contemporary civilization. Subject to all-out attack, civilization thus became the foil that served to highlight the benefits expected from post-civilized "harmonian" society. The lexical pair *civilization-harmony* externalized and projected into an external space (the so-called phalanstery) and future time internal tensions that could not easily be sustained within the single concept of civilization. This new opposition was not without consequence: it not only attached a pejorative value to the word *civilization* but also limited its temporal scope. Civilization ceased to be coextensive with all of human history. It represented only its present phase, with its system of constraints (such as enforced monogamy) on the human passions. The same phenomenon can be observed in the vocabulary of Engels, who drew on the theories of Lewis H. Morgan. For Engels, civilization succeeded savagery and barbarism. Civilization invented the state, private property, the division of labor, the exploitation of the lower classes. The next phase in the historical dialectic would come when this mode of social organization was superseded. The classless society (in which the state had withered away) would do away with the evils of civilization. It would revert, but at a higher level, to the community of property that human beings had enjoyed prior to the advent of civilization.[55] But twentieth-century Marxist writings largely ignore this essentially Fourierist use of the word *civilization*.

From the German world came a far more general concept to rival that of civilization, but one without, at first, direct political or revolutionary implications: the concept of culture *(die Kultur)*. By attaching different names to competing ideas, this innovation triggered a lengthy debate; it brought into the open the contrast between complementary components that Constant and Guizot had attempted to contain within the single concept of civilization.[56] Nietzsche was not the first to take part in the debate, but, true to his genius, he gave vehement expression to the antithetical terms: civilization, he said, is nothing but discipline, repression, diminution of the individual; by contrast, culture can go hand in hand with social decadence because it is the fruition of individual energy:

> Culture versus Civilization: the high points of culture and civilization are remote from one another. Make no mistake: the antagonism between them is abyssally deep. Morally speaking, the great moments of culture have always been times of corruption. By contrast, the eras of man's deliberate and forced domestication ("Civilization") have been times of intolerance for the boldest and most spiritual natures. What civilization wants is not what culture wants; it may even be the opposite.[57]

On the purely terminological level, it is significant that when Freud said he did not wish to differentiate between the notions of culture and civilization, it was in order to locate, within the unified domain of culture (hence also of civilization), an interior threat resulting from a conflict between *two* components: the erotic drive, which seeks to enlarge the community while tightening its bonds, and the aggressive drive associated with the death instinct.[58] Freud's elimination of the culture-civilization antithesis leads to the reinstatement of an antithetical relation, no longer in overt form but in the guise of an inevitable clash between two dynamic intrapsychic principles whose coexistence is made more difficult by the conditions of modern life—despite the fact that our survival depends on that coexistence. Freud, in other words, no longer needs the culture-civilization duality because he has at his disposal another pair of antithetical terms: *eros-thanatos.* What had become a commonplace antinomy was thus eliminated, only to be reborn in the form of a conceptual innovation applicable at the "metapsychological" level.

XI

Civilization is used today in various parallel and contradictory senses, all more or less tiresomely familiar. In spite of its rhetorical pathos, the word *civilization,* as it appeared at the end of Gorbachev's farewell speech in December 1991, should not be dismissed as trivial. Despite the obvious erosion of meaning, the word is a long way from obsolete, and a number of questions can be asked about its use. Has current usage effaced the external and internal antinomies that we noted in tracing the semantic history of the word *civilization?* To be sure, the distinction between culture and civilization is no longer as sharp as it once was, but it does persist. *Culture* sometimes refers to social developments that fall short of the level of a "great civilization." *Culture* is also used to describe distinct systems of values and behaviors within a given civilization: popular culture, high culture, urban culture, "counterculture," and so on. Some writers would go so far as to say that a civilization may include a fairly large number of microcultures.[59] Ethnology uses the term *civilization* in a relative sense: there are many distinct civilizations, each with its own legitimacy. Science must determine the territorial extent, distinctive features, and dates of inception and extinction of each. In mapping civilizations, what matters is the shifting pattern of boundaries and distinctive systems of value, not the qualitative judgment we might make by naively applying our own civilization's values. Civilizations vie with one another like organisms, entering into relations of association, rivalry, and conflict. None can be said to be superior or inferior to any other, though it is a matter of empirical fact that some succeed while others fail. We have only a *scientific* interest in determining why civilizations appear and disappear.[60] In good faith we must recognize, without priding ourselves on the fact, that "our" civilization is the only one to take such an interest in other civilizations, indeed to accuse itself of having frequently done harm to other civilizations when they stood in the way of our lust for power.

The guilty conscience that rather incongruously goes along with our cultural relativism proves that the old antinomies continue to haunt the concept of civilization. They manifest themselves in the guise of threat, danger, and fear. "The ills of civilization" is an ambiguous phrase: it can refer either to the afflictions from which civilization suffers or to the afflictions that civilization causes. In contemporary discourse civilization is perceived sometimes as a source of sickness, sometimes as a victim. Civilization (whether it be technological, industrial, Western, or what have you) is a source of danger to living things, to other cultures and civilizations, to the souls of individuals who enjoy its fruits or submit to its demands. The arguments for and cogency of ecological rhetoric, accusations of genocide, and so forth are sufficiently well known that there is no need to go into them here. The general contention is that "our" civilization is inextricably bound up with a hubris that must be restrained and if possible reversed. Conceiving of civilization as a menace conjures up a series of alarming images of the devastation that civilized technology brings to those subject to its norms (of calculating efficiency, productivity, and so forth). But sometimes we also think of civilization as menaced, and then it is another set of antinomies that troubles us. In such cases the threat is presumably seen as emanating from within civilization itself, because industrial civilization now covers the globe and no longer faces opposition from outside. We feel anxious about the emergence of savage subcultures, about the revival of superstition, about phenomena of intellectual and moral regression that put the tools (and weapons) of civilization into the hands of individuals incapable of controlling them, of understanding their meaning, of recognizing their historical underpinnings. As we witness the disappearance of a dimension of memory that linked the present to the past, we fear that such forgetfulness may compromise the future. We wonder, moreover, whether our science, art, and philosophy still retain the inventive capacity without which our civilization would cease to be what it has been: the theater of a steady transfer of authority based on a wager in favor of the autonomy of human reason as embodied, in principle, in democratic institutions.

Civilization as threat, civilization as threatened: these are just two of many contradictory themes that have gained urgency in recent years. In the clash of opposites, civilization is both threatening and threatened, persecutor and persecuted. It is no longer a safe haven for those who shelter beneath its roof. In an article on the disillusionment of Polish artists of the last generation, Czeslaw Milosz writes:

> The whole heritage of European culture was met with distrust and derision. This explains why, several years after the war, Stanislas Wyspianski's play *Akropolis,* written in 1904, was staged by Jerzy Grotowski in a very peculiar way. The play consists of scenes from Homer and the Bible and thus epitomizes the principal components of Western culture. In Grotowski's version, these scenes were played by Auschwitz inmates in striped uniforms, and the dialogue was accompanied by scenes of torture. Only the torture was real, and the sublime language of the lines recited by the actors was colored by the stark contrast.[61]

As we saw earlier, the marquis de Mirabeau, who introduced the word *civilisation* into the French vocabulary, was already critical of the "barbarity of our civilizations." He also spoke of "false civilization." When the word first appeared, it therefore possessed at least two meanings, and both senses were associated with critical work.

Taken as a value, civilization constitutes a political and moral norm. It is the criterion against which barbarity, or non-civilization, is judged and condemned. By contrast, when used to describe the current organization of industrial society, the word *civilization* is nothing more than a synthetic noun denoting a collective fact to be judged on the basis of other criteria. Instead of a conceptual tool of critical thought, the word *civilization* denotes a fact subject to critical judgment. It is no longer enough for a civilization to be a civilization, it must be a *true* civilization. To make this judgment, a criterion for distinguishing between true and false civilizations is required. That criterion must be taken from some other domain: Mirabeau, for example, in a text cited by the Jesuits of Trévoux, made religion a necessary condition of civilization. But the same Mirabeau, not unduly concerned with logic, proposed the normative pair civilization-barbarity as the criterion of civilization qua fact: the reasoning is circular. Our civilization can be condemned because it is "barbarous," that is, because it is not civilization.

The distinction between de jure and de facto senses of the word *civilization,* which allowed the "noble conscience" to invoke the former against the latter, is challenged by Hegel's analysis, in *The Phenomenology of Spirit,* of *Bildung* and the philosophy of the Enlightenment.[62] Hegel's conclusion is well known: that it is *actual* civilization, with all that appears "barbarous" in it to the moral conscience (that is, to the abstract morality defended by the *philosophe* in *Le Neveu de Rameau*), that constitutes the *truth* of the moment.

The historical moment in which the word *civilization* appears marks the advent of self-reflection, the emergence of a consciousness that thinks it understands the nature of its own activity, that believes it knows how collective reality develops and ought to be regulated. This self-reflection is not self-absorbed: the moment that Western civilization becomes aware of itself reflectively, it sees itself as one civilization among others. Having achieved self-consciousness, civilization immediately discovers civilizations. From then on criticism no longer limits itself to comparing our time *(nostra tempora)* with past times *(pristina tempora)*. It assigns historical tasks to human collectivities, while reserving the right to examine, approve, disapprove, and establish equivalences according to the dictates of enlightened reason. For critical thought, nothing imposed by tradition continues to be obligatory on grounds of longevity alone. Critical thought judges on the basis of its own criteria. It is not unduly paradoxical to say that the appearance of the word *civilization* (at a late stage of what we now call Western civilization), far from reinforcing the intrinsic order of civilized society, marked the beginning of a crisis. The crumbling of sacred institutions and the impossibility of continuing to regard theological discourse as being, in Eric Weil's terms, "concrete and absolute"[63] encouraged most thinkers to embark on an urgent search for substitute absolutes. Civilization proved to be a useful idea. But since it immediately developed an inner fissure, a rift between an (absent) value and a (more or less unpalatable) fact, it turned out to be incapable of filling the role previously played by the absolute in theology. Did the concept "civilization" emerge in civilization's waning hours to herald the impending death of that which it named? I prefer a different interpretation. If critical reason can recognize that it is a product of the very civilization against which its polemic is directed, if it is willing to admit that civilization-as-value can be formulated only in the current language of civilization-as-fact, then one can imagine a new conceptual model in which the opposition between the uniqueness of the absolute and cultural relativism is overcome. This new model would demonstrate the complementary relation of critical reason, civilization as it is (both threatening and threatened), and civilization as a yet-to-be-realized value. Surprisingly, perhaps, this tripartite model establishes a schematic framework capable of accommodating all the debates to which civilization has given rise since the Enlightenment. If it were fully acknowledged and accepted, it would define the basic value of a civilization that one could still support: a civilization in permanent crisis, including within itself the most alert critical freedom and the most independent faculty of reason, a freedom and reason capable of recognizing the real world from which they stem, or, in other words, of recognizing civilization as an accomplished fact, yet against which one could propose, polemically, a project of civilization more amenable to the insistence on universality that undergirds the work of critical reason. I am surprised to find myself theorizing, no doubt naively, on the basis of lexical history, but my final remark will bring me back to the realm of words. The word *civilization* is a powerful stimulus to theory. I find myself in good company. As commonly used the word carries a variety of contradictory meanings, and in particular usages its significance is often clarified by the addition of an epithet: Christian civilization, Western civilization, technological civilization, material civilization, industrial civilization, and so on. Despite its ambiguity, the word clearly describes the human environment in which we move and whose air we breathe every day: *in eo movemur et sumus*. The temptation to clarify our thinking by elaborating a theory of civilization capable of grounding a far-reaching philosophy of history is thus irresistible.[64]

XII

Theorization is certainly a trap. Parable can usefully take its place. In the "Story of the Warrior and the Captive" Jorge Luis Borges tells two tales: one of the barbarian warrior Droctulft who abandons his comrades to defend the city of Ravenna against their attack, and one of an Englishwoman kidnapped by South American Indians, who adopts the "savage" ways of her kidnappers.[65]

What attracts Droctulft and causes him to change sides is the orderliness of the city, the polish of its marble, the values we have summarized under the heads *urbanitas* and *politeness:*

> He came from the inextricable forests of the boar and the bison; he was light-skinned, spirited, innocent, cruel, loyal to his captain and his tribe, but not to the universe. The wars bring him to Ravenna and there he sees something he has never seen before, or has not seen fully. He sees the day and the cypresses and the marble. He sees a whole whose multiplicity is not that of disorder; he sees a city, an organism composed of statues, temples, gardens, rooms, amphitheaters, vases, columns, regular and open spaces . . . Perhaps it is enough for him to see a single arch, with an incomprehensible inscription in eternal Roman letters. Suddenly he is blinded and renewed by this revelation, the City. He knows that in it he will be a dog, or a child, and that he will not even begin to understand it, but he also knows that it is worth more than his gods and his sworn faith and all the marshes of Germany. Droctulft abandons his own and fights for Ravenna.

Borges contrasts this tale with one told by his "English grandmother," who once met another Englishwoman who had been abducted "in an Indian raid." The woman became the wife of an Indian chief, "to whom she gave two sons and who was very brave."

> Behind her story one could glimpse a savage life: the horsehide shelters, the fires made of dry manure, the feasts of scorched meat or raw entrails, the stealthy departures at dawn, the attacks on corrals, the yelling and the pillaging, the wars, the sweeping charges

on the haciendas by naked horsemen, the polygamy, the stench and the superstition. An Englishwoman had lowered herself to this barbarism.

The two individuals thus cross the dividing line in opposite directions. One is a turncoat who abandons barbarism, the other a turncoat who embraces it. Borges's final comment is surprising:

> A thousand three hundred years and the ocean lie between the destiny of the captive and the destiny of Droctulft. Both these, now, are equally irrecoverable. The figure of the barbarian who embraced the cause of Ravenna, the figure of the European woman who chose the wasteland, may seem antagonistic. And yet, both were swept away by a secret impulse, an impulse more profound than reason, and both heeded this impulse, which they would not have known how to justify. Perhaps the stories I have related are one single story. The obverse and the reverse of this coin are, for God, the same.

These lines are troubling: what is said to be the same in both cases is the irrational impulse to cross the divide, to move toward the *other*. Barbarity and civilization thus appear to be identical in the eyes of God. Outside and inside always have value for the other, but in both directions. Today, of course, there are no barbarians or savages outside the walls in the forests, steppes, or pampas. But it is not in a merely contingent sense that the two destinies are said to be irrecoverable. The mirror image of barbarity and civilization is conjured up for us as part of the history of the past, preserved in the memory of the writer and in divine consciousness. Does this mean that civilization has won, that the coin no longer has a reverse? Hardly. What is disturbing about the story is that the passage from barbarity to civilization and vice versa, so far from requiring what historians like to think of as a long period of time, is sometimes just a short step. Although the stories recounted here involve only individuals from the past, the moral has wider implications and could easily be extended to all men at all times. Borges is too civilized, too practiced in the art of ellipsis, to say more. He confines himself to reminding us of the precariousness of boundaries, of the equal facility of conversion and fall. The opposition of civilization and barbarity comes to rest in a question. This leads not to a renunciation of civilization but to a recognition that it is inseparable from its other side.

2

~

ON FLATTERY

The classical doctrine of civility as elaborated in sixteenth-century Italian courts and seventeenth-century Parisian salons laid down this principle: that the reciprocal relations into which men are daily required to enter may, under certain conditions, not only be purified of the risk of violence but also become a source of pleasure. Over the course of an elaborate education the rules of a complex *art* (consisting essentially of language but also including gestures, manners, and dress) may combine with *nature* without suffocating or corrupting it. Once "urbanized" and "polished" in this fashion, the natural becomes compatible with civility; it ceases to be associated with those aggressive features inherent in the idea of the "rustic" (antonym of "urbane") or "crude" (antonym of "polite") individual. What makes pleasure possible is in large part the concerted suppression, the *conventional* repudiation of the potential for aggression intrinsic to all human relationships. A protected space is thus created, an enclosed field where by common accord the partners to a relationship refrain from attacking or injuring one another in ordinary commerce as well as in matters having to do with love. The crucial idea, to use an anachronistic terminology, is one of maximization of pleasure. The loss that the amorous instinct incurs owing to repression and sublimation is counterbalanced, according to the theory of *honnêteté,* by the eroticization of everyday intercourse, conversation, and epistolary exchange. The doctrine of *honnêteté* aestheticizes "instinctual renunciation." Eros is thus "civilized," but at the same time civil relations in general are eroticized and become raw material to be minutely elaborated. The aesthetic value ascribed to "pleasant manners" is credited to the individual, to his or her "personal merit." Thus there is a strong narcissistic component to the process, insofar as it *distinguishes* the individual and destines him or her for a select society. The notion of "good society" or "good company," particularly in the extreme form attached to this idea in the "circles" of the *précieux*, was one characteristic of what would nowadays be called a form of "group narcissism." Surely it is no accident that males in this precise society at this precise moment in history adopted a feminine style of self-presentation, wearing, most notably, wigs with long curls, ribbons, jewels, pumps with sinuous high heels. Nor was it an accident that the portrait and self-portrait originated, as literary genres, in this milieu.

Reason, Judgment, Merit

Much can be learned by examining the language of polite conversation. The science of *honnêteté*, the chevalier de Méré declared, "is properly speaking the science of man, because it consists in living and communicating in a humane and reasonable manner."[1] Thus the first postulate of *honnêteté* is that a person's relations with other human beings are rational. The key role is assigned to judgment. In La Bruyère we find transferred to persons rules that Descartes originally had applied to objects of thought or "truths": "The rule of Descartes, according to which nothing is to be decided about even the least significant of truths until they are clearly and distinctly known, is so beautiful and right that it must be extended to one's judgment of persons."[2] A relationship must be established between the individual who wishes to be judged favorably and the mind of a partner who claims the power to exercise judgment. The ideal of *honnêteté* is perfect reciprocity: the individual who submits to judgment displays his *merit,* and in return the clairvoyant "judicial faculty" of the chosen witness is presumed capable of giving that merit its due. Such a relationship is perfectly reversible: in an instant the person who submits to judgment can assume the role of judge, recognizing as merit the perspicacity of judgment exercised on himself. Roles are exchanged: an equality is established in which each person is by turns the *subject* who judges and the *object* judged. Thus Méré, who professed to teach *honnêteté,* organized his instruction around both the art of *recognizing* merit and the virtues *constituting* it. Being rational, both merit and the judgment of merit held the implicit promise of complete universality. Merit was universally recognizable by right-thinking reason, and, similarly, unclouded reason should be capable of recognizing merit in any guise: "So impervious to prejudice is the *honnête homme* of large views that were an Indian of rare merit and presumed capable of giving an account of himself to come to the Court of France he would forfeit none of his advantages; for no sooner does truth manifest itself than the reasonable mind is pleased straightaway to acknowledge its appearance."[3]

The fundamental structure that, according to the classical scheme, links one person to another through an act of judgment can be discerned beneath several stylistic variants. Sometimes the relation is articulated from the viewpoint of the person who proves his penetrating insight; sometimes it is presented from the standpoint of the person who is the object of others' feelings. One looks, the other exposes himself. The good judge is one who "sees the value of everything," who "esteems" and "approves good things." The *honnête homme,* should he display himself, must know how to "merit esteem" and "receive praise." The clear light of rational judgment thus appears to coincide with the whole range of social intercourse. Things can be appraised at their true worth, measured in terms of a stable schedule of values. Not a single gesture or word goes unremarked or underestimated. The disinterested integrity of the relationship is preserved. The moment a man "gives an account of himself" and is able to make himself understood, appraising judgment intervenes, establishing a relationship of approval or disapproval in which personalities count for less than the tokens they exchange.

But surely there is more to it than that. Everything changes the moment aesthetics begins to color moral judgment, when the operative terms shifts from "worthy of esteem" to "pleasing" or "agreeable," thus introducing an affective component into the relation between the *honnête homme* and his judge. The aesthetic criterion at first sight appears simply to shift the focus of judgment from one order of reality to another, from "good qualities" to "fine manners." But this shift, legitimized by ancient precedents (καλοκἀγαθία), has broad implications. The individual who knows how to "please" immediately becomes "amiable." The relationship is no longer one of pure judgment (or even of that mixed form of judgment that embraces not only a person's "virtues" but also the "attractive qualities" that make him or her agreeable). It is accompanied by a discreet act, by an appeal to which the response is an invitation to join a group or enter into an amorous relationship. When such an invitation is extended, the recipient is said to be "universally welcome" or "wanted everywhere." On the side of judgment the corresponding terms are to "receive favorably," to "prefer," to "wish well," to "seek out," or even to "love," terms that make explicit what the proprieties conceal. What has occurred is a whittling away of the objectifying distance that judgment of merit required as a precondition and that could be maintained only so long as no affective interest interfered. In theory, of course, the rational estimation of merit is by no means ignored when "taste" declares itself. Evaluation substantiates approval and welcome. Acknowledgment of "merit" is coupled with aesthetic "taste" for "fine qualities," with the expression of a "preference" for an "amiable" individual. Once different registers are superimposed in this way, however, their autonomy is hard to maintain. An affective component comes into play right from the start, even as the "disinterested" judgment of esteem is being made. The decision to judge and to be judged is already pregnant with all the virtualities of desire. Recognizing virtue is no doubt a pure form of moral judgment, but to make such a judgment known in the form of praise or of a declaration of esteem is already, in the terminology of the twentieth century, a "gratification" and, for the person who is the object of such a declaration, a "narcissistic gain."

What has become of the perfect balance, reciprocity, and reversibility that seemed to ensure rationality in the judgment of esteem? Judgment is no longer a purely intellectual act predicated on an assumption of universal reason. An element of desire, "polite" and sublimated though it may be, has come into the picture, and the exercise of judgment now finds itself unsettled by the prospect of a new kind of prize: pleasure.

This pleasure by its very nature accentuates the asymmetry between the partners. Only an individual can be welcomed, whereas the favor of a warm reception can be bestowed not only by an individual but even more often by a "circle" or "select society." The individual, in the position of a supplicant, waits to be approved and accepted. The pleasure of acceptance, one suspects, stems not so much from the persons granting the approval as from the sound of their words, from their grant of recognition, and from the self-esteem that such approval authorizes in the person to whom it is granted. It is the pleasure of being "singled out," of being judged worthy to belong to the circle. By contrast, the pleasure of those who "receive," "seek out," or "prefer" stems primarily from the exercise of choice, from the sentiment of being in a position to deny access, and from the application of criteria that require the supplicant to confirm, through his behavior and indeed his whole being, the circle members' idealized self-image. Only candidates who conform to that image, whose merits and qualities reflect the judges' own values, are accepted. A society defines itself as "select" through the very act of choosing its members. Once again the pleasure resides not so much in a "real" relationship with a person (an "object relation") as in the unfettered enjoyment of a well-adapted reflection. This model is exemplified by the Academies, where the relation of candidate to company is regulated by ritual.

The "commerce" that begins in this way is that of like with like. Difference is diminished to the point where it generates not conflict but complicity. This requires the exclusion not only of "bad company" but also of certain topics of conversation (money and wives, for example), "dubious" words, "base" expressions, and so on. The principle of selection is based on "rules" and "correct usage." Preference will go to those who make "elegant," "delicate" use of the resources of language. Their choice of the best words brings them to the attention of the "best society." Diction that is "pure" and "careful" is taken as an indicator of personal virtue.[4]

Marked in this way, language loses none of its referential function but takes on the additional function of characterizing its users, of representing them in a world of conventions where one must be careful to show only one's best side. It may be advantageous to substitute a text in one's place. A letter, for example, can serve as a proxy as well as a source of pleasure. And if a person writes a letter that sets people to talking, he will soon hear of it.

Now we can see all that is theatrical in our two roles: judging and being judged. If one can hide behind a written text, why not hide behind a spoken text, like an actor playing his part to perfection? Listen once more to Méré:

> It is a very rare talent to be a good Actor in life. It takes a good deal of wit and accuracy to achieve perfection . . . Always to do what must be done both in action and in tone of voice, and to perform so accurately as to produce the required effect—that, it seems to me, is the work of a master . . . I am convinced that there are many occasions when it is not a bad idea to look upon what one does as a Comedy, and to imagine that one is playing a character on the stage. Such a thought prevents taking things too much to heart and thus permits a liberty of language and action impossible when one is troubled by fear and anxiety.[5]

Again we see the concern to shun direct confrontation. By not taking things "too much to heart," by avoiding "fear" and "anxiety," one is likely to be protected from the wounds that reality might inflict if taken seriously. The skilled fencer parries every thrust. Wearing a fiction for armor, he feels invulnerable, untouchable. The Stoics long ago advocated such self-protective art as a way of "keeping countenance" in the face of adverse destiny. The trick was to play the role assigned by providence, to accede to and thus simultaneously transcend undeserved misfortune. Disgrace was not avoided. On the contrary, it was accepted, indeed almost embraced, because it allowed a man to assume the heroic role of the sage, steadfastly indifferent in the face of misfortune. But the course recommended by Méré was more likely to result in self-mythologization, in an aestheticized substitute world that allowed for greater freedom than the real world. The point of this avoidance maneuver was to neutralize real dangers, forces beyond one's control. In an age when the essence of theater was its capacity to foster illusion, to advise someone to be a "good actor" was to advocate deliberate deception.

We have come a long way from our original description of value judgment, which required both clarity of mind in the judge and sincerity in the person judged. True, the original definition of merit allowed for growth, for the acquisition of virtue, for the cultivation of qualities. A person's worth was always a product of education. But value was inextricably bound up with "truth." It could not be ostentatiously feigned or put on as a defensive sham. It submitted honestly to judgment, and judgment could therefore be trusted.

The situation becomes much more complicated when the desire to avoid unpleasantness (present from the beginning) develops to the point of encouraging a self-protective playfulness. There is no reason, however, why judgment should not remain unclouded. By tacit consent the parties may pretend to believe in pleasant appearances without being taken in by them. If the implications of the fiction are acknowledged by both sides, there is no danger of deception. Everyone is an accomplice, no one is a dupe.[6] Illusion answers illusion in the common conviction that nothing should be taken too seriously if one is to preserve the possibility of "agreeable commerce." The impossibility of accurate evaluation makes life easier: the moral responsibility of judging individuals according to their true worth no longer exists, leaving only aesthetic judgment, which applies to "looks" and "manners," delights in appearances, and takes at face value each person's self-indulgent approval of his or her own fictive image. Reciprocity, which had seemed to rest on the intellectual act of recognizing "real" qualities, becomes a transaction in which mythical perfections justify one another so as to sustain an equal level of narcissistic satisfaction in all.

Anyone who wishes to remain uncompromisingly vigilant must quit this game and reject it from the standpoint of the "moralist." He must denounce the scandalous blindness of all parties, the mischief wrought by vanity and amour-propre. In classical anthropology the term *amour-propre* covers much the same semantic range as the term *narcissism* in the mythico-scientific language of psychoanalysis. The *blessure d'amour-propre* is the classical equivalent of a "narcissistic injury." The image, that of a wound, is the same. Psychoanalysis, in appealing to the myth of Narcissus, puts on scientific airs while taking a hyperclassicist approach.

In the eyes of the moralist, amour-propre implies a capacity to be deluded. It is rooted in sin, that is, in the work of that great illusionist, the Devil. But amour-propre itself is not an illusion: it is the hidden "reality" that gives rise to and is sustained by a multiplicity of illusions. To name *amour-propre* is thus to ascribe an *origin* to illusion, a beginning as well as an *end,* for it is *through* and *for* amour-propre that illusions come into being.

No one has shed more light than La Rochefoucauld on the *transactional* nature of relations governed by amour-propre: "People usually give praise only to receive it" (Maxim 146); "To shun praise is to court it doubly" (Maxim 149); "When people speak well of us, they teach us nothing new" (Maxim 303). The exchange of praise only confirms each person's overestimation of himself. The rules of the game are tit for tat. What is traded back and forth costs nothing yet is the most priceless thing in the world: "praise," that is, a form of discourse in which a person is presented with an embellished objectification of his own image, a "narcissistic gratification." Praise would not possess this power but for its capacity to reinforce the self-delusion of amour-propre. "Amour-propre is the greatest of flatterers": this fundamental maxim appears second in all editions of La Rochefoucauld's work, that is, in a distinguished place of honor. Amour-propre grants itself the right to speak first among the voices of the inner life.[7] The words of others reach us only through the intermediary of this inner voice. For La Rochefoucauld, self-flattery is essentially the source of all pleasure: "We would experience little pleasure if we never flattered ourselves" (Maxim 123). In the most incisive manner the moralist denounces what he sees as the harm in this pleasure: the exchange of praise, though it appears to be reciprocal, actually costs us something: "If we did not flatter ourselves, the flattery of others could not harm us" (Maxim 152). "Flattery is counterfeit coin, which circulates only because of our vanity" (Maxim 158). Counterfeit currency, as Gide would recall, bears the stamp of our most hidden vice. Would we otherwise stand so complacently for a bargain in which we are always losers? Nothing here remains of the perfect symmetry or reversibility of the judgment of reciprocal esteem, nor is there anything in the way of mutual confirmation of merit.

Flattery

Flattery refers to a type of exchange in which what is given is not of the same nature as what is received. Instead of esteem for esteem, praise for praise, metaphor for metaphor, image for image, illusion for illusion, the exchange is of *words* for *favors*. The aristocratic salon was a unique setting. There, owing to the rules of admission, everyone was of roughly the same "condition." The purpose of love, according to a fiction that was not always easy to sustain, was to effect a mythical transfiguration of "mistress" and "lover," between whom the only apparent bond was one of word and gaze; carnal consent was perpetually postponed. Under these conditions, the ideal could be one of equal exchange in an atmosphere of shared narcissistic elation. The fiction on which this depended, however, was threatened whenever differences of rank and fortune, or the real difference between the sexes, came into play.[8] The moment refined speech—*l'art de bien dire*—was used alone to solicit favor or favors, an asymmetry appeared, equality vanished, and the law of self-interest supplanted or supplemented that of pleasure.

This asymmetry, incidentally, is what makes flattery so important: in classical discourse flattery occupies the place where a psychology of amour-propre comes together with a critique of wealth and power. The concept of flattery has a dual purpose: it makes possible a psychological treatment of certain aspects of social life and a social treatment of certain aspects of psychological life. Flattery simultaneously describes a type of discourse and a mode of circulation of wealth. Broadly speaking, it comes into play wherever a powerful or wealthy individual or person of superior rank maintains a "court" and attracts parasites and/or clients.

Here, too, of course, ancient models are not without importance. Aristotle observes: "The man who exceeds [in pleasantness] is an obsequious person if he has no end in view, a flatterer if he is aiming at his own advantage."[9] To see the ancient flatterer at work we have only to open Theophrastus's *Characters*: "Flattery is a shameful commerce, which is of use only to the flatterer. If a flatterer walks through the marketplace with someone, he says, 'See how everyone's eyes are on you. Such a welcome is accorded only to you. Yesterday you were well spoken of, and there was endless praise of you.'" Flattery knows no limits: it begins with a person's face and reputation and extends to his hairstyle, speech, children, kitchen, wines, residence, and portraits. Nothing about the master's person or possessions escapes praise. In its precise simplicity Theophrastus's text omits none of the aspects of individual character that stand permanently in need of "narcissistic reinforcement." Significantly, the flatterer begins by assuring the "master" that he is *seen* by all, and seen approvingly, and that everyone is *talking* about him and saying good things. The master is thus reassured not only as to the flatterer's personal opinion but also as to his own standing in the eyes of the world: he takes possession of a personal "essence." Since he lends himself to the operation of flattery and therefore consents to take words at face value, there is nothing to prevent him from blindly *overestimating* his own worth. Theophrastus's text does not discuss the response of the flatteree; it simply shows how easily flattery proceeds. It implies sucess: the flattered person sees himself as younger, more handsome, more powerful than he really is. In return for these illusory gains he is prepared to pay hard currency: an appreciable portion of his material possessions and pleasures. He may invite the flatterer to sit down at his table. In the context of the ancient economy the market translates to alimentary gain. The flatterer is a mouth that first speaks, then eats. The theme of the parasite's success in preying on the rich man was incorporated into the classical critique of wealth. If the rich man could be duped so easily, it could only be that wealth does not make for happiness, that money is nothing but a means of obtaining that most illusory of all possessions, the opinion of others and, in consequence, an illusory opinion of oneself. With all his treasures the rich man still is not satisfied so long as he cannot unreservedly approve of his own person. The obstacle that stands in his way is that part of physical nature (the contingency of the body) and of social nature (the judgment of others) which he does not control, and this obstacle the flatterer promises, through specious words, to remove: the rich man falls for an exalted image of himself, while the flatterer, who starts with much less, can content himself with the tangible reality of the feast. The rich man whose house fills up with flatterers may find himself picked clean, as Lucian's and Shakespeare's Timons demonstrate to an extreme degree. Opulence, because it goes hand in hand with dissatisfaction, falls prey to illusion, only to disappear and thus reveal itself to have been an illusion.

This classical asymmetry in the relation of flatterer to flatteree is if anything even more pronounced when the person flattered is not merely a wealthy individual but a tyrant or prince. With a tyrant the stakes are higher and the game is more dangerous: power itself is at issue, and favor translates into immense riches.[10] Flattery's favorite rhetorical device is hyperbole. It apotheosizes the prince, grants him satisfaction of all his desires, and removes whatever obstacles virtue might put in the way. All opponents of the master are delivered up to his wrath: flatterer and slanderer are one. Thanks to the flattery of the imperial senate and freedmen, Nero's sadism, with its narcissistic and infantile aspects, could treat the world as its plaything. Although the distance between the baseness of the flatterer and the apotheosized prince at first seems immense, it diminishes as the spectacle of the prince's "bestialization" progresses. Limitless gratification, made possible by flattering words, amounts to a triumph of animality. The prince's power, which initially seemed unlimited, is ultimately seen to be the slave of "infamous" pleasures. The moral of the story, as Tacitus conceives it, is that this "god" is the unfreest of men. Racine captures the Tacitean psychology marvelously when in order to show how a "monster" is born (and flying in the face of historical probability) he portrays a Nero forced to listen to the speech of the aptly named Narcissus:

De vos propres désirs perdrez-vous la mémoire,
Et serez-vous le seul que vous n'oserez croire?

[Will you lose memory of your own desires,
and will you be the only one you will not dare believe?][11]

The animalization of the flatteree is portrayed in somewhat different terms, using the vocabulary of ruse and capture, in these verses of La Fontaine:

Amusez les rois par des songes,
Flattez-les, payez les d'agréables mensonges.
Quelque indignation dont leur coeur soit rempli,
Ils goberont l'appât, vous serez leur ami.

[Amuse kings with dreams,
flatter them, pay them with pleasant lies.
No matter what anger fills their hearts,
they will swallow the bait, you will be their friend.][12]

The word *bait* takes us back to the "alimentary" theme, but as a metaphor for that which "feeds" the illusions of much-flattered kings. It is in terms of *appetite* that La Fontaine renders the prince's irresistible inclination to believe words that paint him as divine. The verses cited above are the last four lines of "The Lioness's Funeral," in which the flattering stag pretends to have seen the resurrected lioness prancing "among the gods."

Let us consider for a moment the etymology of the language of flattery. Animality is sometimes associated with the behavior of the flatterer, sometimes with the nature of the person who lends himself to flattery. Take, for example, *adulari,* a word that occurs frequently in Latin depictions of flattery: "Originally the verb seems to have had a concrete meaning, like the Greek σαίνω, and to have been applied to animals, especially dogs, which, to indicate pleasure or to flatter their masters, approached *(ad-)* with wagging tails."[13]

As for the word *flatter,* an incorrect etymology (which may have made flattery more acceptable to some) suggested that it originated "with the soft and flowing *fl* sound, which was used particularly to denote pleasant objects notable for their gentleness, especially the breath. Whence the Latin *flo, flare, flatum . . .* Properly speaking, the word means to whisper into the ear words that inflate a person's vanity, praise that stimulates amour-propre."[14] Etymologists today trace *flatter* not to the softness of the breath but to the Frankish **flat* (flat). (*Flatter* thus has the same root as the French hunting term, *se flâtrer,* to crouch down, cower, and as *flétrir,* to brand, mark with a stamp.) The original, intrinsic sense of *flatter* was "to caress with the flat of the hand" or "to pass the flat of the hand."[15] The verb originally conveyed a sense of caressing contact with a body, a light rubbing by the hand. (An even more animal version of the same idea occurs in another trope for reciprocal praise, *asinus asinum fricat.*) The flatterer is therefore a person able to emulate in language the hand's ability to explore a body, to arouse pleasure that reveals a body to itself. In passing from literal, direct action on the body to *figurative* action, however, flattery transfers pleasure from the body itself to a new domain, that of the *image* that appears in the mirror of language: the "ego," always in search of its identity, must find all or part of that identity in the words of the other. The flatteree discovers his image as he discovered his body, through the caress of the other. A painter who paints a "flattering" portrait merely transposes into the realm of the visible a semantic value that has already been extended from the tactile to the verbal. If flattery-as-caress reveals to the body that it can be its own "object," flattery-as-discourse first displaces the object into the glory of a name: renown.[16] Only later is the image finally objectified in the false mirror of a portrait or bust. From elementary pleasure to fatal trap: a whole range of meanings is thus encompassed by the various senses of *flatter* and *flatterer.* "To flatter the senses" is not to deceive but simply to please, to charm. Deception or illusion arises as the immediacy of the caress is lost and the flattered consciousness seeks to find itself, to see itself, in an image with which it aspires to identify.[17] Metaphorically this image, made available for illusory identification, is represented as bait, as a lure, as a trap, as a net into which the animal throws itself under the impetus of an instinctive desire of absorption: the object of flattery "feeds on" the image that is offered to it and thus falls "prey" to the flatterer. The range of meanings runs the gamut from the epidermic superficiality of pleasurable contact to the capture of the deceived animal, which in its eagerness to devour the bait fails to spot the trap.

Once *flatter* can be understood as a representation available to consciousness, the verb can take reflexive form. In French *se flatter* is an ambiguous verb: it can mean to flatter oneself, to delude oneself, to imagine. [*Il se flattait de réussir* means "he felt sure he would succeed." *Il se flatte que sans lui on ne peut rien* means "he flatters himself that he is indispensable," with a connotation, as in English, of self-delusion.—TRANS.] It is an expression of a project, but also of one's commerce with the fictive image one forms of oneself and one's capacities. If the lexicographers are right, the reflexive form first appeared in Corneille, who used it both to signify heroic resolution and to denounce the self-deluded overestimation of the liar and braggart. No one can prepare for or engage in action, we discover, except by first engaging in discourse with himself, and only the outcome of the action will show whether that discourse was "sincere" or misleading. Internalized flattery may be taken for the reflexive form of will—a will animated by the image of future glory or perfection. *Se flatter de*, to feel sure that, is the expression that gives narcissism its chance of glory, leaving it to the event (or effect) to distinguish between what is "solid" and what is "vain" in self-flattery's seductive image. If success proves elusive, that is, if the external objective is not attained, the reflexive action of self-flattery will have remained a prisoner of itself, captive of a hermetic pleasure. The term for this is "to cherish an illusion" *(se bercer d'illusions)*:

> De tous les animaux qui s'élèvent dans l'air
> . . . . .
> Le plus sot animal, à mon avis, c'est l'homme.

. . . . .

Cependant à le voir, plein de vapeurs légères,
Soi-même *se bercer* de ses propres chimères,
Lui seul de la nature est la base et l'appui,
Et le dixième ciel ne tourne que pour lui.

[Of all the animals that rise up in the air . . .
the most foolish, in my opinion, is man.
. . . Yet to see him, filled with insubstantial vapors,
cherishing his own chimeras,
he alone is the bedrock and foundation of nature,
and the tenth heaven turns only for him.][18]

It will come as no surprise that these lines of Boileau's are from the satire expounding the *topos* of man's inferiority to the beasts.

The fable of the fox and the crow in La Fontaine typifies the discourse of flattery.[19] Poet of the relations between hostile forces (and thus a political poet, barely disguised), La Fontaine found the perfect instrument in the fable, where animality symbolizes a world ruled by appetite and deception, by the ruses each creature employs to ensure that its desires will prevail over the desires of others. Everything in this particular fable is uncannily right: the height of the crow's perch, the name of the bird (*corbeau* in French rhymes with *beau,* a rhyme for the ears and an irony for the intelligence), the calculated progression in the fox's discourse from *joli* (pretty) to *beau* (beautiful) and from the familarity of apostrophe *(et bonjour)* to the hyperbolic preciosity of the conceit *(le phénix des hôtes de ces bois).* Everything is marvelously articulated. Note, for example, the rhymes in *age.* The first pair occurs in the narrative exordium: we are in the realm the poet proposes as "real," and what is real is the correspondence between *fromage* (cheese) and *langage* (language). The material prey above is thus opposed to the verbal power which, from below, will take possession of it. The second pair, *ramage* (birdsong) and *plumage* (plumage), occurs within the flattering discourse itself. These full rhymes do not oppose but rather stare at each other as in a mirror: the crow's perfection is richer still if its song matches its plumage. The illusion is based on a hypothetical doubling of physical attributes culminating in a positive affirmation of unique superiority: the "flattered" image having been created, all that is left is for the object of the flattery to *inhabit* that image in reality.

This metamorphosis, this imaginative moult, assumes that for one vertiginous moment self-consciousness is confused and internal perception of physical identity is lost. La Fontaine captures this moment, I think, in marvelous fashion in the first verse of the resumed narrative: "A ces mots, le corbeau ne se sent pas de joie" ["Hearing this, the crow was all rapture and wonder" (trans. Norman Spector); more literally, "The crow, out of joy, does not feel himself any more"—AUTHOR'S NOTE].

The illusory conviction of the "beautiful voice" is born and now asks only to be given the force of reality. The creature wants nothing more than to coincide with the image created by the language of flattery.[20] Opening the beak wide is not singing; it is the action of an *animal* enlarging its oral orifice. Attempting an impossible sublimation in song, the body reveals its ugly corporeal literalness. At the end of the series of four rhymes in *ois* and *oie*, the word *proie* (prey) phonetically sounds the crow's "real" cry and semantically designates the "real" object of the transaction, which falls into the flatterer's clutches. The famous moral "Apprenez que tout flatteur/Vit aux dépens de celui qui l'écoute" [Learn that each flatterer lives at the cost of those who heed] does more than disclose the economic (alimentary) interest dissimulated by the stratagem of a purely aesthetic mode of approbation. It does more than expose the material "infrastructure" that gave rise to the eloquent ruse of the compliment. And it does more than teasingly restore equity to the transaction by substituting for treacherous praise a true and profitable *lesson*, "well worth a cheese." By avowing the aggressive character of flattery, the triumphant fox deepens the wound: he disabuses the victim he has abused, thereby heightening the victim's humiliation.

The Return of Aggression

In its insistence on the harm done by flattery, classical discourse is fully aware of its implicit aggressive component. The flatterer, not content to extort some favor, speculates on the stupidity of the flatteree, who willingly allows himself to be stripped bare. The flatterer is not exempt from scorn for the victims of his deceit. La Bruyère frequently remarks on this: "He has a very poor opinion of men, yet knows them well, who believes it possible to influence those in high position by means of calculated caresses and long, sterile embraces."[21] Or again: "The flatterer does not have a very high opinion of himself or others."[22] The flatterer whose language "praises to the skies" feels humiliated at being forced to "crawl" and exacts vengeance by taking advantage of the "weakness" of others. Should they notice, should the flatterer prove overzealous or clumsy, contempt will be turned against him; he will become the target of aggression all the more dangerous because his adversary will be a man of power. The victim of flattery who cannot accept or identify with the idealized image of himself will for that reason wish to silence his adulator. In "La Cour du Lion" ("The Lion's Court"), the seventh of La Fontaine's *Fables,* the king condemns to death first the "speaker who is too sincere" and later the "insipid adulator."[23]

The inequality of power involved in the distribution of wealth and favor thus reintroduces a violence that the doctrine of civility had done its utmost to repress. When "speaking well" and refinement of language are used to please and acquire, an opportunity for deception arises: what civility would repress returns wearing civility's own mask. Danger, mistrust, contempt all deepen. Men make war beneath a cloak of courtesy: "What a monstrous thing it is, the zest and ease with which we mock, condemn, and despise others, as well as the wrath we feel against those who mock, condemn, and despise us."[24] The moralist, who knows the cost of satisfying amour-propre, is just as conscious of the pleasure "we" feel in doing injury as he is of the pain of being injured. The dupe may seize the initiative and counterattack with an onslaught of contempt: "chased after" like a beast, the man who occupies a high position may, if he avoids the trap prepared for him, counter with mockery: "I do not doubt that a favorite, supposing he has a modicum of strength and nobility, is often dismayed and disconcerted by the vulgarity and pettiness of the flattery, superfluous solicitude, and frivolous attention of those who chase after him, dog his steps, and attach themselves to him as his vile creatures; and that in private he repays such zealous servitude with laughter and mockery."[25]

The situation of the poet in a political and social order in which a writer's material resources still depend in large part on the good will of powerful men is therefore quite embarrassing. He is obliged to praise yet at the same time to defend himself against the imputation of flattery. He must reassure the person to whom he dedicates his work by declaring him too judicious to be flattered. It is within this system of *denial* that Boileau maneuvers, seeking to prevent what I am calling "the return of aggression" by repeatedly asserting his devotion to "truth alone," with the implication that such devotion rules out any abuse of hyperbole.[26] Praise affects humility in order to inspire confidence. With precaution that might well be characterized as rhetorical, it declares itself to be incapable of tampering with the truth or soliciting favor.

> Grand roi, c'est mon défaut, je ne saurais flatter:
> Je ne sais point au ciel placer un ridicule,
> D'un nain faire un Atlas, ou d'un lâche un Hercule;
> Et, sans cesse en esclave à la suite des grands,
> A des dieux sans vertu prodiguer mon encens.
> On ne me verra point, d'une veine forcée,
> Même pour te louer, déguiser ma pensée;
> Et quelque grand que soit ton pouvoir souverain,
> Si mon coeur en ces vers ne parlait par ma main,
> Il n'est espoir de biens, ni raison, ni maxime,
> Qui pût en ta faveur m'arracher une rime.

> [Great king, my vice is this: I know not how to flatter.
> I know not how to place a fool in heaven,
> or make an Atlas of a midget, or a Hercules of a coward;
> or, perpetual slave in the train of the great,
> to burn incense to virtueless gods.
> No one will ever see me force my tone
> and disguise my thought even to praise you;
> Great though your sovereign power may be,
> if my heart in these verses did not speak through my hand,
> no hope of wealth or reason or maxim
> could extract a rhyme from me in your favor.][27]

The idea of the "natural," which Boileau shared with the theorists of *honnêteté*, leads to a profession of absolute sincerity.[28] Yet doubt worms its way in and leads to a self-indictment that quickly develops into a more general accusation:

> Mais peut-être enivré des vapeurs de ma muse,
> Moi-même en ma faveur, Seignelai, je m'abuse.
> Cessons de nous flatter. Il n'est esprit si droit
> Qui ne soit imposteur et faux par quelque endroit;

Sans cesse on prend le masque, et quittant la nature,
On craint de se montrer sous sa propre figure.

[But perhaps, intoxicated by the vapors of my muse,
I deceive myself, Seignelay, in my own favor.
Stop flattering ourselves. There exists no mind so righteous
That it is not in some part an impostor and fraud.
One is always abandoning nature to don the mask,
afraid to show one's own face.][29]

A confession of this kind disarms scornful repartee in advance: the person to whom the epistle, along with the praise it contains, is addressed becomes the poet's accomplice in a common mistrust of human deviousness. This is a compromise position, an armistice in which flattery lays down its arms to forestall counterattack. Meanwhile, in the aesthetic order, we witness the birth of the classical theory of the reasonable compromise, which acknowledges the role of fiction and illusion but dreams of joining it with the "truth," thereby purging its noxious power:

Rien n'est beau que le vrai: le vrai seul est aimable;
Il doit régner partout, et même dans la fable:
De toute fiction l'adroite fausseté
Ne tend qu'à faire aux yeux briller la vérité . . .
La louange agréable est l'âme des beaux vers:
Mais je tiens, comme toi, qu'il faut qu'elle soit vraie.

[Nothing is beautiful but the truth: the truth alone is likable;
It ought to reign everywhere, even in fable:
The clever falseness of all fiction
tends only to make the truth luminous to the eyes . . .
Agreeable praise is the soul of beautiful verse:
But I hold, as you do, that it must be true.][30]

A fiction that is not deceitful but an embellishment of the truth: therein lies a possible justification of "dedicated" poetry, whose intention is that it be read without mistrust by the dedicatee and which claims not to succumb to the laudatory perversion of "fine style." Seeking another target, the aggressive energy thus contained turns against the world from which the poet has detached himself. Henceforth the poet's aggression will be directed toward the spectacle of flatterers and their dupes, of impostors and their undeserved success.

He exempts himself, along with the person to whom his work is addressed: together from on high they look down on the ignoble comedy. The targets of satire's laughter are to be found in a world of false brilliance, bedazzled inanity, painted faces. The "truth" toward which Boileau and many another writer turned is that of the face revealed when the masked is torn away:

> En vain par sa grimace un bouffon odieux
> A table nous fait rire, et divertit nos yeux:
> Ses bons mots ont besoin de farine et de plâtre.
> Prenez-le tête à tête, ôtez-lui son théâtre;
> Ce n'est plus qu'un coeur bas, un coquin ténébreux:
> Son visage essuyé n'a plus rien que d'affreux.

> [In vain with his grimace an odious clown
> at our table makes us laugh and diverts our eyes;
> his witticisms have need of flour and plaster.
> Take him tête-à-tête, take away his theater;
> he is nothing but a vulgar character, a shady scoundrel:
> Wipe his face and what remains is frightful.][31]

Courageous unmasking is the new form of judgment. Despite the tone of connivance with the recipient of the epistle, this judgment is clearly the act of a solitary consciousness that has detached itself from a world in which it no longer finds reciprocity. It breaks with the vanity of the present and takes refuge in its own certitude. Significantly, Boileau's critique of deceitful characters is immediately followed by a lengthy excursus (inspired by Juvenal and anticipating Rousseau's first discourse) in which a critique of luxury and civilization is coupled with "primitivist" nostalgia:

> Jadis, l'homme vivait au travail occupé,
> Et ne trompant jamais, n'était jamais trompé.

> [Once, man lived occupied by work,
> And, never deceiving, was never deceived.]

The animus, partially dictated perhaps by a commonplace tradition, is directed against a style of living, toward which the poet adopts the stance of disgusted witness:

> L'ardeur de s'enrichir chassa la bonne foi.
> Le courtisan n'eut plus de sentiments à soi.

Tout ne fut plus que fard, qu'erreur, que tromperie:
On vit partout régner la basse flatterie.

[Ardor for riches drove out good faith.
The courtier had no more private feelings.
Everything was mere disguise, error, or deceit:
Vulgar flattery reigned everywhere.][32]

The poet, who knows the difference between truth and falsehood, good and evil, discovers that the virtues he holds dear are not to be found in the world. For him that is sufficient reason, if not to withdraw from the world entirely, at least to take his distance, to speak from outside or above it. The act of judgment, which no longer has much hope of reward, now intervenes not to cement bonds of esteem but, in Hegel's words, to "characterize energetically the glaring discord between the real world and the principles of an abstract morality." In Boileau, of course, enough playful amenity remains to limit the satire to a literary exercise in which "sorrow" and "bile" must enter into combination with "laughter." For him there are limits that must not be exceeded; one must always "please." If necessary he can always "disavow" a satire or, when addressing the king, "learn to praise within satire."[33] The enemy of harmful masks and illusions carved out a habitable place for himself in the world as he found it. He actually set one cliché against another: that of the ubiquity of masks against that of the inevitable triumph of truth over sham and misleading ostentation:

Le monde, à mon avis, est comme un grand théâtre,
Où chacun en public, l'un par l'autre abusé,
Souvent à ce qu'il est joue un rôle opposé.
Tous les jours on y voit, orné d'un faux visage,
Impudemment le fou représenter le sage,
L'ignorant s'ériger en savant fastueux,
Et le plus vil faquin trancher du vertueux.
Mais, quelque fol espoir dont leur orgueil les berce,
Bientôt on les connaît, et la vérité perce.
On a beau se farder aux yeux de l'univers:
A la fin sur quelqu'un de nos vices couverts
Le public malin jette un oeil inévitable.

[The world, in my opinion, is like a vast theater,
in which people deceive one another, each one

playing in public the opposite of what he is.
Every day one sees people wearing false faces,
the madman impudently playing the sage,
the ignorant man pretending to be magnificently learned,
and the vilest scoundrel pronouncing on what is virtuous.
But no matter what mad hope they may nourish in their pride,
one soon knows them, and the truth shows through.
It does no good to paint one's face before the world:
in the end the shrewd public casts an unerring eye
on each of our hidden vices.][34]

The satiric poet is thus reconciled with the world, with the "public," and regains a function in the established order as the active agent of disillusionment, of the reinstatement of truth and reason. In compensation for this moral role he expects a tribute of recognition.

The hint has been sounded, however, of a more radical break, a more uncompromising attack on deception—and hence of a more pronounced solitude for the judgment that unmasks. Satire is turning "misanthropic." Misanthropy extends anger against the "vices of the age" to the whole "human race." Its attention is on present-day relations, on the way in which men live "among themselves," for which it places the blame on "human nature." Unlike Boileau, who is no longer read, Molière's *Le Misanthrope* (The Misanthrope) is too well known for me to cite here the lines of the play that evince a demystifying passion, a hatred of masks. Alceste speaks the language of satire, and when he denounces the calculating material interest that cloaks itself in laudatory civility, the tenor of his remarks is already familiar: politeness, far from implying respect for others, is a feigned caress; the flattery of some meshes perfectly with the vanity of others, which thrives on illusion; bounties, promotions, and positions always go to scoundrels in disguise. Alceste is an outraged spectator of a play in which people are vulnerable to the schemes of the dishonest because they begin by deceiving themselves.

But the heart of the matter is elsewhere: the comedy in this play is aimed at the champion of sincerity, at the "demystifier" himself. This was clearly perceived by Rousseau, who began his intellectual career by demystifying the aggressiveness hidden beneath the mask of courtly manners: Rousseau knew full well that he was Molière's target, that Alceste was himself before the fact. The "lesson" of *The Misanthrope*, for anyone who pays close attention, is to disclose the trap hidden in any attempt to unmask. Molière in fact reveals the unseen contradictions that force the enemy of the world unwittingly to become part of the world he denounces. Professing disinterested love of the truth, vituperating against the seductive embraces and protestations of respect that feed the illusions of amour-propre, Alceste himself exhibits his own amour-propre, ever more sensitive and difficult to please: "I want to be singled out." The virtuous censor is a disappointed Narcissus. Molière makes him no less haughty than the rest.[35] What blindness makes the enemy of masks love Célimène, the woman whose mask is the most perfect of all? Molière introduces a devastating contradiction between the conduct and principles of this man who wants to be immune to illusion. In order to bring his conduct into harmony with his principles he must make a definitive break and retire to the "desert." But the very extravagance of those principles makes them suspect. Molière clearly implies that they are a product not of serene judgment but of an effervescence of bile, or, more precisely, of atrabile: Alceste, with his "black humor," is a melancholic in the technical sense in which the word was used by contemporary physicians.[36] Molière attributes to Alceste the temperament that Boileau ascribed to himself and that he apparently considered part and parcel of the satiric institution.[37] Black bile and the desire to write are one and the same:

> . . . Depuis le temps que cette frénésie,
> De ses noires vapeurs troubla ma fantaisie.
>
> [Since the time when that frenzy
> disturbed my fantasy with its black vapors.][38]

Contemporaries did of course believe in the existence of a generous melancholy, which was associated with contemplation, ecstatic visions, and poetic inspiration. The medicine of humors posited a range of intermediate conditions between an excess of atrabile and a proper mixture with blood, yellow bile, and phlegm. If atrabile dominated the other humors, the resulting "distemper" could take either of two forms, hot or cold, furious or languid, and each form exhibited its own range of intermediate conditions. Alceste's "black sorrow" could range from despondency to rage. His melancholy found its adversity in the salon and not, as in the case of Quixote or Hamlet, beneath the vast night of the world. Within the confines of the well-to-do bourgeoisie in which Molière places him, however, Alceste is at war with himself and others, and that war is bitter enough that his final solitude bears the marks of a defeat: a tragic interpretation is permissible. Alceste is nonetheless a laughingstock because all along he has been the plaything of his "temperament."

The spectator of *The Misanthrope* is invited to believe that the "critical" protest against the mores of the age, against social corruption, and against the fundamentally animal interest dissimulated in the transactions of flattery stems from a physical disorder and not from an act of moral reasoning. Alceste professes a disinterested love of truth, a passion for sincerity, but that passion is subverted from within by the ineluctable workings of the humors. The rebel subjectivity takes a stance of violent opposition to the world as it is yet fails to achieve independence; it remains subject to the laws of physical necessity. The object of Alceste's attack lies within himself. He claims to have seen through the fraudulent illusion of "proprieties" but falls victim to the impassioned illusion that Hegel called "abstract morality."

This can of course be seen as a "conservative" stratagem aimed at defusing or discrediting an intolerably acerbic critique of the success of scoundrels and of the political system that has put them on top. In this way the most mordant of satires can make its statement, reach its audience, and still count for nothing, since the person making the statement is the victim of a distemper of the humors, himself the butt of ridicule. The rhetorical device is the familiar *argumentum a persona:* there is no better way of discrediting dangerous opinions than to declare the person who holds them to be "out of his senses." Some activists hold that psychoanalysis proceeds in the same way: it discredits rebellion by calling it neurosis and brands pathological what it sees as "maladapted" behavior, which allegedly ought to be hailed as the manifestation of liberating impulses. But this type of criticism, whether directed toward Molière or toward psychoanalysis, is in essence theological: it implies that, since the existing order is fundamentally wicked, any act of refusal or insubordination bestows a sanctifying grace, and that to criticize such an act in any way is to abet evil.

Regardless of whether the force that drives the sworn enemy of flatterers and masks is the narcissism of amour-propre or the effervescence of a "black humor" or both together, classical discourse invites us to ask if the energy of demystification does not itself stem from a "mystifying" source. It encourages doubt: he who *speaks* of sincerity is not exempt from error. He who laughs at a world in which fraud everywhere lays its traps and snares risks falling into traps both within himself and in the world. Consciousness cannot attain a place safe from passion, error, and illusion no matter how much it repudiates or withdraws from the world. It always runs the risk of being taken by surprise, and the more it thinks it has seen through the false tinsel that impresses men of commoner stamp, the more vulnerable it becomes. Alceste can readily make out covetous desire, ambition, and hatred even when hidden beneath the most exquisite manners. But in order to combat an illusion of civility that covers up violence instead of repressing it, Alceste himself becomes violent and therefore "unsociable." Everything must therefore begin anew. Society must be reinvented. The only alternative is to accept the illusion, to master it, to exorcise it if possible, and to consent in full foreknowledge to the ubiquity of doubt in human relationships. To do so means tolerating weakness and complacency, but better that than to break all contact with one's fellow man.[39]

3

~

EXILE, SATIRE, TYRANNY: MONTESQUIEU'S *PERSIAN LETTERS*

Most fiction writers in the period when *Les Lettres Persanes* (The Persian Letters) first appeared pretended to be nothing more than editors: they claimed to deliver to the public, for its instruction, secret memoirs or other interesting papers that had come into their possession. It was easy to invent some pretext to explain how the material had come their way. Montesquieu was no exception. His preface, or rather anti-preface, set the tone. He took even more precautions than usual, claiming to be the adaptor of the letters but refusing to satisfy the curiosity of the reader by giving his name.

The author hid or pretended to hide himself from view. Anticipating criticism, he ducked. Such amusing letters would not be deemed worthy of a serious man. The work might seem out of keeping with the "character" of the magistrate. Better to let the letters speak for themselves, without anyone to vouch for them. Anonymity would in any case make them more provocative.

Protecting the author was not the only purpose of choosing anonymity. His identity could not have been much of a mystery to the regime's efficient police. The desired effect involved not so much the author as the very structure of the work.

To pretend to publish documents received from Persian travelers along with secrets allegedly obtained without their knowledge was above all a way of claiming the authority of real life, of bestowing upon the work—the day's novelty—the prestige of stemming from outside any literary tradition. It was to deny, if only in a flourish of style, that the work was a work of the imagination. Through vigorous effort the actual existence of the characters and their adventures had to be made *credible*. The author therefore worked hard to eliminate all trace of his invention. Montesquieu, pushing the technique to an extreme, eliminated the author himself. The classical system of verisimilitude encouraged blotting out the author in favor of "historical" texts of which he claimed to be the indiscreet repository.

In the case of the *Lettres Persanes* the effacement of the writer has the effect of bestowing apparent autonomy on each person who wields a pen within the text. Presented as an anthology of letters, the book has as many authors as there are letter-writers. Noble travelers, eunuchs, wives, distant friends, and dervishes all have their turns to speak. The work is one of plural consciousnesses, of diverse points of view and beliefs. Like stage heroes, the characters thus allowed to express themselves in writing can have their own subjectivity and give free rein to their passions and prejudices. They can plead their case, in good or bad faith, with arguments inspired by their mood of the moment.

The reader, however, quickly comes to feel that these plural voices and subjects, each right within the confines of his or her own private reason, are fronts for a hidden but omnipresent author, who confronts passion with passion, dogma with critique of dogma, in such a way that the perception of *relations* leads imperceptibly to the triumph of reason. But this triumphant reason is not the possession of any of the characters, not even the reasoner Usbek; rather, it manifests itself wherever there is clear and intolerable contradiction. Thus the reader comes to sense a clear need for a principle of non-contradiction, of universality.

Contradiction is present everywhere. It exists first of all within the world of the Persians, the writers of the letters in the collection. It also divides the competing religions, whose rival dogmas are so similar that they cancel each other out. Montesquieu, moreover, is keen to use the visitors' astonishment to demonstrate that contradiction also exists in the West between observable facts and alleged values, between actions and pretexts for action.

Yet while Montesquieu is determined to turn the conflict between incompatible contradictions into a victory for reason, he is also determined to see that the reader's pleasure emerges victorious from the battle. From the liberties the translator-adaptor admits to having taken with the original to the piquant, at times blatantly comic form in which the most serious critical ideas are couched, every effort is made to ensure that the reader will never be bored: the "pleasure principle" is all-powerful yet never in conflict with the insistence on reason. Pleasure requires that things be prepared and dressed up to our liking. It also requires, as Montesquieu points out in his *Essai sur le Goût* (Essay on Taste), variety, surprise, and asymmetry. The hidden author, who pretends simply to be reporting on arguments that have been brought to his attention, is able to bestow these literary virtues on his work.

The travelers are interested in everything. Everything they see is food for thought. The principle of variety is thus satisfied, and the work is further enriched by the diversity of female voices and by the great castrati "arias." Diversity, carefully prepared, creates surprise. To cite just one of many possible examples, consider the totally unpredictable way in which the gossipy letter about Suphis's marriage (letter 70) immediately follows Usbek's letter on the attributes of God (letter 69). The reader's mind has to change gears quickly, and the slight shock of incongruity that attends these rapid shifts is not without pleasure. (Compare the predilection of rococo decorative art for changes of scale.) Surprise, moreover, is the state of mind that the tone of the *Letters* is continually meant to suggest, at least at the beginning of the book. The author tips his hand as he apologizes for his audacity: "These barbs *(traits)* are always linked with the sentiment of surprise and astonishment." The reader feels a *stab* of pleasure, an unexpected sting that causes both pain and laughter. And the best justification for the satirical barb is the pretense that the West is subject to the scrutiny of Eastern eyes, of men from beyond the Danube less uncivilized than the virtuous Peasant.

Montesquieu shifts responsibility for his irreverent observations from himself to the ostensible translator and editor of the letters and from the translator to the Persians themselves. The transparent excuse of blaming the most mordant barbs on the Persians' surprise justifies uninhibited frankness. Insolence benefits from the immunity accorded to outsiders unfettered by bonds or obligations of any sort. (This had been the function of the court jester and was still, in Montesquieu's time, the function of Harlequin. Later it would be the function of Voltaire's Ingénu and Beaumarchais's Figaro.)

The fiction thus serves as a filter. It requires writing about only those things that an Oriental observer would have found striking or singular. Montesquieu thus obliges himself to say nothing without a certain verve, to write nothing that does not indicate a considerable ignorance on the speaker's part regarding the object under consideration and that does not abolish that ignorance by some unforeseen oblique thrust that goes straight to the heart of the matter. Propositions and ideas that would have been nothing more than echoes of classical morality or superficial perceptions of the new philosophy if expressed in the form of an academic treatise or discourse (at which Montesquieu often tried his hand in youth) were given *electric charge* by attribution to the Persian letter-writer. For the ostensible writer these ideas are *discoveries:* they are being thought and written down for the first time. The writer who formulates them clearly feels the pleasure of surprise. The fiction of the Persian traveler thus rejuvenates not only the external objects that he sees and describes (as the Turk in the book of Marana and several others did earlier) but also the truths that he reveals. Certain important principles, already well known, indeed too well known, yet forgotten, could thus be recalled by the device of ascribing them to a newcomer who sets them down in the very instant his mind grasps them. This manner of presentation gives rise to a style: the usual subject matter of an essay is reduced to a letter or a series of letters. This justifies brevity, omission, cutting, elimination of preambles and excurses. The Persian letter-writer can go straight to the heart of the matter without getting bogged down in the secondary issues that a Western writer would inevitably have had to face. The only objections that occur to him are those of the Muslim religion, toward which it costs him little to declare his obedience in an ornate rhetorical style that affords ample scope for leisurely poetic diction. The vivacity of *new* ideas is thus counterbalanced by the sinuous formulas of an *inherited* language, of which the French reader knows, from the Introduction on, he will find an imitation adapted to his taste. The Persian fiction thus forces Montesquieu to write differently, and indeed better. This felicity of style is felt in the speed with which the axioms of reason are established as well as in the ornamental parody of oriental rhetoric.

*　*　*

The *Lettres Persanes* had no author and no epistle dedicatory (hence no privileged reader). But the obliteration of names did not end with the title page and introduction, and its function was not simply defensive. The reader quickly notices that none of the individuals whom the Oriental visitors meet in France have names. Anonymity concerning everything to do with the West is an integral part of the literary system of the work. The only individuals named in the 161 letters of the collection are the travelers, their friends, their wives, and their slaves. Names belong to the realm of the Oriental fiction. As for the West, only countries, cities, and institutions are named: Venice, Italy, France, Paris, and even Pontoise; Parlement, the Académie Française, and so on. It is virtually an absolute rule that no Frenchman is named or even identified by a fictional or authentic Christian name and/or patronymic. Louis XIV, Philippe d'Orléans, and John Law, though clearly identified, are designated only by function or origin: "the king of France," "the regent," "a foreigner" (or "the son of Aeolus"). Apart from these outstanding figures, the Persian visitors fail to perceive the identity of any individual; they remark only the typical forms of behavior and speech that identify the individual as the representative of a group. The eclipse of the person's name reveals his social role, function, and generic behavior. The "sociological revolution" that Roger Caillois rightly perceives in the *Lettres Persanes* consists in omitting the distinguishing features of individuals in order to bring out their membership in distinct social subgroups: whether corporations such as the parlements and other courts, religious groups such as the Capuchins or Jesuits, or the personnel and habitués of public places such as theaters, operas, and cafés or hospitals (such as the Quinze-Vingts and Invalides); whether distinguished aristocrats, women, journalists, or scholars. Montesquieu clearly wanted his Persians to focus nearly all their attention on the various groups that could be observed in the capital. When there is a portrait of an individual, the singular always implies a plural. The personage portrayed invariably belongs to a category sufficiently important to be catalogued: alchemist, geometer, judge, fop—none is alone of his kind.

Is the book therefore an exhaustive survey of French society? Hardly. Certain types of work are not represented. Aside from a mention of the liberal arts, almost nothing is said about the professions. Psychological and emotional types are also left out, because Montesquieu reserves the emotional register for the East. It is there that we find jealousy, anger, and dissimulation. A sharp line divides the world of feeling, the Orient of the soul, from France, whose multifarious surface activities Montesquieu satirizes through the cunning curiosity of the Persians.

In France the Persians make no commitments, form no attachments, and need meet a person only once to paint his portrait. All their encounters are first encounters, which immediately yield definitive descriptions that brook no appeal. The French reader is thus encouraged to adopt the foreigner's point of view to examine his own country and its customs; meanwhile he is initiated into the innermost secrets of bodies and souls in far-off Persia. He is taken out of his own setting and indiscreetly introduced into an absent world. In the erotic imagination Persia is close, while observant irony makes France, anonymous and caricatured, a remote continent. The equilibrium of the *Lettres Persanes,* the often neglected relation between the book's Western and Eastern parts, reflects a mathematical equivalence: if one multiplies the geographical distance by the moral distance the product is the same for the Persian plot (in which the soul's secrets are entrusted to letters) as for the sweeping critique of French society (which reveals only external *appearances*).

The Persians are struck by the extraordinary. They know nothing of the "connections" among ideas, customs, and practices. Their *astonishment* not only filters but also fragments what they see. Montesquieu's sociological reduction therefore does not lead to a global view of French society. Instead it yields a discontinuous, fragmentary apprehension of a series of surprising sights. Each letter presents some new object of curiosity, some new fragment of the social whole. The fragmentation of time required by the epistolary form accords well with the fragmentary description of social types and institutions. Nearly every missive, including even the salvos of letters on Troglodytes, the depopulation of the globe, and books, establishes a boundary, signaled by a final period. Within letters, moreover, each paragraph tends to start briskly and end with a barb. Even the sentences are structured like well-tuned machines, which is why they frequently give an impression of corseted elegance, of grace pinched in at the waist. Successive instants stand out, each substantial in its own right and full of renewed surprise. The "ignorance of connections" that Montesquieu attributes to his Persians leads them to perceive illogicality and inconsistency in France and among Christians. The assumed texture of Western beliefs and institutions is unwoven strand by strand. Close connections do not exist or are no longer effective. Seams are exposed as imaginary (or, in Valéry's word, "fiduciary"), so that an unbiased observer can perceive the holes and gaps in the fabric. Not only does Montesquieu take apart, analyze, and "deconstruct," but he perceives, in all simplicity, separate things as separate. *Non sequiturs* become apparent.

It should come as no surprise that in writing a book whose characters fail to perceive connections, whose vision in a sense generates discontinuity, Montesquieu should have felt the need to balance things out. He therefore has his characters evolve so as to "take their place in a chain that binds them together." He creates a "secret chain" tying together the various themes of his book. The discontinuity that emerges everywhere is subdued by a writer bent on establishing a new continuity in the construction of the book itself.

Hence discontinuity is not synonymous with disorder. Working, like the anatomist, *a capite ad calcem,* the Persians first turn their curiosity on the king and the pope. They begin with the crucial question of political and religious power, with power's psychological basis in the credulity and vanity of "peoples" and its economic basis in wealth and the manner of its acquisition. But when they move on to other levels of society, the Persians do not methodically examine the inner workings, such as they are, of French institutions. They focus instead on disruptions and accidents, on the most glaring sources of discord and scandal: actresses, coquettes, Don Juans, gossips, financiers and nouveaux riches, casuists and confessors, newsmongers, academicians, quarrelsome men of letters: in the astonished eyes of Usbek and Rica, a long list of types and groups appears useless and parasitic, not to say downright harmful to the social order.

The suppression of names, the mythological mask, makes it possible to mention things that if named would have been taboo. (It is as if taboos applied to the names of things more than to the things themselves.) But how could things be designated without being named? By being described. If one pretends not to have a word with which to name a person, object, or type of behavior, one has no choice but to define the thing in terms of recognizable characteristics. Homer becomes "an old Greek poet." A rosary becomes a string of "little wooden beads." These periphrases are riddles, easily solved by the reader who knows the unmentioned names. Montesquieu's ruse is to mimic the Persians' lack of vocabulary for things of which they are ignorant. This voluntary aphasia requires him to talk around things, sometimes by rediscovering their tangible qualities, sometimes by introducing foreign equivalents for French words: priest becomes dervish, church becomes mosque. This makes it possible to refer to things that it would have been dangerous to name directly; it also desanctifies previously sacred objects and persons by capturing them either in secular language or in the vocabulary of a rival religion. Once the linguistic code in which religious conviction is inscribed has disappeared, nothing remains but a description of ritual actions deprived of the justification provided by the "chain" that previously linked ceremony to dogma and "other truths." An act of faith, a belief *(croyance),* is reduced, in its external appearance, to a credit *(créance)* without evident collateral, just as the credits of John Law's Compagnie des Indes Occidentales, once considered substantial, proved to be worthless. Thus a papal bull is nothing but "a grand script *(écrit)*" (letter 24), and Law's promises are contained in a "poster *(écriteau)*" (letter 142). The parallel exposes the foolishness of those who allow themselves to be taken in. The job of criticism, of demystification, is to do away with prestigious names to demonstrate the emptiness of things invested by language with a deceptive prestige. Outside the code that consecrates them these things are no longer worthy of respect. Their effects on the mind can be termed magic, fraud, charlatanism. Usbek, who is an enemy of masks even before he sets out on his journey (letter 8), strips off a series of masks and false faces in conjunction with his partner Rica: among the things he exposes are the honors sold by the king of France, the lies of coquettes, the deception of "the man who represents," the nouveaux riches who ape the nobility, and the impostor "disguised as the Persian ambassador." Counterfeit is everywhere, and the Persians, whether naive or enraged, denounce it by stripping objects of faith of their respectable names and leaving them only the scant surface available to naive perception. The book ends with the spectacle of a bankruptcy.

Yet as severe as the foreign visitors' explicit or implicit criticism is, as glaring as Western recourse to camouflage and hypocrisy may be, compared to Persia Christian France is a country where people go without veils, where women dare to appear in public, and where, in select company, gaiety prevails. As for honor, which Montesquieu even before *L'Esprit des Lois* called the "principle" of the monarchical state, it was of course often a hilarious thing, yet its public and private consequences were less dreadful than were the consequences of the fear that reigned in Persia, Muscovy, China, and wherever despotism triumphed.

Usbek, Rica: the Persian characters' names are carefully coined as if to convey a sense of character and temperament. The aesthetics of variety, which calls for difference and nuance, requires that the Persians, while similar in background, differ in sensibility.

Rica is the younger traveler, the one who laughs *(rire),* sometimes derisively *(ricaner):* the very syllables of his name thus convey to the French reader a sense of his gaiety and freedom. We learn from the fifth letter that he has left an "inconsolable" mother at home in Persia, but this does not seem to concern him unduly. Since he has no wives and no harem to administer from afar, he can give himself body and soul to the new world, which receives him with intermittent curiosity (letter 30) but whose manners, banter, and mocking tone he quickly adopts. Nothing prevents him from yielding to the present moment, savoring its surprises, or recounting it in such a way as to relive its pleasures. He does not expound; instead he tells stories, he vividly describes sensations. His style is well suited to satire and bawdy tales (as in letter 141, the "Story of Ibrahim and Anaïs").

Rica merely complements Usbek, who plays the leading role. From nothing but the two vowels of his name—vowels not found in the name Rica—we know, from the effect of contrast, that Usbek is a somber, meditative man. The letter *k* at the end of his name augurs ill for the end of his story: it can be read as an emblem for the punitive cruelty to which he is driven by his rage at being cuckolded. Rica and Usbek are constructed according to the traditional theory of temperaments. Rica is sanguine, juvenile, and jovial; Usbek is melancholic, with all the attributes of "generous" melancholia: imprudent truthfulness, hostility toward masks and false appearances (letter 8), nobility of spirit, reflective detachment, and a taste for speculation and grand abstractions, yet relatively slow in thought (letter 25), inclined to prolonged suffering, and rather cold and indifferent in love (letter 6), though this does not protect him from the rages and torments of jealousy. The character of Usbek, as Montesquieu imagined it, can be many things at once: the mature man who has a hard time getting used to a foreign environment; the reasonable Muslim who, as he gains experience, gradually discovers affinities with deism and Cartesianism; the putative author of moral and political miscellanies that Montesquieu plucked from his satchel of contributions to the academy of Bordeaux; and the morose master of an unruly harem.

The use of differences and contrasts in the invention of Persian names is actually wider than I have suggested. The vowel *o*, not found in either Usbek or Rica, is the property of proud Roxane and of Solim, the eunuch who serves as executioner. Usbek's other wives, less heroic than Roxane, are designated by the sinuosity of the letter *Z*, which had exotic associations in rococo literature: the initial letter of their silky names implies bodies subject to sensual anxieties and deviousness behind an appearance of obedience. Zachi, Zéphis, and Zélis are interchangeable and all but confounded in the ardor of their appeals and reproaches to their absent master. The slighter, thinner sound of Zélide, the slave, suggests her sometimes rather too close attachment to the various mistresses who compete for her services. Somewhat set apart from the others, Fatmé has a name that suggests opulent beauty and ardor. All the names mentioned thus far, male and female, consist of two carefully balanced syllables. Double names, signifying dignity, are bestowed on the two venerable dervishes, Méhémet-Ali and Hagi Ibbi.

Usbek appears initially on his way to a world other than his own (letter 1). He does not tarry in Persia. His pilgrimage to Qum is a mere formality. He hastens toward knowledge. The importance of distance and time in the *Lettres Persanes* can be seen from the very first letter. Isfahan, Qum, Tauris, Erzurum, Tokat, Smyrna, Livorno, Paris: space is clearly delineated, marked off in plausible segments that might well have corresponded to the stages of an actual journey and of course following an itinerary opposite to that of the Western travelers whose accounts Montesquieu studied. For Usbek the pursuit of knowledge implies mobility, openness to the outside world, and above all refusal to submit solely to the authority of his native "culture." "We were born in a flourishing kingdom, but we did not believe that its boundaries were also the boundaries of our knowledge or that we ought to be enlightened exclusively by the light of the Orient." Usbek renounces

"Iranocentrism" in all its forms. Does it follow that the true center is henceforth in Paris and the West? Not at all. Note that Usbek's words are perfectly reversible. This reasonable Persian's resolutions force the French reader to make a similar, reciprocal decision. Hasn't the time come to venture outside the territory illuminated solely by the light of the Occident? One way to do this, perhaps the first that would occur to anyone interested in undermining confidence in inherited custom, is to imagine the surprise of a visitor from another continent. The bold questions of the intruder who has set aside the prejudices of his own land pose a challenge to Eurocentrism. (Note, by the way, that only European culture has run the risk of casting doubt on the righteousness of its own standards, that only Western intellectuals have suspected that other cultures might have an equal claim to legitimacy.)

In fact, the geography of the *Lettres Persanes* encompasses more than just the two opposing capitals, Paris and Isfahan. It includes cities, some of them stopping places along the route of travel, in which various correspondents and informants reside: Ibben in Smyrna, Usbek's nephew Rhédi in Venice, Nargum in Moscow, Nathanael Levi in Livorno. News arrives from Spain, Sweden, and Tartary. English politics are abundantly represented. At the end of the book, when Usbek examines the reasons for the depopulation of the globe, his letters are not an unwarranted excrescence on the body of the work but a natural outgrowth of an expansive curiosity interested in all humankind, over the entire surface of the globe and the whole extend of recorded history: China, the Americas, Africa all come under scrutiny. The geographical scope of the *Lettres Persanes* is extremely wide. Usbek's letters on global depopulation (113 to 122) have an ironic counterpart in Rica's letters (133 to 137) on his visits to the monastery library. The description of the *orbis terrarum* is complemented by that of the *orbis litterarum*: all the sciences, all the histories, all the literary genres constitute a literary synthesis *(totalisation)* that is the bookish counterpart of the geographic synthesis.

By the end of the *Lettres Persanes* the reader has been treated to more than just a comparison of Parisian mores with those of Isfahan. He or she has completed a mental trip around the world. All the most illustrious historical sites have been visited: Judaea, Greece, Rome. Confronted with the relativity of the absolutes that people have revered in different times and different places, the reader becomes aware of the need to rise to the level of the universal and experiences the awakening of a cosmpolitan concern for the happiness and prosperity of all peoples. The groundwork has been laid for the triumph of the universal concepts of Reason, Justice, and Nature, in whose name local fanaticism and regional prejudice can be condemned.

One cause, one motive, hides another. Montesquieu is a past master at the art of recognizing multiple determinations and complex causalities. He knows that in the realm of human actions, determinism is plural. The depopulation of the globe, for example, is the result of many physical factors as well as many moral ones.

Usbek's journey is no different. The reason stated for it in the first letter, "the desire to know," initially seems both necessary and sufficient. But the moment he crosses the border from Persia into Turkey, Usbek tells his friends from Isfahan "the real reason for [his] journey" (letter 8). At the court of Persia he had demonstrated rather too much zeal for "unmasking vice." As a result he not only failed to gain "the favor of the prince" but also aroused "the jealousy of the ministers." In serious danger and in fear for his life, he initially chose retirement. "I pretended to feel a great devotion to the sciences, and out of my pretense came the real thing." But to save his head he eventually chooses exile. Although the desire to know is a sincere motive and not a mere pretext, the need to escape tyranny is at least equally important. The conflict between the ethical requirement of truth (unmasking vice) and the hypocritical violence of the courtiers is the fundamental political determinant of the work. Had the threat been less serious, there would have been no journey to France. This background justifies the many letters on justice, government structure, and the like. They are written by a person whose senses have been steeled by circumstance.

The role of deception in this fictional structure is considerable. Montesquieu pretends that the letters are actually written by a Persian, while the Persian, in order to save his head, pretends to be a scholar (and soon develops a real taste for the part). Montesquieu dons a Persian disguise to foil the censorship of the Church and the powers-that-be; Usbek, as if mirroring this choice, flees his homeland to escape the wrath of an angry despot manipulated by his ministers. Usbek's journey can be seen as a hyperbolic reflection of Montesquieu's incognito, each invoking the other. Similarly, the oriental despotism that threatens Usbek's life can be seen as a hyperbolic image of the French monarchy's abuse of power. Montesquieu, whose distrust of centralized absolute monarchy is well known, constructs the *Lettres Persanes* by slipping an image of the despotic Orient beneath that of France. The resulting superimposed portrait brings out the risks inherent in the "orientalization" of the French monarchy. Writing of Louis XIV Usbek says: "He was often heard to say that, of all the governments in the world, the two that pleased him most were that of the Turks and that of our august sultan—such was his admiration of Oriental politics" (letter 37).

At the end of the work, when Rica tells of the Paris Parlement's banishment to Pontoise, he briefly describes the function of the parlements, which, put simply, is to tell the truth. This is exactly what Usbek had tried to do on his own, thereby endangering his life. Comparison brings out the parallel. In letter 8 Usbek says: "As soon as I recognized vice, I fled; but then I went back in order to unmask it. I took the truth to the very foot of the throne, where I spoke a language previously unknown. I baffled flattery and astonished both the idol and its worshipers." Letter 140 discusses the parlements of France: "These corporations are always odious. They approach kings for one reason only, to tell them sad truths, and while a mob of courtiers invariably portrays the people as happy under the king's government, the parlements confound this flattery and bring to the foot of the throne the baleful and tearful plaints confided to them." The striking parallelism reveals Usbek as the alter ego of Montesquieu the *parlementaire*.

The image of despotic government, with its Turkish, Muscovite, and Japanese models, among others, would again form a menacing background in the *Esprit des Lois,* where the unlimited power of a single individual reigning through fear is presented as the end of a degenerative process to which all societies are subject. Montesquieu repeatedly warns against this danger: "Most of the peoples of Europe are still governed by custom. But if, through a long abuse of power or a great conquest, despotism were to establish itself at some point, neither custom nor climate could resist; and in this beautiful part of the world human nature would suffer, for a time at least, the insults to which it is subjected in the three others" (*Esprit des Lois,* 8.8). Usbek makes much the same point in letter 102: "Most of the governments of Europe are monarchical, or, rather, are so called: for I do not know if there has ever been a genuine monarchy there. It is difficult in any case for a pure monarchy to subsist for long. Monarchy is a violent state, which always degenerates into despotism or republic."

Usbek left Persia in the grip of fear (the principle of despotism). The question of violence is thus the source of the entire work. Even if avoided or checked for a time, violence can suddenly rear its head either through a caprice of the prince or in a rebellion of his subjects: "Even with the unlimited authority our princes possess," Usbek observes, "if they did not take precautions to protect their lives, they would not last a single day. And if they had not in their pay countless troops to tyrannize their subjects, their empire would not last a month" (letter 102). The disasters suffered by the Turks, mentioned in letter 123, stand as a warning. Paradoxically, however, the best example is the disaster that befalls Usbek's harem.

As he leaves his homeland, Usbek cannot refrain from a backward glance. Although he describes in his first letter his pleasure in crossing boundaries and seeking knowledge in far-off lands, his second letter, addressed to the first black eunuch, reveals a very different concern: to maintain an unchanging order in the private domain over which he is sovereign. Usbek too has troops in his pay. He has his guards, not around himself but around his most precious possessions: his harem, his women. In his domestic life he is therefore an Oriental despot. Even though the prince's treatment of him has made him aware of the evils of absolute power, Usbek holds a power of life and death over his wives. He wants to be obeyed. He tells his eunuchs and his women that they are to tremble when they open his letters. Himself a victim of terror, he exercises terror in turn. Though he boasts (in letter 1) of being the first to give up "the pleasures of a quiet life," he has not given up his absolute possession of his wives, whom he continues to rule, body and soul, from afar. He attempts to retain power over their minds by reminding them of their duty and by issuing veiled or overt threats of the consequences should they forget.

Usbek's absence lasts for nine years, long enough to enable Montesquieu to explore, in the shadows of the seraglio, all the variants of frustrated desire, all the ruses of compensation, all the versions and perversions of substitute pleasure. Since the inmates of the harem are not free to roam like their husband, they flee in another way. They take refuge in the imagination, hoping that one day the figments of their imagination may come to life and consummate their adultery. And perhaps they did not have to wait nine years. In the first letter written by the first eunuch (letter 9) the rumor of a "young man" is mentioned. Is it the same young man who makes a fleeting appearance in two subsequent letters (147 and 149) and who, surprised in Roxane's arms, is beaten to death by the eunuchs (letter 159)? Montesquieu leaves it to the reader to decide.

Montesquieu fashioned his Usbek as an enemy of masks, a traveler enamored of rational knowledge, yet also a true representative of Persian domestic customs (based on detailed information provided by Chardin, Tavernier, Ricaut, and others). He therefore created a character with two sides, or, rather, with two functions: to observe Western institutions and to be the nervous master of five wives and seven eunuchs, a tyrant who never questions the validity of his rule. Usbek is therefore both the author of judicious descriptions of France (addressed to his male friends) and the jealous husband who issues imperious commands to subjects over whom he wishes to perpetuate his domination though he is all too well aware that his absence has made them potential rebels to his rule. Thus Montesquieu, not content with having created two contrasting characters in Usbek and Rica, makes Usbek himself a man with two faces, one turned toward the anonymous generalities of French society, the other involved in a private intrigue in which the characters have names. Did this choice make Montesquieu's hero less plausible as a character? Was it asking too much to have him bear the burden of two such contradictory roles? How could the serene observer of the French monarchy and of world history turn, from one letter to the next, into the anxious recipient of letters from Isfahan, letters to which he responds in terms of mounting alarm and violence? How could the detached observer turn into the ferocious husband, fiercely jealous of his possessions?

Readers, however, must accept the character as written. More than that, they must try to understand Usbek's contradictions, and not merely by blaming them on the inconsistency of an author keen to combine the pleasures of fiction with the more substantial attractions of philosophy and moralizing. The very ambiguity of Usbek's contradictory, "divided" character requires an intepretation that fully justifies

Montesquieu's decision to make him as he is. The contradiction between Usbek's intellectual predilections and his private behavior is significant; it is an object lesson. His appeal to universal reason is sincere and heartfelt (as can be seen from the views he expresses about justice, truth, virtue, and many other topics), yet he remains in some respects the product of a particular civilization and moral code, a man educated and shaped by a historical tradition. His viewpoint, particularly in regard to what used to be called *mores,* is not disinterested but conditioned. Montesquieu may have wanted to bring out this often neglected truth: that one must inevitably adopt a particular point of view even if one aspires to transcend the particular, even if, by confronting incompatible orthodoxies in the hope of annihilating them, one seeks to promote the triumph of what is generally and universally human. To transcend the relative we must begin with the relative. A melancholy tyrant in thrall to Oriental prejudices about male honor, Usbek aspires to a philosophy that seeks, in good faith, to free itself from all prejudice. He comes to understand that the king's or the pope's claims to absolute power are unfounded, yet he has no doubt whatsoever about his own claims to domination: his eunuchs are nothing more than his "base instruments," and their job is to guard "the most beautiful women of Persia," who are treated as mere possessions, as a "precious trust." The wives are captives, just as the subjects of the king of Persia or the tsar are captives. They need their master's permission to leave the kingdom (letters 8 and 51). Usbek has suffered, and he makes his women suffer. There are inherited certainties he has not yet learned to question. We must not make the mistake of thinking that when he speaks to his wives of order, virtue, and nature, he is deliberately using deceptive language designed to subject them to permanent subjugation. As Usbek uses them, these abstract words awaken no doubt about the legitimacy of "domestic servitude" but in fact constitute its justification; the self-deception involved is perceptible only to the Western reader, not to Usbek. Montesquieu intends this as yet another warning: there are words so grand, so abstract, or so vague that the things they denote on different occasions are inevitably dissimilar. The word *nature* can mean anything. In Usbek's mistaken reasoning nature is what dissuades Parisian women from adultery: "When it comes to taking the final steps, nature rebels." In the protest of rebellious Roxane the same nature justifies adultery: "I reformed your laws on the model of Nature's." Rebellion strips the oppressor of his moral and philosophical vocabulary and turns it back against the hated master.

The relative that Usbek is incapable of seeing in relative terms is exemplified by "domestic government," the customs and laws that govern relations between the sexes. It is significant that, for the individual caught up in it, this archaic realm, in which custom is more constraining than any deliberate policy, is the area that reason has such difficulty making sense of. While Usbek's reflections on law and history immediately (with the story of the Troglodytes) attain the loftiest of viewpoints, the realm of sexuality remains subject to an ancient system of authority. It is virtually a separate order, an irrational and violent unconscious that underlies the quest for rationality and nonviolence, something counted out: but Montesquieu is well aware that what was counted out in the past must be reckoned with in the long run. If, having shown that no one can escape the need to begin from a point determined by history and education, Montesquieu had also wanted to show that the philosopher who would reflect on society and history must also consider his own situation, must not exclude himself from critical examination, he could not have improved on the structure of *Lettres Persanes,* in which the final disaster may be viewed as the punishment for blindness and ignorance. Roxane's revolt, in the final letter of the collection, against traditional domination and Koranic (hence particularistic) custom, which Usbek had tried to enforce *in absentia,* also invokes universal values, and with greater justice than Usbek. Dying yet triumphant, Roxane associates the words *delights, pleasures, desires* with the authority of "Nature." The imminence of death reveals the prospect of a universally liberating reason. Usbek was able to formulate and live by only some of its precepts. Roxane's courage in the face of death attests to the legitimacy of what we nowadays call (somewhat ponderously) the libidinal impulse, which she numbers among humankind's inalienable rights. Until this final letter true love had not found a place in the *Lettres Persanes,* except perhaps in the story of Aphéridon and Astarté, which tells of the love between brother and sister. This absence is no accident, for it permits the objective observation, close scrutiny, and ironic distancing that are hallmarks of the book's style. The nameless, almost ghostly youth who is taken from Roxane's arms and beaten to death by the eunuchs stands for true love, whose part in the drama is shadowy but indispensable and whose immolation leads to the death of the principal characters.

In Usbek desire is nonexistent. Easy satiety has put it to death. Speaking of his wives, Usbek writes to his friend Nessir: "It is not that I love them, Nessir. In that respect I find myself utterly insensitive and without desire. In the many seraglios I have lived in, I have anticipated love and used it to destroy itself" (letter 6). The ground is thus cleared for reflection, particularly on human society. "I spend my life in examination" (letter 48). But the fissure thereby instituted between the pleasure of seeing and the disused domain of the flesh is not radical enough to count as asceticism. When a man who thinks he can no longer love nevertheless wishes to remain master, his thoughts are no longer free. They dwell on his poorly guarded wives, and he suffers at the loss of a possession though it scarcely means anything to him. He succumbs, in other words, to that retrospective and unhappy form of reflection, jealousy: "Out of my very coldness comes a secret jealousy that devours me" (letter 6). The spirited enthusiasm of intellectual curiosity, which discovers and describes a new world, is counterbalanced by morose reflection, which dwells on lost possessions and which, through torment and worry, aggravates the loss. When Usbek announces his imminent return to Isfahan in letter 155 to his friend Nessir, he says that he expects to remain a prisoner of jealous reflection even after he has returned to the arms of his wives. Reflection thus becomes a source of woe. The effects of the division that it brings about are as baleful as the violence that, when inflicted on the bodies of eunuchs, "separated them from themselves" (letter 9): "I shall immure myself behind walls more dreadful for me than for the women held within. I shall take all my suspicions with me. Their eagerness will hide nothing from me. In my bed, in their arms, I shall enjoy nothing but my own anxieties. My jealousy will find food for reflection in the most unsuitable of moments. Refuse of human nature, vile slaves whose hearts have been closed forever to all the sentiments of love, you would cease to bemoan your own condition if you knew the unhappiness of mine" (letter 155). This last letter from Usbek is the mirror image of the first (and the eighth): the book began with a centrifugal movement, toward knowledge, beyond the reach of mortal enemies; it ends with centripetal nostalgia ("happy is he who . . . knows no land other than the one in which he was born") and resignation ("I am going to bring my head back to my enemies"). The reversal is complete when we read Roxane's letter. When we first meet Usbek, in letter 8, he is an implacable enemy of masks, a demystifier able to penetrate to the heart of French credulity. In the end we see that he himself is the victim of illusion, the dupe of appearances. It is he who has been too credulous, who has allowed himself to be taken in by a mask: "But for a long time you had the benefit of believing that a heart like mine was obedient to you. We both were happy: you believed that I was deceived, and I deceived you" (letter 161). Roxane's letter, which reestablishes the reign of absent love and announces the violent end of the eunuchs, gives the whole book its unexpected yet necessary *point* in the form of an angry revenge. (The rhetorical figures used to accomplish this combine antithesis and hyperbole, antithesis to mark the reversal, hyperbole so that a single letter can, by its intensity, stand up against the hundred and sixty letters that precede it). We are consequently forced to *reread* the entire book in search of a blind Usbek who, from an impossible distance, preaches an inhuman virtue to his wives and complacently ascribes Roxane's behavior, which we now know to have been motivated by hatred, to her virginal modesty (letter 26). Already he is lost, having ceased to see clearly. In his philosophical justification of suicide (letter 126) we find a premonitory excuse of Roxane's final act. The ironic dimension of the *Lettres Persanes* becomes fully apparent only on second reading, after we have been enlightened by the sudden revelation of what had remained hidden for so long.

Everything reverses itself in the *Lettres Persanes*. Reversal, the *style à renversement*, is Montesquieu's favorite image for tyranny and its consequences. Tyranny is power carried to excess (hyperbolic power), and its very extravagance inevitably results in a sudden swing toward the opposite excess. Speaking of despotism in general without realizing that he is also describing his "domestic government," Usbek writes: "I even find the prince, who is himself the law, less in charge than anywhere else" (letter 130). Yet he had read an analogous remark, couched in a series of antitheses, in a letter from Zélis about the impossibility of subduing a consciousness that refuses to be treated as an object: "In the prison in which you keep me I am freer than you are. Were you to redouble your efforts to hold me, I would take pleasure in your anxiety" (letter 112).

Because the eunuchs are instruments of tyranny, they are the embodiment of paradox. Men but no longer truly men, they are reversal incarnate. They are its pivotal locus. To the first black eunuch Usbek writes: "You command them and obey them. You blindly carry out all their wishes and by the same token enforce the laws of the seraglio . . . Bow down before the women who share my love, but also make them aware of their utter dependence" (letter 2). The eunuch wields awesome power but by delegation, and he can never forget that the very act that raised him out of nothingness also destroyed his virility. He thus experiences to the full the contradiction of a self-negating power, of a physical negation that is transformed into power. The loss inflicted by emasculation is counted as part of a transaction. Radical alienation is supposed to find compensation: "Tired of serving in the most arduous of employments, I hoped to sacrifice my passions in favor of tranquillity and fortune" (letter 9). But did the transaction fulfill this wish? Were material and moral benefits (fortune and tranquillity) acquired in exchange for sexual wholeness (passions)? Far from eliminating all desire, the physical inability to seduce and possess a real person gives free rein to vain desires, regrets, and fantasies. Power, once gained, makes the separation that was its condition painful to bear: "Woe unto me! My mind made me see the compensation, not the loss. I hoped that I would be delivered from the pangs of love by my inability to satisfy them. Alas! The effect of the passions was extinguished but not the cause, and, far from being relieved, I found myself surrounded by objects that stimulated them constantly" (letter 9). The eunuch suffers because, though dependent on the forbidden object, he can now relate to it only in perverse ways: terror, intimidation, punishment. Suffering endured is transformed into suffering inflicted. A notion of *reciprocation,* of turning round and round, appears, significantly, in this context, as the reversal repeats itself indefinitely, like a machine that runs on indefinitely:

These same women, whom I had been tempted to look at with such tender eyes, I now envisaged only with the severest of looks . . . Although I guard them for another man, the pleasure of making myself obeyed fills me with secret joy. When I deprive them of all they have, I feel as though I am doing it for myself, and I always experience an indirect satisfaction . . . Yet I am forced to endure infinite unpleasantness, and every day these vindictive women try to pay me back for what I do to them: they have awful ways of turning the tables. Between us there is an ebb and flow of empire and submission. (letter 9)

For the eunuch the only compensatory path to revenge is that of intelligence and ruse. By developing a highly specialized science—by *penetrating* the women in his safekeeping with his gaze and by sowing division and slander—he can consolidate his power over the harem and even impose his will on his master. The chief of the black eunuchs claims to have learned this from the person who schooled him in the secrets of the art:

> With this great teacher I studied the difficult art of command and learned the maxims of inflexible rule. I studied the heart of woman. He taught me to take advantage of women's weaknesses and not let their haughtiness surprise me . . . He possessed penetration as well as firmness. He read women's thoughts and ruses. Their studied gestures, their false faces could hide nothing from him. He knew their most hidden acts and their most secret words. He used one to know another, and he was wont to reward the slightest confidence. They went to their husband only when called, and the eunuch called whomever he chose and focused his master's eyes on the one he designated in reward for the revelation of some secret. He had convinced his master that it was best for discipline that he should be allowed to make this choice. (letter 114)

A remarkable mechanism of domination was thus established in the heart of servitude by combining the psychology of unmasking with a proven technique of rewarding informers. The master himself was not far from becoming a tool of this sophisticated administration, this *corps intermédiaire* indispensable to the maintenance of discipline and order. "In the seraglio I am, as it were, in a tiny empire, and my ambition, the only passion left to me, is a little satisfied" (letter 9). This comparison, formulated by the first eunuch, suggests that while "domestic despotism" is described accurately according to the available sources, it can also be interpreted as an eroticized trope for political despotism as it existed in the East and as it threatened to overtake the French monarchy. Absolute power could maintain order only with the aid of a class of privileged yet frustrated, authoritarian yet alienated functionaries who derived a substitute for erotic pleasure from lording it over the people. These functionaries had the power to mete out favor and disgrace, reward and punishment, to the individuals over whom they wielded authority. They enabled the despot to impose his will from afar. Guided from afar, they served him as propaganda agents and organizers of amusement: "See to all their pleasures, provided they are innocent. Deceive their anxieties. Amuse them with music, dancing, delicious drinks. Persuade them to gather often." It has been rightly remarked that the police and propaganda agencies of the seraglio-state establish an order that is in constant danger of collapse.[1] And should seniority (that great bureaucratic principle) confer power on an unfit eunuch the risk to the master is obvious. An example of this comes at the end of the *Lettres Persanes,* when the weak and credulous Narsit allows indiscipline to get out of hand. By the time Solim is invested with authority it is too late, and his harsh repressive measures only spur further rebellion. The situation has reached a stage where nothing the eunuch-functionaries can do can stem the disaster. Revolution is inevitable. The fiction thus incorporates a political theorem, a hyperbolic metaphor of the danger that threatens France. A general theory of power has been tested in the laboratory of the erotic imagination.

Montesquieu was increasingly concerned with the nature and form of power in relation to the time and place in which it was exercised and with the consequences of the way in which decisions were made and carried out under different systems of government. Given today's widely held belief that the only kind of injustice is economic, we would do well to take a fresh look at Montesquieu, for the effects of political injustice are incalculable.

Montesquieu likes to measure the cost, the profit or loss, of every situation. The cost of exercising absolute power from afar, as Usbek wants to do, is that of terrorizing the eunuchs who will in turn terrorize the women of the harem. Not only is the price heavy, but it still leaves the master in a state of anxiety. What is the value of security acquired at such a price? What is the value of professions of obedience obtained under such circumstances? If the women of Persia owe their beauty to the disciplined life they lead, and if that discipline requires constant surveillance by the eunuchs, is the cost not too high? In such a society the educators are slaves, hence lame educators. A Frenchman asks Usbek: "What can one expect of an education received from a wretch who stakes his honor on guarding another man's women and prides himself on the vilest of human employments?" The moral problem is compounded, moreover, by a demographic problem whose seriousness Usbek does not hide: "A man who has ten wives or concubines is not overdoing it if he has an equal number of eunuchs to guard them. But so many men dead from birth represents an incalculable loss for society. The risk of depopulation is great" (letter 114). The price is surely heavy, far too heavy when judged in the light of reason. And what is the cost to the Troglodytes of concerning themselves solely with their self-interest? The community cannot survive: selfish anarchy brings on collective destruction. Usbek's letters on the depopulation of the globe total up the heavy cost of Christian monasticism, of banning divorce, of Muslim polygamy, and of colonial conquests. The price is reckoned in terms of human lives, but in arithmetic, quantitative terms. When Rhedi (anticipating Rousseau) worries about the harmful effects of the arts and sciences, Usbek for once responds by arguing that, all things considered, the price paid for technical progress is warranted. The positive balance is measured in the numerical language of economic prosperity.

In evaluating any policy, it is necessary to weigh not only the consequences of that policy but the cost of putting it into effect. Action equals reaction, to put it in Newtonian terms. Montesquieu is determined to keep all this in mind in evaluating the cost of each form of government (and particularly despotic government). The *Lettres Persanes* was a way of putting the tyrannical model to the test and showing that over the long run it cannot endure. The notes for the *Esprit des Lois* contain the following sentence, which curtly but powerfully sums up the results of the experiment: "The kings of Europe must not expose themselves to the despotism of Asia; the minor pleasure of expressing irrevocable wishes is purchased at a cost so dear that no sensible man can covet it."

For all its varied registers, fragmentary letters, and reversals, Montesquieu's book in the end has only one theme and pursues only one question: If man wishes neither to suffer nor to inflict division, and if, though rejecting the disorder and violence that are the necessary consequences of liberating individual appetites, he nevertheless rejects an oppressive order that can be maintained only at the cost of amputating part of his flesh and his intelligence, how should he organize his life and his institutions? To what authority should he appeal if he wishes to sacrifice neither his desire nor his reason? Usbek's answer, in a book in which all external authority is challenged, is an act of faith in an innate and universal norm opposed to all external injunctions: justice is at once an "inner principle" and a "conventional relation" between things. It is a yoke that we cannot throw off without abandoning our wish to survive. Authority resides in man's conscience, duly qualified judge of the moral as well as the physical world—but only on condition that it knows where its certainty ends. Although that authority is inseparable from our idea of a just God, it is an idea that originates in man himself. Man's task is to calculate the balance of forces required to assure a rationally perfect government capable of achieving "its goal at the lowest cost" (letter 80).

Usbek, who states these principles and who knows that men become unjust the moment they "prefer their own satisfaction to that of others," is incapable of perceiving his own injustice. He exemplifies a persistent separation between the domain of reflection and that of action. The example was embarrassing and would remain so. It cannot be evaded by asserting that the separation in question is a flaw inherent in "idealist" philosophy, as if a disparity between actions and principles were a failing of idealism alone. Montesquieu is actually well aware of the importance of material factors in history, not the least important of them being the preference that men give to their "own satisfaction." Through the many voices of his book, some of them frivolous, others grave, he urges us to recognize a need that we are not yet close to knowing how to satisfy: the need to bring ideas into harmony with actions within the context of a liberating rationality, the need to reject tyrannies that imprison peoples and mutilate individuals. We are as far from fulfilling this need as Montesquieu. It is therefore well worth our while to reread the *Lettres Persanes* with some care.

4

❧

VOLTAIRE'S
DOUBLE-BARRELED MUSKET

I. On the Philosophical Style of Candide

A narrative? Of course. But even more, the simulacrum of a narrative, a parody, a pared-down reflection. The fiction in *Candide* is a caricature of fiction, an exaggerated version in which all generic conventions are combined: those of the adventure story (of Hellenistic origin), of the picaresque novel and—even more hospitable to the improbable— the fairy tale. If forced to give *Candide* a genealogy, I would begin with Lucian and Petronius and continue by way of Rabelais and Cyrano. The events in *Candide*, and even more the manner in which they succeed one another, do not simply defy all probability; because they are so disparate they clearly do not require the reader's confidence, they leave the reader free: apparent deaths, unexpected discoveries, ultra-rapid concatenations, fabulous lands, boundless riches—these elements tell us that we are not to pay serious attention to the story itself. They also point toward extremely well-known literary models, which, through caricature, are deliberately transformed into a parable whose moral is to beware of all morals.

Is this a game, then? Certainly. But a game in which none of the situations being parodied lies outside the reality of the present: in Germany there are war, massacre, and rape; in Portugal heretics are being burned; in America savages eat their captives; in Paris gamblers cheat and prostitutes rob unwary travelers. In many respects Candide is merely a front, the minimal identity that must be conferred on a character whose primary function, as he goes about his business, is to encounter the world and thus reveal it as it is.

Candide is thus a stew, a grab-bag, and not just because of the dizzying succession of episodes. I am thinking even more of the mélange of self-annihilating fiction and inescapable truth, of the unstable amalgam of narrative whim and obtrusive ambient violence. The variety of content parallels the obsession with the ubiquity of evil. Wherever one turns, senseless violence crushes freedom. The implausible rapidity of Candide's journey turns it into a more or less comprehensive review of the countries of the world. The narrative economy of time hastens us from place to place and allows us to accumulate experience of stupidity, intolerance, and tyranny. Because the narrative is not realistic, the earth can be traversed in any direction and horrifying realities can be witnessed one after another, yet none can be called into doubt or attributed to the author's fancy.

Voltaire, whose method is systematic mockery and whose invincible hero narrowly escapes every peril he faces, is thus able to describe the wickedest of abuses. His strategy is one of repeated denunciation. The writing is full of cuts, ellipses, litotes, of all varieties of *subtraction,* for indignation would have inflated the style, drawn out the accusation, taken time to mark the "truth" of the sentiment. Emotional time is thus abbreviated; feeling is accelerated. By deliberately "playing false," Voltaire avoids the dangers of sentimental excess and misdirected eloquence. The wickedness of the world stands out all the more sharply, all the more tenaciously in a climate of dryness that leaves no room for either pity or consolation. None of the atrocities in *Candide* is invented. Voltaire gives us a documentary, somewhat simplified and stylized to be sure but still a catalogue of atrocities about which any interested European could read in the gazettes. In *Candide* we encounter, in the mode of fiction, what is perhaps the first example of something that has become commonplace in the West today as a direct consequence of the diversity of sources of information: the perception of all of humankind's woes by a suffering sensibility whose nervous system extends across the surface of the globe. Voltaire trembles with the world's suffering. He knows, or claims to know, all the perpetrators of injustice, all the banners that hide oppression. He catalogues them, compares and contrasts them. He is too intelligent to denounce the wrongs of just one party. He sees the same crimes committed by rival princes, by antagonistic churches, by "civilized" peoples and by "savages."

*　　*　　*

If the sinuous line, with its suggestion of unexpected caprice, is one of the typical figures of rococo taste, the travels of Candide, the old woman, and Cunégonde are its clearest possible transcription onto the map of the world: chance, desire, and repeated persecution are responsible for such endless detours that in the end nothing seems a detour and no direction is preferred over any other. Yearning for the new and "piquant," another characteristic feature of rococo taste, is also abundantly present.

Playfulness, parody, satire, denunciation of the world's violence, philosophical inquiry: these are the ingredients of what is not only a composite work but a text without precedent, a text whose only relation to earlier compositions is by design polemical. *Candide* combined all the formulas for producing a spicy saga: the diversity, unpredictability, and scandalousness of its adventures, the unpredictability of its itinerary, the succession of surprises, the telling brevity of each episode. The result was that ultimate stimulant, novelty. The visit to Pococurante's library (chapter 25) provides an opportunity for reviewing older models, for casting a retrospective glance at the entire literary institution, of which the disgusted booklover speaks with nothing but disdain. Literature appears to have reached a dead end. *Candide* is a supernumerary production, an inventory of the past, a post-literary work: it stands outside literature, outside philosophy, and mocks them both. Of course it can do nothing but propose another literature and another philosophy in their stead. "It is a great pleasure," Cacambo says, "to see and do new things."[1]

It is not difficult, however, to see *Candide* as an exemplar of an age-old type: the comic narrative (or pantomime) that employs the utmost virtuosity of style to conjure up a character of the utmost clumsiness and incompetence.

So many critics have remarked on Voltaire's exuberant, light, unclouded style and superb use of repetition, contrast, and ellipsis that further comment is superfluous. Syntactic patterns are varied at will to reinforce or disrupt the equilibrium of the sentence. This stylistic mastery, which does little to conceal itself and indeed displays its resources so boldly, is not by itself a source of comedy. What makes it comical is that so much mastery is expended on the subject of lack of mastery: the story of a guileless boy who cannot master his own fate and so proceeds from misfortune to misfortune. His adventures, like those of so many clowns, begin with kicks in the behind. We laugh while he cries, sighs, and falls into despair.

The style of the narrative, supremely *active*, calculates and governs all its effects, the chief of which is to represent its opposite by depicting Candide, almost to the end of his adventures, as *passive* and amazed.[2] Although Candide at first speaks and acts at the behest of others, he witnesses the disproportionate consequences of his words and deeds. He is always being carried farther than he hoped or anticipated. The narrator slyly allows us to witness the misadventures of a person who is easily duped and whose fate is not in his own hands, except at the end of the story, which seems to mark the beginning of a stable and active period. Candide is like those stage characters or circus clowns who endure repeated failures, choreographed as carefully as a ballet, only to amaze us in the end with an astonishing recovery. The sight of such technical mastery employed to mimic the plight of a hapless victim is pleasantly unsettling.[3]

Candide, however, is not so much a victim as a person whose desire fails to attain its object. He loses what he wants or finds only some degraded remnant bearing little or no resemblance to the vivid image of his desire. Although he is no longer persecuted after his visit to Eldorado, he remains fundamentally frustrated: deprived of Cunégonde's companionship, he has only one thought, which is to find her again. But when he finally does, she has become so ugly that he recoils "three steps in horror." Gilles and Pierrot are swindled in the same way: circumstances conspire to deprive them of what they believe they are on the verge of possessing. They come away with empty hands and heavy hearts. For Candide, all that will remain of the Westphalian paradise is the memory of a furtive caress behind a screen (a caress, please note, that is enjoyed at Cunégonde's behest). This "tempting" fruit, offered willingly, will remain forbidden. It is destined to pass through many hands, and of the most brutal sort: violated, stabbed, sold, kept, humiliated, profaned in every way, Cunégonde will eventually be redeemed by Candide, but not before being branded with the stigmata of physical and moral evil, the imprint of a wicked world and the mark of destructive time. The woman whom Voltaire presents as the cause of Candide's peregrinations—his expulsion, wandering, and search—is a figment of those perishable qualities, freshness and youth.

Desirable as long as she is absent and because she is absent, Cunégonde regained is nothing but an ugly shrew with whom life would be intolerable were it not for the garden to be cultivated, the productive flight into labor. Candide is duped by love: foremost among the ideals the narrative seeks to destroy is the myth of passion. Candide, the object of an experiment, is motivated by an illusion that vanishes at the precise moment when the beloved object ceases to be an image and a name and becomes a "real" person. The comedy lies in making the long-delayed possession an occasion of intensified disappointment.

A clairvoyant, omniscient, free writer and a naive, clumsy, long-deluded hero subject to the law of violent men: the relation of author to hero is one of irony. This is indicated, right from the start, by the frequent use of the figure known as irony according to the narrow classical definition: destructive antiphrasis, the use of words in a sense opposite to one's intended meaning, as in "a *beautiful* auto-da-fé."

What is the function of irony here? It is not to assure the author (and reader) of a facile victory over the ignorance of a schematic hero. Nor is it to exalt the writer's consciousness of a freedom that stands above all finite reality. Voltaire does not aspire to the disengaged freedom of "romantic" irony, whereby spirit attempts to guarantee its own separate realm. The irony in *Candide* is an offensive weapon. Aimed outward, it carries on reason's battle against whatever usurps the authority that only rational thought ought to possess.

The authority of theology and its successor, metaphysics, can be seen to be usurped once the difference between the world as it is and the world according to optimistic theodicy has been demonstrated. As much as *Candide* is a critique of contemporary reality, it is also a critique of smug theory's abstract assertions about the nature of the world. In their singularity the events of the journey contradict Pangloss's lecture on point after point. It is scarcely necessary to allow the Anabaptist Jacques and the Manichaean Martin, proponents of opposing philosophies, to have their say. The *facts* alone educate Candide. The result is illustrated by the difference between the first chapter, in which Candide listens respectfully to his master's peroration, and the last, in which he cuts him off. Voltaire's irony conspires with the world's riposte to the euphoria of the system. The "point" and "edge" of ironic diction gleefully add hyperbolic ferocity to the cruelty of reality. So energetic is the refutation that it is hard to distinguish its vehemence from the unconscionable violence that is also one of Voltaire's targets. Mutilations, castrations, and amputations contradict, in living flesh, all the affirmations of a perfect Whole. Pangloss loses an eye and an ear and the old woman loses a buttock. The depredations of disease, war, and the inquisition are narrated with a verve that conveys pleasure in the destruction of optimism's illusions. The characters' bodies are surrendered to the savaging of imperfection and unreasoning brutality. The very style of *Candide* (what I have called a style of subtraction) mimics the way in which afflictions physically diminish the body of their victims, and thus it mimics the world's reply to what optimism thinks it has to say. Against a metaphysics that postulates the eternal presence of a global meaning of the universe (a meaning that we only inadequately perceive), Voltaire erects a reason that sees the requisite clarity lacking everywhere and that finds in this very defect, this scandalous deficit of meaning, the spur to its own militancy.

But irony, having allied itself with the ferocity of the world in order to refute the preconceived system, now turns against violence and injustice. Despite all the alacrity with which Voltaire shows how easily syphilis, storms, Bulgarian heroes, black pirates, and inquisitors win out over the Leibnizian system's articles of faith, he is nevertheless outraged by the infliction of suffering. And despite the overtones of sadism in the manner in which the triumph of cruelty and intolerance is described, he does not believe, as Sade does, that evil in all its forms is the expression of natural law, or, to put it another way, he does not believe that natural law ought to be celebrated as benevolent. The determinism that produces gallstones, pox, and earthquakes attests to no solicitude for man on nature's part. But these unavoidable evils, which must be endured in pain, are compounded by the unnecessary evils that people inflict on one another—and that cannot be described without disgust. Voltaire does not accept them. He does not assent to the miseries that he so cheerfully allows to rain down upon his characters' heads.

The irony is turned up one notch, the vigor of the reaction is intensified. Having refuted optimism by allowing images of evil free rein, Voltaire, horrified by injustice and fanaticism, now speaks out. His style, usually characterized as "witty," "incisive," and "sarcastic," owes its specific character to the twin targets it is called upon to attack. Most of the events narrated in *Candide* are *bivalent:* they joyfully demonstrate the absurdity of Pangloss's system, but once the polemical point is made they come to seem intolerable. Events that denounce the illusions of optimism are themselves denounced for their atrocity. They belong to the category of facts about which Voltaire cannot think without "trembling with horror" (an expression that occurs frequently in his correspondence and historical writings). The "gnashing" that Flaubert rightly discerned in Voltaire is a consequence of the coexistence of polemical verve with shudders of horror. It is a consequence of the fact that each of the "realities" that contributes to the undermining of Pangloss's system becomes in turn the target of an unsparing critique. The atrocity that contradicts antecedent dogma is subsequently repudiated on moral, aesthetic, and affective grounds.

In order to achieve such effects the act of writing must be granted the privilege of the *last resort*. Voltairean "mockery" implies an *a posteriori* view, an experiment that has run its course, a perspective that comes from knowing how things turn out. The game is over, and irony is applied in hindsight. Against the background of the past Pangloss's first speech is already ridiculous: as "reported" it is derisively stigmatized and dismissed from the standpoint of superior wisdom, the result of reality's contradiction of metaphysics and of practical reason's criticism of reality. Consider, for example, the role of the hero's and his companions' reflective commentaries following the many episodes that make up *Candide*. These commentaries, detached from the narrative, would be categorized in rhetorical terminology as *epiphonema*. Their function is to impose a *general* judgment, reflecting self-assured knowledge, on a series of *particular* facts or feelings. Though the term may seem somewhat pedantic, I think its use is called for here: an epiphonema is the exclamatory conclusion of a lesson, which sums up its content in the form of a maxim or "moral." Whenever we encounter this rhetorical figure, we know that a rational power, a faculty of judgment, is at work, a power capable of abstraction and generalization. Candide's final exclamation—"We must cultivate our garden!"—remains tied to a particular situation (exile and farming on the Bosphorus) yet serves as an epiphonemic conclusion to the entire narrative—a "sage" conclusion, a discovery of universal significance, which confirms what was said about the hero at the outset ("his judgment was rather good"), while the ensuing trials and tribulations have confirmed the accompanying characterization ("combined with the simplest of minds"). Irony can now be directed toward the past with the benefit of the knowledge and education acquired along the way: the naive adventurer's wanderings and illusions are narrated from the standpoint of relative stability and security gained by the conversion to productive labor. We know *a posteriori* (but Voltaire, as he took up his pen, knew in advance) that despite all the losses, deceptions, mutilations, and the like, the resource of work always remains intact. What is more, the remark about the function of epiphonema and retrospective irony in *Candide* can be applied to the function of *Candide* in Voltaire's life. After the betrayal and death of Madame du Châtelet (whose philosophical leanings were toward optimism of the Wolfian or Panglossian variety), after Voltaire's experience in Prussia, after his arrest in Frankfurt, after his search for asylum and purchase of land near Geneva and Lausanne, *Candide* was in a sense a recapitulative entertainment: in the same breath Voltaire invents, parodies, caricatures, and expresses his resolve. In this way he delivered himself from the past by means of a comic magic that transformed experience into fiction.[4] The responsibilities of the country gentleman on the shores of "the Bosphorus," meaning Lake Leman, were not fictional, however: this lesson, learned late in life, became a general maxim, a touchstone for distinguishing true from false, illusory from solid. *Candide* was an epilogue, an epiphonema, a figurative profession of faith in a belatedly discovered practical wisdom. The transmutation of personal disasters into tragicomic fiction became part of wisdom itself and cleared the way for productive activity.

Candide's experiences reveal a transfer of authority that propels the narrative from episode to episode. Authority is asserted, then challenged, then reasserted in a new form, challenged again, and so on. Abstractly formulated, this is the tale's dominant dynamic. Any analysis that aims to capture not only the style but also the point of *Candide* must deal with the concept of authority.

Initially, within the enclosed world of the tiny Westphalian barony, the hero is in no doubt about the sources of authority: dynastic preeminence, aristocratic birth, and the philosophical system of Pangloss, according to which the world has a meaning and exists for the benefit of man. At first Panglossian metaphysics appears to be allied with the status quo: it justifies and reinforces the authority of the master. But the cleverness of the narrator, who knows better, immediately undermines this alleged authority. As a bastard, Candide is living proof of love's interference with aristocratic imperatives. Candide's very birth attests to the fragility of the conventional order: the quarter of nobility he lacks is an original lacuna, a void at the heart of the imposed rule. The narrator also loses no time in denouncing the verbal artifice by which the baron pretends that his country seat is a veritable court: by sleight-of-hand "barnyard dogs" become a "pack" of hunters, "stable boys" become "huntsmen," and a "country vicar" becomes a "chaplain." Similarly, by affecting Panglossian knowledge of the suffix *nigology* Voltaire immediately devalues it: he bells the cat with withering scorn. The preceptor's lecture, which claims to celebrate the world's comprehensible logic, exemplifies the most egregious illogicality. Intellectual authority is sabotaged even as it is being asserted (for anyone who knows how to read). But Candide is full of admiration.

The kiss behind the screen allegorizes the furtive intrusion of traditional authority's stubborn rival: sentiment, desire. Cunégonde is prepared to repeat with her cousin the act of derogation to which he owes his birth. But authority's eclipse is brief: kicks and cuffs—the first occurrence of violence in the story—promptly restore order. When it comes to violence, however, minor potentates and minuscule states are by no means assured of retaining the upper hand. Noble titles, vestiges of an ancient military order, are as nothing against princes with large armies whose soldiers drill every day. In a world whose principle of political authority is princely sovereignty, military might plays a decisive role. Thus, the province, the castle, and the baron are promptly reduced to their proper place, although Candide, the naive and credulous pupil, had at first taken the preceptor at his word and looked upon them as absolutes. The facts—massacres and ruins—take on the burden of proof. If nothing that exists wants for *sufficient reason,* then whoever has the best army can lay claim to sufficient reason. Power rapidly changes hands. The use of force triggers a "chain of events" whose end is uncertain. Voltaire likes to subject the violent to violence, to cause tyrants to perish at the hands of equally tyrannical enemies or fall victim to victorious rebellion. The baron who sends Candide away disappears in the disasters of war. The Bulgarian soldier who rapes Cunégonde is killed on the spot by his captain. The kidnappers of Urban X's daughter are slaughtered by a rival faction. The Grand Inquisitor, who holds Cunégonde and who orders the hanging of Pangloss, is killed by Candide. The Dutchman who robs Candide is sent to the bottom. And so on. These episodes are too sporadic and too blind to be interpreted as immanent justice. Violence is not visited exclusively on the violent. The innocent too die, and brutes go unpunished. Even worse, good and sincere individuals like Candide are caught up despite themselves in the cycle of violence. In such circumstances it is not easy to find one's way: in the game of slaughter no one holds true power for long, and with the fall of the baron succeeded by that of the Grand Inquisitor, the Reverend Father Commandant, and the English admiral, the story takes on a sense of general destruction, which affects not only those who wield civil and religious authority but authority as such, or whatever principles legitimate the exercise of power. Neither the Church nor the monarchy emerges unscathed: while Candide is in Paris an attempt is made on the life of the king, and all foreigners are arrested. Except in Eldorado no representative of supreme power is exempt from danger: the dinner of the fallen kings in Venice, with its extraordinary comedy of repetition, carries this frenetic lèse-majesté to its ultimate degree. The target, clearly, is not only the vanity of grandeur before the caprices of fate but even more the ultimate powerlessness of those who wield or or hope to wield sovereign authority. One need not be a high priest of psychoanalysis to see that throughout *Candide* Voltaire is bent on inflicting a sophisticated variety of humiliations on endlessly multiplied images of the father: what satisfaction, what revenge, when one can mock "his miserable Highness"! Nor is it difficult to recognize a similar attack, this time on literary authority, in Pococurante's judgment of the great authors. Never mind that the disrespectful judgment is that of a tired dilettante. Its effect is to strip of rank, to refuse to pay the traditional homage, to cut down (yet another mutilation) illustrious works by discrediting their weak parts.

When the young baron, the last representative of inhibiting authority, is sent to the galleys, there are no longer any rulers: no more high and mighty inquisitors, no more reverend fathers are left in Propontide. The survivors are foreigners, who own a "little farm." Political power is far away, and we assume that it is respectful of property rights and reluctant to intervene through its administration. Where is authority now? Has it been reduced to this non-intervention, this laissez-faire, which benefits all who are willing to keep their distance from the court? Have Candide and his friends come through their ordeal only to discover a place where authority is of no further concern to them, where it has forfeited the right to scrutinize their actions? Or will they themselves institute a new authority, different from the one of which they had been subjects, which they had tested, and which they had found sometimes laughable, sometimes tyrannical, and sometimes both at once?

Let us reconsider the problem from a philosophical angle. The original question concerned the harmony of the world, its purpose as reflected in all things. The doctrine of optimism affirms not only that such a purpose is clearly legible but that to interpret that purpose is our primary duty. The debate over theodicy assumes that man gives priority to the search for contemplative knowledge, to the apprehension of meaning. The important thing is to understand the world, to recognize its order. The optimist believes that this goal has been attained. Nothing remains to be *done*. The question of theodicy is interesting only if, as an ancient injunction has it, man finds happiness through *theoria*, through the contemplative apprehension of meaning. In that case, as Pangloss postulates, authority lies in the intrinsic logic of the world, which is revealed by the unfolding of events. A will, an intelligence, an absolute power (that of God, about whom Pangloss has little to say but who is always implicit in his arguments) has chosen the highest perfection for the universe. Man's task is not to intervene in the course of events but to decipher, even in the woes that afflict him, their unfolding meaning: Pangloss is content to be an interpreter. Before evil can be combatted it must be understood as one of the transitory means that a just Creator needs to arrive at his ends, which are the general good and, in the future, universal happiness. Panglossian optimism is inclined to forget Leibniz's argument against "idle sophism."

The method of Voltaire's critique is to omit from the chain of putative causes those that cannot be seen by the innocent (in French: *candide*) eye, namely, the divine source and harmonious finality. He polemically denounces as chimerical the wish to discover a primary cause and the presumption to pronounce on various final causes. It is idle to pretend to know each event's place in the divine plan. The perfection of the whole is an illusory consolation, refractory to refutation and at odds with the "reality principle."

Candide's history unfolds in a series of brief episodes, each governed by a short-term causality that is the exact opposite of the causality invoked by Pangloss with its endless chains of causes. The presumption here is in favor of a radical empiricism that refrains from making any conjecture not subject to verification, so that only proximate causes and their consequent effects are taken into consideration. The principle of sufficient reason is thus reduced to efficient causality alone. The extreme restriction that Voltaire imposes on the range of causality is deliberate: his strategy is to isolate the event, to separate it out from the project that might have given it meaning, to force it to exist on its own. The absurdity then becomes immediately apparent. Consider, for example, the chapter on the battle. What are the political intentions of the Abar and Bulgar kings? Voltaire intentionally says nothing about them. The omission of the war's ultimate causes and goals leaves only the *fact* of war: slaughter, weapons, bodies. The war seems horrible, particularly since Voltaire makes it appear that it is literally being waged for no reason. Only the mechanics and the arithmetic of combat remain: "The cannon first cut down roughly six thousand men on each side." Here, to be sure, we have cause and effect: instrumental cause, murderous effect. But we are treated only to the spectacle of "twitching limbs," in the absence of any "deep reason." And we witness only one day of battle. (The *Poème de Fontenoy*, in which Voltaire assumes the role of official bard of the king's victory, is quite another matter. In this case the battle is justified by a grand political design: the victorious king "will bring order to Europe, will calm the Empire.") What disgusts Voltaire more than anything else is the way in which men excuse the absurdity and brutality of their actions by attributing them to a providential will that watches over their destiny: the battle (an effect of short-term causes) is nonsensical, but the two kings order *Te Deums* as though the event has its place in the long-term causality of the divine plan. When religion sanctions absurdity in this way, Voltaire can scarcely conceal his outrage.

In order to accentuate the critical effect achieved by fragmenting the causal chain, Voltaire occasional introduces terminology borrowed from systematic philosophy. He does so in order to test the borrowed terms against finite reality. Uprooted, detached from their theoretical moorings, and set in a trivial context, such concepts as experimental physics, cause and effect, sufficient reason, and the best of all possible worlds inevitably wither. Their incongruous appearance in this artificial setting tends to discredit them generally. They seem fundamentally inadequate, devoid of all authority. Hence the infinite chain, the "great chain of beings and events," does not exist, or, to put it more precisely, the chain grows by sprouting new branches, and surprisingly many of the branches turn out to be broken or to bear no fruit. Everything is not the cause of everything else. See the entry under "Chain" in the *Dictionnaire Philosophique,* where Voltaire sets forth his arguments in the clearest possible terms:

> Make no mistake: every effect obviously has its cause, and so on from cause to cause all the way back into the abyss of eternity. But not every cause has an effect, and so on to the end of time. I admit that all events are produced by other events. If the past was pregnant with the present, the present is pregnant with the future. Every child has a father, but not all people have children. It is exactly like a genealogical tree: as everyone knows, every house can be traced back to Adam, but in any family many individuals die childless.

Thus some events are dead ends, without consequences, and we therefore cannot say that they are necessary links in a causal chain leading to some "future good."

Ultimately what one has in *Candide* is not a chain but a disconnected series, a series of mishaps and absurdities that follow one another according to the dictates of chance: in the genealogy of syphilis and the list of assassinated kings there is succession but not progress. Sickness—moral as well as physical—merely repeats itself in never ending, sterile repetition. Pangloss, in his attempts to justify providence, merely maunders on. One of the final images of procession in the book comes as Candide looks upon an endless stream of vessels sailing to and fro with disgraced, beheaded, and otherwise fallen Effendis, Pashas, and Cadis on board. The chain is absurd, a senseless cycle in which tyranny repeats itself indefinitely. In the face of this spectacle ("there is a dreadful lot of evil on earth"), the dervish, the final representative of religious authority, falls silent. He orders the System, in the person of Pangloss, to hold its tongue. The last external master abdicates, or at any rate refuses to interpret the will of God, whereupon God retreats into the unfathomable outer reaches of the universe, leaving man alone, without the comfort of universal order, exposed to the "convulsions of anxiety" and the "lethargy of boredom." The world is no longer governed by rectifying Reason. It is subject only to the unbenevolent law that governs the effects of the natural order. All that is left is to *understand* that merciless law, not to celebrate it in resignation but to command it, as Bacon suggested, by obeying it. Individuals, living in the finite space allotted to them, in their tiny garden, find in themselves, and in the quantitatively measurable results of their productive efforts, the new authority that will occupy the place left vacant by the old. "The small farm yielded a great deal." When Martin exclaims, "Let us work without reasoning," he is stating the imperative of the new human order, and he links it directly to the repudiation of reasoning, that most unreasonable activity whereby men in the past had attempted to construct an image of the universe that they might contemplate with approval. Authority, henceforth, is nothing outside of man; it comes down to the necessity of labor, which now enjoys absolute primacy. There is no order to contemplate, there is only land to work.

Is this simply a matter of the symbolic advent of the bourgeois morality of labor and productivity? Things are not as simple as contemporary literary sociology would have them. In Candide's formulation of the imperative of labor we also recognize a precept that Christian moralists preached as a remedy for the boredom of cloistered monks: manual labor is the cure for *acedia,* for *taedium vitae.* And acedia is definitely the psychological affliction of the survivors in Turkey: "When there was nothing to fight about, the boredom was unbearable." At the end of *Candide* work is proposed as a psychological remedy.

Of course it is also a response to economic necessity. Voltaire had fun portraying Candide at first as extremely poor (when he leaves his first "paradise") and later as extremely rich (when he leaves Eldorado). He loses all his treasures, partly through the dishonesty of his fellow men and partly through his own generosity, for having ransomed nearly all his enslaved companions. Eventually his reserves of "yellow mud" and effortlessly gathered "pebbles" are depleted, and he must find a way to live.

In poverty Candide discovered that in this world everything is not for the best. No sooner does he become fabulously wealthy than he begins to ask new questions: Who is happy? How does one become happy? Without Cunégonde wealth does not bring happiness. Nor does Cunégonde herself, found too late, bring happiness. In the end work disguises the absence of happiness and substitutes other goods in its stead—goods undoubtedly less precious but in the absence of which emptiness would carry the day: "Cunégonde was in truth quite ugly; but she became an excellent pastry chef."

A more accurate way of registering the transfer of authority that takes place in *Candide,* I believe, is to note how the accent shifts from the world's *order* to man's *happiness.* In linking happiness to labor Voltaire offers a quick sketch, drawn with a light touch, of what Goethe would later explore more fully in part two of *Faust.* The widely used concept of the "bourgeoisie" is insufficient to define the new age: what we witness, in fact, is the moment when man ceased to be an admiring spectator of an all-encompassing totality and asserted himself as the producer of his own world—a world finite, fluid, and forever unfinished.

There is as yet no inkling, however, of the coming industrial revolution and man's technological domination of nature. What Voltaire sketches in miniature is an agrarian society that draws the bulk of its income from the soil, with sumptuous textiles as its only modest luxury. And is it really a *society?* Is it not rather a withdrawal into private life? The group around Candide does not constitute a state or even a family. It is at most a tiny enclave in a world given over to evil; a refuge, an "asylum" (as contemporaries called it) for a group of cripples brought together by chance and misfortune. None of the farm's residents is a native of the place. They reconstitute a homeland in miniature in a place where they can live better than anywhere else, and that is a place subject to no religious or political authority. Significantly, these exiles form a cosmopolitan group: the Westphalians (Candide, Cunégonde, Pangloss, Paquette) are joined by Italians (the Old Woman, Brother Girofleo), a Dutchman or something of the sort (Martin), and the half-breed Cacambo. The group is thus something very like a symbol for all humankind, with the variety in shades of skin and opinion that Voltaire considered precious and whose protection he advocated in all his appeals for tolerance. The group is marginal; it is so small that there is no need to consider the problems of political organization. The emphasis on the need for productive labor is meant to curb any tendency toward utopianism. This tiny society is in no sense a model. "The small farm yielded a great deal." That is all—and some considered it to be not very much, but it was enough for Voltaire. (Rousseau, for his part, would portray Clarens as a place offering a greater abundance of emotional and social goods.) Voltaire reserved his variations on the utopian theme for his portrait of Eldorado, implying perhaps that the best of political organizations is conceivable only as an attribute of a place that does not exist. In Propontide, at the end of a disappointing odyssey, we are a long way from perfection. There a bastard, assisted by a prostitute, a renegade priest, a pox-ridden pedant, a hideously abused baronette, and a half-breed valet—impure, guilty, corrupt individuals when judged from the standpoint of traditional morality—take charge of their own destiny and, through what they undertake to accomplish, what they do with their own hands, hope ultimately to make themselves less unhappy. They settle for second best, for something that will never be able to hide the sheer difficulty of life. A political interpretation of *Candide* would have to ask whether the small farm is any more likely to endure than was the minuscule barony—that Eden in miniature which was swept away by violence at the beginning of the story. If small feudal states are simply swallowed up in the conflict of great nations, why should a private estate survive in a country ruled by despotism? Does this compromise solution have any future? Perhaps Voltaire's intention was to make us aware of the fragility, the eccentricity intrinsic to anything that might seem to offer hope of stability.

To interpret *Candide* in this way, however, is no doubt to reason too much about a text that warns against excessive reasoning. One can treat *Candide* as a parable, but it is a parable only in its general outline and in some of the issues it raises and judgments it offers. These are all but swamped, however, by whimsicality and even folly—not without hidden relation to the book's central lesson. How, for example, is one to interpret the paired figures, the ballet of minor characters who enter and exit as couples? There is a long series of such pairs: two recruiters, two enemy kings (Abar and Bulgar), the servant of the inquisition and his attendant, the Grand Inquisitor and Don Issachar, Cunégonde and the Old Woman, two girls pursued by two apes, Girofleo and Paquette, two serving girls employed by Pococurante, the young baron who is chained alongside Pangloss, the two sons and two daughters of the "good Old Man," and so on. And this brief list records only some of the instances of simultaneous duality in the text. A second list could be compiled of pairs of successors: the Protestant preacher followed by good Jacques; the Spanish kingdom in South America followed by the Jesuit kingdom; the Parisian experience followed by the English experience; the dervish followed by the "good Old Man." These pairings allow Voltaire to achieve both the comic effects of symmetry and the unsettling effects of disparity (where more important characters are involved or when there is a succession of episodes). Disparity, contrast, and difference, thus arranged in paired figures, bring out an image of a world irregular in its regularity (I am thinking of Pangloss blinded in one eye or of the Old Woman's lost buttock), subject, yet at the same time refractory, to geometric law. Nothing matches, nothing fits the harmonious *pattern* discussed by metaphysicians and theologians. In order to make this point Voltaire must indulge in excess, in wild fancy: the Grand Inquisitor, who consigns marranos to the flames, shares his mistress with a Jew; priests, unafraid to mete out the harshest of punishments, including hanging and burning, debauch themselves with young girls and boys; and every woman, willing or unwilling, is a prostitute. *Candide* is not a representation of the world, not even remotely. The elements of reality it contains are grossly caricatured. But here, too, the principle of disparity comes into play: *Candide* makes its point by pairing itself off with the world. The resulting couple is deliberately asymmetrical, and the fictional image, concise and extreme, forces us to see the perverse earnestness, inflexibility, oppressive meanness, and dogmatic intolerance that we accept as the inescapable human condition.

II. The Innocent on the Beach

In memory of Leo Spitzer

The Huron hastens to his beloved. Naively he tries to wed (in the physical sense of the term) *"la belle Saint-Yves."* But this pleasure is one that the institutions of the civilized world are unwilling to grant so readily. Though in love with the Innocent (*l'Ingénu*), Mademoiselle de Saint-Yves "struggled with all the decency of a person of breeding." And there is a further impediment to this "marriage": the Huron has recently been baptized, Mademoiselle de Saint-Yves is his godmother, and "marriage with one's godmother is forbidden" without "a dispensation from our Holy Father the Pope." In order to protect *la belle Saint-Yves* from the Huron's advances, her elder brother, "who was also her guardian," sends her away to a convent. The Innocent is plunged into despair.

L'Ingénu plongé dans une sombre et profonde mélancolie se promena vers le bord de la mer, son fusil à deux coups sur l'épaule, son grand coutelas au côté, tirant de temps en temps sur quelques oiseaux, et souvent tenté de tirer sur lui-même; mais il aimait encore la vie à cause de Mlle de Saint-Yves. Tantôt il maudissait son oncle, sa tante, et toute la basse Bretagne et son baptême. Tantôt il les bénissait, puisqu'ils lui avaient fait connaître celle qu'il aimait. Il prenait sa résolution d'aller brûler le couvent, et il s'arrêtait tout court de peur de brûler sa maîtresse. Les flots de la Manche ne sont pas plus agités par les vents d'Est et d'Ouest que son coeur l'était par tant de mouvement contraires.

Il marchait à grands pas sans savoir où, lorsqu'il entendit le son du tambour. Il vit de loin tout un peuple dont une moitié courait au rivage, et l'autre s'enfuyait.

Mille cris s'élèvent de tous côtés; la curiosité et le courage le précipitent à l'instant vers l'endroit d'où partaient ces clameurs; il y vole en quatre bonds. Le Commandant de la milice qui avait soupé avec lui chez le Prieur, le reconnut aussitôt; il court à lui les bras ouverts: Ah! c'est l'Ingénu, il combattra pour nous. Et les milices qui mouraient de peur se rassurèrent, et crièrent aussi: C'est l'Ingénu, c'est l'Ingénu.

[The Innocent, sunk in a deep and somber melancholy, headed for the shore, his double-barreled musket on his shoulder, his great cutlass at his side, firing occasionally at some birds and frequently tempted to turn the gun on himself; but he still loved life because of Mademoiselle de Saint-Yves. One moment he cursed his uncle, his aunt, all of lower Brittany, and his baptism too. The next moment he blessed them because they had introduced him to the woman he loved. He resolved to burn down the convent and stopped short for fear of burning his mistress. The seas of the Channel are not more lashed by east and west winds than his heart was tossed by so many contrary emotions.

He was striding along in no particular direction when he heard the sound of a drum. In the distance he saw crowds of people running, half toward the shore, the other half in the opposite direction.

Shouts filled the air. Prompted by curiosity and courage he hastened toward the source of the noise, reaching it in four bounds. The commander of the militia, with whom he had dined at the prior's, recognized him immediately and ran toward him with open arms. "It's the Innocent, he will fight for us." And the militiamen, who were frightened to death, took heart and shouted too, It's the Innocent, it's the Innocent.]

These three paragraphs, which open chapter seven of *L'Ingénu*, exhibit a sharply defined style, a pattern so typical and a form so fraught with significance that the closest possible reading is warranted. *L'Ingénu* is Voltaire's last story, and we may therefore expect to find in it the quintessence of his thinking, the final form of his philosophy.

The first sentence of the passage is asymmetrical. Its first part moves forward in a series of phrases, each more forceful than the last, as if mimicking the Huron's progress as he walks toward the coast. The second part is astonishingly simple: there is no internal subdivision, except perhaps a slight "breathing" pause (without punctuation) after the word *life*. Note that the statement of the cause (Mademoiselle de Saint-Yves) comes after the statement of the effect (he loved life). The significance of this inversion of cause and effect will become apparent later, when we examine more perspicuous instances of the same device.

This asymmetry in the morphology of the sentence coincides with a difference in the content of the two parts. The first part, with its several components, points toward death by way of a gradation that runs from melancholy to a precise specification of two lethal weapons and culminates in a temptation to commit suicide by a method that is clearly spelled out. The brevity of the sentence's second part thwarts the somber design and affirms the Innocent's attachment to life, Mademoiselle de Saint-Yves being so important to him that the mere thought of her is enough to cancel out or at least offer temporary compensation for the desire to die. Despite the asymmetry of the sentence, balance is restored: the brief statement following the *but* provides the necessary counterweight. Its concision reveals the intensity of the passionate energy associated with the memory of Mademoiselle de Saint-Yves. The ear hears the syllable *Yves* as a mirror image of the syllable *vie* (life). The two are secretly synonymous and reinforce each other. The asymmetry of the two parts of the sentence is the stylistic means by which Voltaire tells us that the beautiful captive is first the pretext for a *series* of desperate actions and then the *unique* reason for the Innocent to go on living. The pattern is so clear, the reversal so sudden, that it strikes us as somewhat mechanical. The sentence takes an abrupt turn, it makes rapid play with the antithesis of life and death. The beginning of the next sentence takes us back to the initial melancholy: "One moment he cursed." The blessing follows. We are caught up in a to-and-fro that has no reason to stop.

Look once more at the first part of the first sentence. It is divided up into distinct components. Various kinds of pairing exist: words are coupled by syntactic equivalence, repetition of terms, parallel syntactic structures. Semantically, these pairings conveys first identity, then difference, then contradiction. The contrastive function increases.

The first pairing, redundant and almost pleonastic, occurs in the epithet *sombre et profonde* (somber and deep) modifying *melancholy*— a commonplace. Next, in segments of almost equal length (nine and eight syllables, respectively), Voltaire symmetrically evokes the Huron's two weapons: the double-barreled musket and the great cutlass. These are followed by two more segments, both eleven syllables, in which the same verb, *tirer* (to shoot) is used in two different ways, one pertaining to action (shooting birds), the other to intention (the Huron's temptation to shoot himself). Each verb is modified by an adverb or adverbial phrase: *de temps en temps* (occasionally) follows the verb, *souvent* (frequently) precedes it. The objects are placed symmetrically at the end of each phrase: *sur quelques oiseaux* (at some birds), *sur lui-même* (at himself).

Although the paired epithets are not semantically dissonant, the paired weapons are. The double-barreled musket is the weapon of a "civilized" man, whereas the cutlass is that of a "savage." The two weapons are mentioned at the same grammatical level, and the only contrast comes from the connotations. The fact that the Innocent carries both a musket and a cutlass is a sign of his dual origin: he is the child of Breton parents but was raised by savages; he is a Huron but has been baptized. In any case, musket and cutlass are species belonging to a common genus: both are lethal weapons. Civilized people make war, and savages engage in their own forms of battle: only the technical means are different. Voltaire of course did not believe that savages were peaceful people; he is making fun of Rousseau, who saw warfare as a consequence of socialization. The two different weapons, named in syntactic segments of equivalent function, make us feel the comedy in the pairing of inequivalent objects, in the disparity hidden behind what seems to be mere innocent repetition. But it also hints at the identity of human nature, at man's essential violence, behind its variable cultural expressions. In the two participial phrases that follow (*tirant de temps en temps,* shooting occasionally, and *souvent tenté de tirer,* frequently tempted to shoot), the metrical equality and the apparent equivalence indicated by the repetition of the verb *tirer* are immediately undermined by the contrast between the externalized act (shooting) and the still internal intention (tempted to shoot). This opposition is further emphasized by the radical qualitative difference between the objects of the two verbs, which are symmetrically placed at the end of each phrase *(sur quelques oiseaux, sur lui-même).* Voltaire maintains the equivalence of diction and grammatical function as long as possible so as to dramatize, in the final moment, the incommensurability of the actual targets (birds) and the potential target (a man tempted to turn his gun on himself). The direction of fire is radically reversed: the change in the object of the verb "to shoot" rotates the line of fire one hundred eighty degrees. Thus in the first part of the sentence Voltaire uses numerous paired structures to indicate a variable but steadily increasing degree of opposition. But after the suicidal reversal of the direction of fire, we witness yet another reversal, a reversion to the love of life that seems all the more sudden and vigorous because it comes as the Innocent reaches a low point of despair. The antithetical meaning is no longer insinuated into the deceptive symmetry of the language but is now intended to be manifest, engendering a morphological contrast, a single, short proposition that serves as counterweight to the whole previous thesis. In other words, asymmetry is introduced to make explicit the contradiction previously implicit in the deceptive symmetry. Voltaire simultaneously satisfies the aesthetic need for variety. After so much formal regularity, a segment of markedly different length was required, thus confirming the asymmetry of the entire sentence. It should come as no surprise that Voltaire almost instinctively obeyed one of the "laws" of rococo style. Our pleasure stems from the fact that for a brief instant equilibrium is reestablished in the guise of disequilibrium.

Clearly, then, duality is present in every possible form and in all the various combinations made possible by different levels of language (form, meaning, and so on). This is not the place to attempt a systematic classification of Voltaire's stylistic devices. Note, however, that duality is not limited to the use of morphologically equivalent or inequivalent pairs or of semantic binomials establishing different degrees of contrast (ranging from pleonasm to antithesis). It can also take the form of clear contrast between the implicit and the explicit or between understatement and hyperbole. It exists, too, in the contrast between inwardness (melancholy) and externals (shore, equipment, birds); between the broadly sketched setting (seacoast) and the minutely detailed weaponry (musket, cutlass); between act (shooting) and intention (temptation to shoot); and between indeterminate plural (some birds) and determinate singular (himself).

A text with such a clear structure could easily be diagrammed so as to reveal features that become clear as the reader proceeds. (The blackboard is a seductive temptation, at best a subterfuge for summing up what takes place as one reads.)

What is the effect of this use of duality? Parallel propositions, symmetrical in structure but contrasting in meaning, are certain to produce a comic effect, especially if certain words are repeated with different meanings. Yet expressions such as "sunk in deep and somber melancholy" or "tempted to turn the gun on himself" are surely expressions of pathos. Taken out of context, they would not make anyone smile. (More precisely, they would not make any eighteenth-century reader smile; "deep, dark melancholy" later became a cliché, but can we be sure that Voltaire meant to amuse us by joining the two adjectives?) When such phrases are "set in parallel," however, as parts of paired structures, they become amusing. Their pathetic significance is not abolished but is, as it were, confiscated by the comic significance established by the pairing. To put it more precisely, the pathos is chilled by the disparity expressed through the incongruous pairing. An alternation is established between the pathos of certain components of the structure and the comedy that surrounds and lightens thems. This is an effect of the rhythm that Voltaire impresses upon the narrative, of the highly variable tone that the narrator favors. Certain statements are undeniably tragic, but the outpouring of emotion is limited to a fleeting moment before it is caught up in and dissolved by the free irony of a composition that plays with all the resources inherent in binary systems. What witnesses tell us about Voltaire's extraordinary psychic lability at the time he wrote *L'Ingénu*—his moods ranging from tearful emotion to indignation and from indignation to sarcasm—tends to confirm this idea of a constant alternation between brief bouts of emotion and ironic jibes.

More generally, the same alternation constantly turns our attention from the hero's misadventures to the writer's devices and back again. The narrator never effaces himself for the sake of his character. Voltaire makes his presence felt everywhere; we share his company far more than we do that that of the fictional Huron. The story may be about the Innocent and Mademoiselle de Saint-Yves, but the carefully contrived mechanics of the style remind us constantly of the watchmaker-creator. The ingenuity of the writer is responsible for arranging semantic contrasts in parallel grammatical or syntactic positions. The narrator is not trying to create an illusion. The comic alternations are obviously an effect of the writer's pen, and this prevents us from mistaking them for the deep thoughts of his improbable hero. The schematic nature of the contrasts is a clear indication of Voltaire's indifference to psychological plausibility and realistic illusion. Consider this example from the very first sentence: "But he still loved life *because* of Mademoiselle de Saint-Yves." Is this the hero's own explanation, or is it an explanation provided by Voltaire? We hesitate, and that hesitation is significant. Love of life is no doubt an attribute of the Huron's consciousness, but such a succinct statement of the reason for it brings us closer to Voltaire (as omniscient as he is omnipresent) than to his hero. It is not the Huron who is suffering here, it is Voltaire who is commenting. Thus in this case the duality is between the writer and his character, between the level of the narrative (where we pay attention to the fate of the hero) and the level of style (where we admire the dexterity of the writer). This duality prevails throughout the story; it is in fact one of the laws of the philosophical tale.

The rest of the text only confirms what we have already discovered in the first sentence. Duality next takes the form of temporal alternation and morphological parallelism (*tantôt il maudissait,* sometimes he cursed, *tantôt il bénissait,* sometimes he blessed). These two sentences of contrasting meaning are roughly similar in length (23 and 21 syllables, respectively). After this we encounter duality in yet another setting, within a single sentence that is divided by a comma into two equal parts, each fifteen syllables long: *Il prenait sa résolution d'aller brûler le couvent, et il s'arrêtait tout court de peur de brûler sa maîtresse* (he resolved to burn down the convent and stopped short for fear of burning his mistress). Once again there is an opposition between thought (the resolution) and action (he stopped short), between the hostility of things (the convent is a prison) and the only person who counts (his mistress, prisoner of the convent). The repetition of the verb *brûler,* to burn, brings out the contradictory nature of the heroic act and its disastrous effects (burning the convent, burning his mistress), or, in other words, the disparity between the imagined means and the catastrophic end. This is an excellent example of inequality in symmetry, inequality whose inconsistency becomes clear only at the end of the sentence. Voltaire is clever enough to use the conjunction *et* (and) to indicate opposition: this muting technique paves the way for the ironic effect. To be sure, there is nothing unusual about this use of *et.* Voltaire deliberately avails himself of a resource that allows him to accentuate the disparity between the resolution and its result, the burned convent and the mistress dead in the flames.

The paragraph ends with a comparison between the Innocent's heart and the seas of the English Channel. The comparison establishes a slight quantitative inequality between the two terms. By using the phrase *pas plus que,* no more than, Voltaire implies that the agitation of the Huron's heart might have been more intense than that of the ocean waves. The two components of the first sentence of the paragraph are here developed into a trope and inverted in a chiasmatic pattern appropriate to contrary emotions:

A	The Innocent, sunk in deep and somber melancholy	headed toward the shore	B
B′	The seas of the Channel are no more lashed by east and west winds	than his heart was by so many contrary emotions	A′

The sequence of psychological and geographical terms has been inverted, so that the paragraph begins and ends with descriptions of the Innocent's emotional state. In the final sentence the principal and subordinate clauses share the same passive verb (to be agitated), which ascribes the same passion to the natural world as to the hero's heart. The comic effect of projecting the abstract, geometric opposition of east and west into the psychological sphere scarcely needs emphasizing. While it was common for poets in the classical tradition to compare internal conflicts to violent natural storms, Voltaire treats the metaphor in the schematic manner of a cartographer: he evokes measurable space rather than a vivid impression of tumultuous seas.

Note, too, the words used to end the first and last sentences of the paragraph. The final sentence ends with the phrase *mouvements contraires* (literally "contrary motions," translated more idiomatically in English as "contrary emotions"), which makes explicit the duality we have previously detected at various levels of the text. The four previous sentences all end either with the name of Mademoiselle de Saint-Yves or with a fairly direct allusion to her:

Sentence 1: Mademoiselle de Saint-Yves
Sentence 2: his baptism (since Mlle de Saint-Yves was the Huron's godmother, she cannot marry him)
Sentence 3: the woman he loved.
Sentence 4: his mistress.

Now look ahead to the final words of the chapter. They are: *et se recommandant à sa maîtresse* (and commending himself to his mistress).

Clearly, Voltaire uses this insistent and somewhat mechanical repetition to associate an obsessive idea with the dualistic system. This single idea, this idée fixe associated with frustrated desire, runs through the entire paragraph. The emotional duality is the result of an absurd set of prohibitions: desire is obliged by human malice and religious regulations to forgo gratification. Initially that desire was a simple expression of nature: the Huron does not suffer from internal conflict until he runs afoul of social obstacles. To be sure, this conflict is merely the internalization of the story's primary given: the presence on French soil of a man born in Brittany yet raised according to Huron custom. The whole story is based on the contrast between an isolated individual and a community, each a stranger to the other. Their incompatibility becomes a source of conflict for the hero, but from the narrator's point of view it also becomes a source of reflection on man in general, on the savage, and on the abuses of contemporary society.

The binary rhythm, the two-beat motion of the text, is not limited to the evocation of the Huron's psychological states. Analysis of the rest of the passage will show that dichotomies and oppositions that at first seem to be a schematic formalization of the hero's conflicting emotions in fact correspond to the worldview that Voltaire wants to get across.

Il marchait à grands pas sans savoir où, lorsqu'il entendit le son du tambour (he was striding along in no particular direction when he heard the sound of a drum). The action is reflected in a sentence consisting of two equal clauses, each ten syllables long. Their symmetry is further emphasized by the assonant rhyme: *où, -our*. Another action is about to unfold on the same shore, this time involving not an individual but a whole group of people. These people are in motion, and, because the writer's unfettered irony decrees it so, the mass of human beings is divided into two equal halves moving in opposite directions. This motion thus mimics exactly the contrary "motions" evoked previously. The same dynamic scheme is thus repeated in a new key—an echo or reflection in form, although the content presumably has changed.

The need for rapid development of the narrative forces Voltaire to abandon his binomial sentences. He now juxtaposes discontinuous moments in the unfolding of the event. Things move quickly: "There are shouts on all sides." The Innocent arrives on the scene. Translated literally, the text reads: "He flies there in four bounds." He is already in the grip of powers other than melancholy, powers evoked by a pair of abstract nouns: curiosity and courage. Voltaire is not careful about emotional transitions. *Il y vole en quatre bonds* is a double hyperbole: not only does the Huron fly, but he covers the distance in just four bounds. We need not go so far as to presume that Voltaire chose the number four because it is twice two. But note the repetition of the exclamation, "It's the Innocent!" Like sheep, the militiamen echo first their commander and then one another. This refrain marks a sudden reversal in the troops' morale: fear turns directly into confidence. Voltaire expresses this reversal in a dizzying series of verbs (*qui mourai-ent de peur se rassurèrent, et crièrent,* [the militiamen] who were frightened to death, took heart, and cried out). Equilibrium is restored by means of an unanticipated counterweight (the principle of equivalence in asymmetry). Just as the image of Mademoiselle de Saint-Yves by itself counterbalanced a welter of melancholy emotions in the Innocent, the mere presence of the young savage is enough to halt the flight of half the crowd and, for some mysterious reason, restore the courage of the militia. The foreigner will save the fatherland. Yet the rulers of the fatherland (the men of the Castle) will persecute the courageous Huron.

The time has now come to consider more closely another dichotomy, namely, Voltaire's separation of cause and effect. One device that Voltaire uses regularly to point up the ridiculousness and absurdity of human affairs is to give effects priority over causes (effects are singular, odd, sometimes trivial, and above all devoid of justification). Made perceptible in some unexplained fashion, the effect, as in the case of the crowd's agitation here, is a pure phenomenon, foolish and pointless. Only later is the cause of the commotion revealed: "Do you not see the English coming?" Since the ridiculous effect has been shown first, the cause, not specified until later, is spattered with the absurdity of what we have just witnessed. As Sartre perspicaciously pointed out in his study of Camus's *L'Etranger* (The Stranger), humor in the philosophical tale aims at decomposing a situation into a series of "discrete" acts or states scattered in time. The significance of the overall event is "atomized" in a series of small, concrete facts, which are perfectly grotesque when taken one by one. The asyndeton (omission of the conjunction) is astonishingly effective. All we see is a scattering of moments unconnected by any vector of meaning or rational coherence. Each instant is isolated as if in its own hermetic world. Instead of texture there is an absurd graininess. Of course the effects become intelligible once their cause is finally revealed. Everything becomes clear, but this retroactive intelligibility cannot make up for the destruction of logical sequence. In our text this destruction results in the presentation of numerous consequences whose cause (the approach of the English) is relatively simple. The discontinuity of isolated instants thus reflects an opposition between the complex and the simple, reinforced by an inversion of logical sequence. Voltaire frequently resorts to this kind of rearrangement of cause and effect. He wants to create a sense of disproportion, of dissonance, among events which, though dependent on a causal link that they ultimately reveal, nevertheless attest to the incoherence of the world as it follows its course. Note, too, that Voltaire allows himself considerable freedom in the representation of cause and effect. If the contrast between the two is large, he does not need to invert the logical sequence. The opposition of the simple and the complex can also take another form: instead of a multitude of small effects deriving from a single cause, Voltaire sometimes implies that a large effect can be the result of a host of trivial causes, or that an immediate cause is itself the grotesque effect of a still earlier cause.

Consider once more the inversion of cause and effect in the story of the English landing. If the narrative inverts the intelligible order of events, it nevertheless respects the chronology of their apparent succession. The Innocent perceives before he understands. He hears the sound of the drum, he sees a crowd of people running in opposite directions, and he hastens to the spot. Voltaire pretends not to know any more about what is going on than his character does. Nothing in this account is incompatible with sensualist theory: perception precedes apperception which in turn precedes reflection and comprehension. Voltaire presents his hero's "natural" experience in schematic form. If he inverts the logical sequence, he does so for the sake of empirical sequence, following the order of sensory experience. But Voltaire's irony amuses itself by widening the gap between the moment of perception and that of comprehension. Events are unfolding rapidly on the beach but in such numbers as to delay revelation of their cause. And not only is the revelation of the underlying cause delayed until later, but the Innocent must have it explained to him twice. First he is asked if he does not see the English approaching. Not having learned to look upon the English as enemies, he sees nothing alarming in this and responds that they are good people. The commandant must therefore explain the significance of the landing: "The commandant explained to him that the English were on their way to pillage the Abbey of the Mountain, drink his uncle's wine, and perhaps abduct Mademoiselle de Saint-Yves." In other words, the cause must be explained in terms of a series of concrete, short-term effects. The event is explained in terms of simple motives but with the implication that the Innocent may lose what he cherishes. He responds by invoking an abstract principle: "Oh! If that is the case, they are violating natural law. Leave it to me. I lived among them for a long time, I know their language, I will speak to them." Just as it took two explanations to make the intentions of the attackers intelligible, so too will the Innocent react with equal vigor in two radically different ways, one after the other: first with words, then with violence. The young savage, who takes the principles of ethics literally, thinks he can invoke those principles by talking to the people who taught them to him. He is naive enough to assume that English behavior conforms to the theories expressed in English books. But principles are one thing, actions another. When he boards the command ship to talk to the attackers, they laugh in his face and treat him as a harmless madman: "The admiral and his crew burst out laughing, served him some punch, and sent him on his way." The savage, until then a good pupil, can no longer believe in the power of the word. The English, teachers of political morality, are waging an undeclared war. He is left with no choice but to join the Breton militia and, in a second phase of action, repel the English invaders. The law of two stages (or, to use Voltaire's own image, the double-barreled musket) is fully verified: talk fails, violence succeeds.

This law will become clearer if we look at the seventh chapter of *L'Ingénu* in its entirety. Between a desperate prelude (the solitary walk on the beach) and a conclusion full of hope (the projected journey to Versailles, the illusory idea of seeing the king and receiving a reward), the chapter recounts two actions. The first is triumphal: the battle with the English. The second, despite its apparent ease, is a miserable failure: the attempt to rescue Mademoiselle de Saint-Yves:

Le Bailli qui s'était caché dans sa cave pendant le combat, vint lui faire son compliment comme les autres. Mais il fut bien surpris quand il entendit Hercule l'Ingénu dire à une douzaine de jeunes gens de bonne volonté dont il était entouré, Mes amis, ce n'est rien d'avoir délivré l'Abbaye de la Montagne, il faut délivrer une fille. Toute cette bouillante jeunesse prit feu à ces seules paroles. On le suivait déjà en foule, on courait au Couvent. Si le Bailli n'avait pas sur-le-champ averti le Commandant, si on n'avait pas couru après la troupe joyeuse, c'en était fait.

The bailiff, who had hidden in his cellar during the battle, came to pay his respects like the others. But he was quite surprised when he heard Hercules the Innocent say to the dozen well-meaning youths who were with him, "My friends, rescuing the Abbey of the Mountain was nothing, we must rescue a girl." The impetuous youths were inflamed by these words. A mob immediately set out after him, headed for the convent. If the bailiff had not alerted the commandant at once, if they had not run after the jolly troop, it would have been done.

Talking to the English had proved of no avail. Forced to meet violence with violence, the Innocent had easily gained the upper hand. Now, however, the words of the coward who happens to hold the office of bailiff prove extraordinarily effective. The bailiff's word to the commandant stops the whole escapade in its tracks. Two phases of action are thus clearly delineated, and the difference between them could not be more complete. The failed rescue attempt is of course a much briefer episode, and it makes it clear that it is infinitely easier to win a victory on the battlefield than to rescue a victim of social and religious prejudice from a convent.

The distinctive structure of the chapter's opening sentences is thus mirrored in the structure of the chapter itself. It can also be found in the next chapter (chapter 8): the Innocent, on his way to Versailles, stops at an inn in Saumur. He converses freely and naively with Huguenots on their way out of France (phase one, five paragraphs). Among those present, however, is a Jesuit spy, who sends a letter of denunciation to Versailles (phase two, just one paragraph, the shortest of all). The event narrated in phase two proves more important: the Innocent and the letter arrive at Versailles at the same time. The naive hero and the slanderous piece of paper follow a parallel itinerary: this duality governs the composition of the next chapter (chapter 9), whose ironic title consists of two phrases: "Arrival of the Innocent at Versailles. His reception at Court." The chapter consists of two roughly equal parts (four and five paragraphs, respectively). The first part recounts the Innocent's fruitless activities as he is refused audiences with the king, Louvois, and the first secretary and received only by the first secretary's secretary. The second part relates the quick and decisive consequences of the letter's reception by the king's confessor. Along the way we discover that not one but two letters have arrived simultaneously in Versailles: the bailiff has written another letter intended to harm the Innocent. As a result of these two letters of denunciation, he winds up in the Bastille.

This should come as no surprise: the Bastille offers the Innocent an opportunity for an asymmetrical dialogue. He shares his cell with a companion in misfortune, the Jansenist Gordon. The man of nature is a partner in captivity with a theologian who rejects nature in the name of the doctrine of efficacious grace. No contrast could be more stark, but the antithesis raises the possibility of permutation. Gordon has many books, and he becomes the Innocent's teacher. The Huron loses his instinctive spontaneity and develops reflective understanding; he sheds his ignorant individuality in favor of rational universality. While the "savage" thus acquires the resources of culture, his teacher undergoes a change in the opposite direction. The educational dialogue also transforms the educator from a fanatic theologian into an adept of natural philosophy. We witness a double evolution, and the imprisonment takes on a double meaning, signifying both governmental tyranny and retreat fruitfully employed for the expansion of knowledge. Through an irony that is merely a caricature of a fundamental process, the acquisition of enlightenment is the reward for frustration, for loss of the freedom of movement. For the two prisoners in the Bastille, the dialogue is therefore an opportunity to move from a first to a second view of reality: hence the prison, although it inflicts the worst separation, takes on the opposite value of an experience of amical communion.

If we now consider the story as a whole, we can easily recognize the "law of the double-barreled musket," which we observed first in the structure of a sentence, then of a paragraph, and then in the architecture of a series of chapters. Mademoiselle de Saint-Yves is at first locked up in a convent, as the Innocent will later be locked up in the Bastille. The Innocent attempts to rescue Mademoiselle de Saint-Yves, as she will later attempt to rescue her "lover." The Innocent fails in his attempt, but he sets out full of hope for Versailles. Mademoiselle de Saint-Yves succeeds, but it costs her her honor and she dies of despair. We thus have a series of similar but inverse situations in which certain elements remain invariant: the mutual and unalterable love of the two young people and the knavery of those in power. For the heroine the heartbreaker is that the Huron did not marry (read: rape) her without formalities and that she was forced to endure the shame of surrendering herself to the highly civilized minister, a man she does not love.

To be sure, it would be a simple matter to demonstrate the presence of a series of minor oscillations in the story as a whole: oscillations between good and evil, happiness and misfortune, light and dark motifs. The Innocent is recognized by his parents, but because of his baptism he cannot have the woman he loves. He defeats the English, but because of the denunciations by the Jesuit and the bailiff he is thrown in prison. He is rescued by Mademoiselle de Saint-Yves, but she, on the advice of Father Tout-à-tous (whose name, which might be translated as All-Things-to-All-Men, is based on an arresting repetition), gives herself to the minister Saint-Pouange (whose name juxtaposes *pou*, louse, with *ange*, angel) and dies of having consented to her own dishonor. In each case, owing to religion or a priest (an obsessive idea that insinuates itself between the two phases), the happiness that the Innocent believed was his collapses and misfortune prevails—or seems to prevail.

Is *L'Ingénu* a pessimistic story? No more than *Zadig* is an optimistic one. To be sure, in the alternation of negative and positive, Zadig always seems to progress from apparent misfortune to real happiness. But if misfortune is the necessary condition of good fortune, the price of happiness is rather high. Looked at more closely, *L'Ingénu* teaches the same lesson. The Innocent's parents were killed by savages, but the same savages raised the child with affection. Mademoiselle de Saint-Yves has been locked up and the Innocent plunged into despair, but the situation offers him an opportunity to display his bravery. He is imprisoned in the Bastille, but there he meets a Jansenist (the "good Gordon," ready to give up fanaticism) with whose help he can complete his education and "develop his genius" (chapter 9). Mademoiselle de Saint-Yves dies, but on the day of the funeral Saint-Pouange, whose love has been rekindled, turns up by chance and is moved to repair the misfortune he has precipitated. The Innocent, having become an officer, will be "both a warrior and an intrepid philosopher." If evil is the work of religion, prejudice, and tyranny—that is, of abusive institutions—good is something that can always be accomplished by a man who resolves himself to the purpose, and despite misfortune. Voltaire suggests that his work can be read simultaneously in two different ways. This hint can be found in the two closing sentences, whose structure is once again dual, a "double-barreled musket": "He [Gordon] took for his motto the saying, Misfortune is good for something. How many decent people in the world have been able to say, Misfortune is good for nothing!" Here again there is asymmetry in duality. Gordon expresses a singular opinion, but the contrary assertion is attributed to an indeterminate number of decent people. Quantitatively, at least, misfortune prevails. The relative happiness accepted by the sage does not compensate for the absolute unhappiness of others. It is possible to lose everything. It is also possible to play loser take all.

The law of the double-barreled musket is clearly the expression of a worldview. There is no good without evil or evil without good, and the amount of one need not compensate for the amount of the other. The world is imperfect. Evil appears to have the upper hand because of its absurd institutions. But the triumph of evil, however inevitable it may seem, can be turned into its opposite. The proof is that even as things stand, there are already compensations for philosophers. What should be changed? The reasons for the misfortunes of the Innocent and Mademoiselle de Saint-Yves are pointless or absurd: an article of canon law, a spy's letter, a junior minister's sensual caprice. Crush the power of the Church, diminish the tyranny of those who govern, and the balance might tip to the side of happiness. Of course plenty of iniquities would remain on the other side of the scale. Human happiness requires institutions, and none is immune from abuse. One thing is certain: Candide and the Innocent will not find happiness in love.

Logic is not satisfied by this reasoning. True, human beings are not often happy. They are nevertheless capable of happiness. Voltaire's thought owes its mobility to the repulsive and propulsive force of the concessive conjunction *but:* Saint-Pouange behaves like a monster, but "he was not wicked." Gordon is a fanatic, but he is capable of embracing ideas more reasonable than that of efficacious grace. There are evil priests; there are also good ones. Mademoiselle de Saint-Yves dies of guilt, but the Huron would not have regarded what she did as a sin. The touching victim may be a fool. The contraries are so truly contrary that in contradicting one another they contradict the law of the excluded middle (which states that p and not-p cannot both be true). Carrying the contrasts of duality to an extreme means precisely that the excluded middle prevails: what is true is precisely "p and not-p." Each of the contradictory propositions is true in turn, or both are true simultaneously. In the binary rhythm of this imperfect world, where perfect consistency is impossible, neither the positive nor the negative represents the definitive truth: philosophical irony finds that you cannot have one without the other, and that if the world did not limp along with its imperfect gait it would not move at all. We had best not scorn the small happinesses that we are granted in place of the one large happiness. The Voltairean tale offers us an accelerated, caricatural image of this constant motion, of this oscillation between nature and culture, vice and virtue, laughter and tears, pessimism and optimism, and leaves us in a state of overall confusion despite all the clarity of the individual details. The final duality is this: while Voltaire's irony gives us the impression of dominating the world and doing with it as it will, its passion, its anxious energy are caught up in the world and carry us along with it. So goes the world, says the ironic consciousness—free, playful, and detached. And so we go too, for we are in the world, and not even ironic consciousness can escape its flux.

5

∾

THE ANTIDOTE IN THE POISON: THE THOUGHT OF JEAN-JACQUES ROUSSEAU

I. Achilles' Spear

Rousseau, speaking of his childhood, found affliction inherent in it from the beginning: "I was born weak and sick; I cost my mother her life, and my birth was the first of my misfortunes."[1] This initial injury (or, rather, conviction and narration of injury) elicits and mobilizes all available reparative energies, all the faculties of compensation. An entire life is not too much to devote to the search for a cure when the disease is intimately bound up with one's arrival in the world. Afflicted with a congenital malformation and guilty of having killed his mother, Rousseau is at once the victim and the cause of an evil fate, yet it is a malady that he neither deserved nor wanted. In recounting his life with the intention of "telling all," he immediately blames his destiny on his initial injury, whose primary presence he would continue to feel at times owing to its aggravated effects, at other times to its surprising disappearance during intervals of good health. The reader is implicitly invited to pity a man afflicted by misfortune from the first yet also to feel amazement at all that was gloriously accomplished in spite of illness and in the face of an adversity that marked Jean-Jacques's existence in its very commencement.

In the *Confessions* the theme of a primitive injury is almost immediately coupled with that of therapy (in the broad sense of the term). Disease and its treatment enter into combination. The very possibility of survival depended on a saving intervention, yet this same intervention allowed the disease to persist. Rousseau does not hesitate to yoke opposites in his narrative, to join them inextricably. Aunt Suzon's care saves him, but the initial evil is only reinforced. Jean-Jacques barely escapes death; his survival is a miracle. But at the same time his sickness only gets worse. Astonishment and compassion are doubly warranted: "I was almost born dead. They had little hope of saving me. I carried the germ of a disorder that the years have reinforced and that now allows me moments of respite only so that I may suffer more cruelly in some other way. One of my father's sisters, a woman kindly and wise, took such good care of me that I survived."[2]

Rousseau wants very much to be able to mention in the same breath both the saving of his newborn life and the implacable crescendo of the illness he brought with him into the world. He invites us to envision in a single glance images of disease along with images of attempted remedies and cures. It is therefore essential that we try to understand how he compares, contrasts, and combines these images in a work that is among the most astonishing accounts we have of the *curable* and the *incurable*.

The Ills of Civilization

The *Discourse on the Sciences and the Arts,* which marked the debut of Rousseau's literary career, is an indictment of the disease—the poison—that overtakes civilized societies as "fatal enlightenment" and "idle knowledge" progress. Can the progress of this disease be reversed? For a while Rousseau allows us to believe that it cannot, but he is only setting the stage for a final effect. In his conclusion he mentions the possibility of extracting a therapeutic principle from the poison itself, and since he has written the essay in the hope of winning a prize offered by the Academy of Dijon, he uses this as an argument to justify the existence of academies. But even though Rousseau's purpose here was to compliment the academicians who would sit in judgment of his work, his argument was of the utmost importance and would later serve him in very different contexts: "I admit, however, that the evil is not as great as it might become. Eternal providence, by placing salutary simples alongside noxious plants, and by endowing the substance of certain harmful animals with remedies for their wounds, has taught the sovereigns who are its ministers to imitate its wisdom."[3]

The idea is expressed in the broadest possible terms: remedies are to be found near where poisonous plants grow and in the very flesh of dangerous animals. In one case the noxious agent attracts its antidote; in the other it contains it. The intervention of a therapist—in this case Louis XIV, the protector and founder of the Academies—is required to *extract* the remedy from the poison. By following the example of Providence, Rousseau asserts, "this great monarch drew from the very bosom of the sciences and arts, the sources of a thousand aberrations, . . . those celebrated societies charged with the safekeeping of human knowledge and with the sacred trust of morals."[4] The image of the remedy is here patterned after that of a select society of men bound by a mutual insistence on purity of morals and concern to safeguard a perilous treasure.[5] Thus the remedy is to entrust the ambiguous privilege of knowledge to a small number of men, who will seek to perpetuate and even increase that knowledge while limiting its diffusion. We recognize the Rousseauist ideal of a closed community, which can be as large as a city-state but which can equally well be limited to a small "elite society" of noble souls *(belles âmes)*. The antidote is the poison itself, provided it is kept under strict surveillance by exceptional men certain not to be corrupted by its deleterious power. The society of Clarens is a perfect example.

The evil of which Rousseau accused the sciences and the arts was that of dissolving the truth of human relations. By contrast, one could reconstitute an island of transparency by gathering together a community of equal individuals, all virtuous, who would form a select society devoting itself to "cultivation of the sciences." Of primary importance was that each member of this society should be a *true* scholar. The members of academies, as idealized by Rousseau, were people in possession of abundant and authentic knowledge, radically different from the "idle science" he denounced as the work of "charlatans." This deceptive and pretentious brand of learning had only the appearance of knowledge. Around it the gap between appearance and reality spread like an epidemic. The true science of the academicians repaired, among themselves at any rate, this ontological tear; it overcame alienation and restored the unity of external appearance and internal reality.

Was the remedy reliable, however? Was it powerful enough to overcome the disease? Because Rousseau does not wish to diminish the pathos of his indictment, he hints that the outcome may be uncertain and of limited effectiveness. At a time when medicine had few effective weapons at its disposal, the metaphor of a "remedy" left the way clear for skepticism: "The intensity of the care only demonstrates the need, and no one looks for remedies for nonexistent diseases. To be sure, the available remedies are inadequate. But is that not the case with all common remedies?"[6]

Indeed, there was a danger that the prestige of the academies might make the sciences attractive and thus, rather than confine them within a safe zone, help spread them dangerously abroad, leading to relapse. Rousseau refuses to retract his accusatory warning that the disease may be irremediable, but he is equally unwilling to relinquish whatever appeal he may exercise on the reader who, having been made to feel his guilt, is instructed on the means of achieving a difficult salvation and the price that must be paid. In the course of the lengthy polemic triggered by the first discourse, Rousseau continually invoked the remedy metaphor, but he varied it in every possible way as if experimenting with its latent possibilities. In one text he starts out by stating that "no more remedies can be hoped for," but ultimately he leaves the question open.[7] He leaves it to others to provide an answer: "I have seen the ill and tried to find its causes; others bolder or more foolhardy than I may search for a remedy."[8]

In the *Observations* (which Rousseau addressed to the king of Poland, who had ventured to take part in the debate) and later in the preface of *Narcissus,* the remedy was downgraded to the status of a palliative. Compromise with the disease is the only hope that remains:

I have praised the academies and their illustrious founders, and I gladly repeat that praise. When the disease is incurable, the physician applies palliatives and administers remedies in proportion not so much to the patient's needs as to his temperament.[9]

The same causes that have corrupted peoples serve sometimes to prevent even greater corruption. Thus a person who has ruined his temperament by unwarranted use of medicine must look once more to the physicians to save his life. And the arts and sciences, having given birth to many vices, are needed to prevent them from turning into crimes. At least they cover them with a varnish that prevents the poison from being exhaled so freely . . . My advice is therefore . . . to allow academies, colleges, universities, libraries, spectacles, and all the other amusements that may divert men from their wickedness to exist, and even to devote much care to their maintenance.[10]

Note that here the recourse to medicine (and its remedies) is itself described as a kind of poison; the palliative extracted from the primary poison is a drug of the second degree. But the relation between illness and remedy can also be cast in more dramatic fashion as a choice between incurable disease and heroic cure, now called "revolution," which risks provoking a disease even more serious than the one it is meant to treat. Is Rousseau proposing a potential cure, or is he pushing pessimism to an extreme by suggesting that the heroic cure magnifies the disease to the ultimate degree?

> No one has ever seen a corrupted people return to virtue. You may pretend to destroy the sources of the disease, but to no avail . . . You may restore men to the primordial condition of equality, but in vain . . . Their hearts, once spoiled, will remain so always. No remedy is possible, except perhaps some great revolution almost as much to be feared as the disease it is meant to cure, and which it is blameworthy to desire and impossible to foresee.[11]

Note the rhetorical precautions employed here to evoke, hypothetically, a remedy that can be described only in terms of the ambivalent feelings it inspires before the fact. Rousseau does not tell us whether a "revolution" that by some miracle does exert a curative effect is derived from the substance of the poison itself. It may rather be one of those dramatic changes that take place when things are at their worst: a reversal brought about by the disease but not necessarily of the same nature. But it makes no difference: Rousseau sees the malady as reintroducing itself via the "revolution," so that an intimate relation persists between disease and response.

It is a matter of some moment, however, whether the remedy is conceived on the homeopathic model as being inherent *in* the cause of the disease itself or on the allopathic model as coming from *outside* to combat the disease through administration of a contrary agent. If, through improvements of a practical order, the disease can somehow be made to cure itself, the way is open to a great reconciliation, and none of what human beings have acquired over the course of history need be totally rejected. If not, the disease must progress to a point of crisis before a liberating rupture can occur and a new order be established to replace the one that has succumbed to terminal corruption. In either case the disease will have been useful, but in the former it will have demonstrated its aptitude for transformation from evil into good, whereas in the latter its very severity will have called down the forces of destruction and led to its replacement by an antagonistic power.

LITERATURE JUSTIFIED

One of the first objections raised by Rousseau's adversaries (who in so doing availed themselves of a familiar figure of legal rhetoric known as retortion) was to ask how it was, since he condemned the arts and sciences, that he came to write such eloquent discourses. Rousseau defended himself by invoking the image of using evil to combat evil, a theme on which he rang countless changes:

> On this subject I might mention what the Church Fathers said about the worldly sciences they despised yet used to combat the pagan philosophers. I might cite the comparison they made with the Egyptian vases stolen by the Israelites. But I shall limit my final response to this single question: if someone came to kill me and I were lucky enough to catch hold of his weapon, would I be forbidden to use it to drive him from my home before disposing of it?[12]

When he published the comedy *Narcissus,* however, Rousseau could not avoid explaining his participation in an activity that he had so loudly condemned. Among the reasons he gives at least two belong to the order of argument that concerns us here. He says, first of all, that what he is doing is merely a diversion, a palliative. For once he expresses this in a nonmedical metaphor: "The question is no longer to induce people to do good but simply to distract them from doing ill. They must be occupied with foolishness in order to dissuade them from wickedness. They have to be amused, not preached to."[13] Yet soon the figures of injury, venom, and poison are again being invoked as metaphors for the disease in question, which must therefore be treated with the appropriate therapy, namely, the poison itself: "Although these things have done much harm to society, today it is highly essential that they be used as a medicine for the ills they have caused, or in the manner of those harmful animals that must be crushed on the very wound they inflict as they bite."[14] Later he addressed Voltaire: "But there comes a time when the illness is such that the causes from which it stems are necessary to prevent it from increasing. It is like the arrow that must be left in the wound lest the victim die from plucking it out. As for myself, if I had followed my original vocation and neither read nor written, I would no doubt have been happier. If letters were now abolished, however, I would be deprived of the only pleasure I have left."[15]

In the dialogue that serves as a second preface to *La Nouvelle Héloïse,* Rousseau has his interlocutor pose the following questions: "Is it enough that [the moral of your book] goes to the source of the ill? Are you not afraid that it will cause further harm?" Rousseau answers: "The source of the ill? Whose ill? In a time of epidemic and contagion should the distribution of drugs helpful to the sick be prevented on the grounds that they may be harmful to healthy people?"[16] The novel is indeed an ill, as the first of the two prefaces states: "No chaste girl ever read novels . . . Any girl who, despite this title, dares to read a single page is lost."[17] Yet Saint-Preux writes Julie: "Novels are the only instruction that remains for a people so corrupt that no other instruction can do it any good."[18]

Rousseau develops a similar casuistry when he considers the value of theater in various types of society. Though pernicious for states that have preserved their moral health, the theater may be useful in large cities, where it interferes with more harmful activities:

> Reason demands that amusements of people whose occupations are harmful be encouraged and that those whose occupations are useful be dissuaded from partaking of those same amusements. Another general consideration is that it is not good to allow idle and corrupt men to choose their own amusements lest they conceive them in the image of their vicious inclinations and become as obnoxious in their pleasures as in their affairs.[19]

Clearly Rousseau has in mind some form of government intervention, and it is difficult to say whether that intervention would have had more in common with old-fashioned religious censorship or with the state-sponsored cultural policies of our own day. But this voluntaristic conception is itself a consequence (or corollary) of the idea of history as decline or as the progress of evil. The virtually constant metaphor of a remedy administered by a therapist is linked to the metaphor of social change as decline, as akin to the decay of a living organism. The "morals" of a people are subject to "the inevitable accidents that attack them," to "the natural tendency that deforms them."[20] When salutary action is possible, it consists essentially in prohibiting certain things or delaying certain changes: "All that human wisdom can do is to prevent changes, to halt long in advance everything that brings them on."[21] If the disease is not too advanced, preventive measures can be recommended. But by the time corruption has progressed in "large cities," it is too late for anything but diversion, carried out in deliberate fashion by an informed government:

> Government policies (la police) cannot do enough to increase the number of permissible pleasures or to make them even more agreeable so that private individuals are not tempted to seek out even more dangerous recreations.[22]

> In some places [theatrical spectacles] may be useful for attracting foreigners; for increasing the circulation of currency; for stimulating artists; for varying fashions; for occupying those who are or aspire to be excessively wealthy; for making them less harmful; for distracting the common people from their miseries; for turning their attention to mountebanks and away from their leaders; for preserving and improving taste when decency is lost; for varnishing over the ugliness of vice; in short, for preventing bad morals from degenerating into brigandage.[23]

In other words, having stated that "the moral effect of plays and theaters can never be good or salutary in itself," Rousseau now admits that "when the people are corrupt, spectacles are good for them."[24] Concerning Geneva, the final pages of the *Letter to d'Alembert* begin with what appears to be a definitive denunciation: "With plays, all that may be useful to those for whom they are created may become harmful to us."[25] But just when it seems that Rousseau has banished the theater from Geneva once and for all (on the grounds that the people of the city still have "morals" and would therefore stand to lose if they tolerated such a seedbed of corruption), he proposes a surprising remedy, and one that relies on the dramatic art, that is, on the disease itself. The therapeutic approach is to accept the evil inherent in the theater (which is distortion, alienation, separation of consciences) and use it to effect a reconciliation of the self (retour à soi):

> I see only one remedy for so many drawbacks: in order to appropriate the dramas of our theater, we must write them ourselves, and we

must have playwrights before we have actors. It is not good for us to be shown all sorts of imitations; it is good for us to be shown only those decent things appropriate to free men. It is certain that plays derived, like those of the Greeks, from the past misfortunes of the fatherland or the present defects of the people could offer useful lessons to their spectators.[26]

It will, however, be difficult, Rousseau admits, to build a great national theater, since the heroes that it would celebrate would be obscure men with "common names." At his wits' end, Rousseau therefore asks Voltaire (who is the implicit enemy throughout the *Letter to d'Alembert*) to write new tragedies on Roman and republican themes. Voltaire is thus invoked against Voltaire himself. This part of the text is not intended simply to mollify the great man. As usual it proposes treating the disease with a remedy derived from the disease itself: "May M. de Voltaire deign to compose tragedies on the model of *The Death of Caesar* or the first act of *Brutus*. If we absolutely must have a theater, let him pledge to fill it always with his genius, and to live as much as his plays do."[27]

Ultimately Rousseau comes to favor other kinds of spectacle: popular celebrations in the open air (for summer) and dances (for winter). Is the festival really the negation of the theater, however? Isn't it rather the generalization, the extension of the theater to the entire community? If so, then Rousseau is proposing to treat the disease of exclusive theatrical presentations not by eliminating the theater but by transforming it into something more inclusive. In that way it can incorporate the entire population of the city, as each person becomes simultaneously actor and spectator. The festival is the theatricalized version of the act of voluntary alienation performed by the parties to the social contract: obedience and submission, which are evils as long as they remain partial, become the cornerstone of legitimacy when no one is exempted. The alienating effects of the theater can be eliminated by transforming the theater into something like a "group in fusion" [to borrow Sartre's terminology—TRANS.]. The effects of appearance and imitation could be denounced as corrupting as long as they implied isolated consciousnesses. As if by a stroke of the magic wand, however, appearance becomes beneficial as soon as everyone is drawn into the business of viewing everyone else in a universal exchange of gazes.

Clearly, the terms of the problem had simply been shifted. Evil—*true evil*—revealed itself most fully in the guise of non-reciprocity. In the development of Rousseau's thinking, non-reciprocity vanished when the theater, initially stigmatized as a perverse entertainment, was generalized to a universally shared experience. In other words, the remedy's medicinal value lay in the move toward self-reconciliation (which is what Rousseau has in mind when he speaks of "appropriating the dramas of our theater") and egalitarian universalism. This move strikes at the root of the illness and opens up a new perspective. Read the celebrated exhortation that inspired Robespierre and many others in more recent times: "Go one better: make the spectators themselves the spectacle. Make them actors themselves, see to it that they see and love themselves in one another for the greater unity of all . . . All societies are one, all things are common to all men."[28] Compare this with the doctrine attributed the the Gnostics, that the best way to free oneself from evil is to extend it, to push it to the limit. In Tertullian's *De pudicitia* (I, 16) we read: "Incontinence is necessary to continence; fight fire with fire."

EXTENSION OF THE SYSTEM

It should come as no surprise, therefore, that, twice and in almost identical terms (in the *Political Fragments* and in the Geneva manuscript of the *Social Contract*), Rousseau used the metaphor of "the antidote in the poison" to formulate the fundamental insight of his political philosophy: "Let us strive to draw from the poison itself the antidote needed to counteract it. If possible let us correct through new associations the defect in the general association . . . Let us demonstrate . . . in perfected art the cure for the ills that inchoate art *(l'art commencé)* inflicts on nature."[29] Although Rousseau blames human history for having developed the alienating faculties of reflection, amour-propre, abstraction, imagination, and intellectual dependence, he expressly warns against any attempt to turn back the clock. The development that has made us unhappy must be carried even further: reflection must be perfected, amour-propre put to work, the imagination channeled. Alienation must be made reciprocal and complete. This is our only chance of rediscovering in a new (political and moral) form our original (natural and animal) wholeness, which has been destroyed by the onset of our affliction. In *Emile* he writes: "It requires a great deal of art to prevent social man from being entirely artificial."[30] And: "Our only grip on passion is through the passions. Their tyranny must be combatted through their power."[31] The name for the disease is also the name for the antagonistic force.

The imagination, which is to be feared if it obtrudes on life too early, takes on a positive value when it serves to distract Emile from "real objects," namely, women encountered "in the world." In book IV of *Emile* Rousseau recommends smothering "the first flames of the imagination." But later, in order to prevent his adolescent pupil from succumbing to corrupting influences, he calls upon the imagination to invent an ideal "model." Initially suspect because of its power to "awaken the senses," the imagination is now invested with the power to "repress the senses." There is nothing contradictory about this. The argument is based in large part on a therapeutic model: an active substance ceases to be dangerous depending on the individual, the time, the danger to be met, and so on.

In fact, the whole ethical program that immediately precedes the discussion of religious education in book IV of *Emile* is aimed at assigning amour-propre the positive role it was absolutely denied at the beginning of the same book. Earlier Rousseau wrote that "love of self, which looks only at myself, is content when my true needs are satisfied; but amour-propre, which compares, is never and can never be content, because in preferring myself to others this sentiment also requires that others prefer me over themselves, which is impossible. Thus the gentle and affectionate passions stem from love of self, and the hateful and irascible passions from amour-propre."[32] But Emile cannot be prevented from making comparisons, and he thus comes to experience amour-propre. The reader then learns, not without surprise, that not all the passions stemming from amour-propre are hateful and irascible. Some of them may be "humane and gentle" and can develop in the direction of "benevolence" and "commiseration."[33] Emile's education thus enters a new phase, which makes use of a properly guided amour-propre. Accordingly, an activity that had been described as harmful in an earlier stage can now be useful, namely, profiting from the "experience of others" by reading history.[34] Emile can now be permitted to covet first place, to prefer himself to others, and thus to expose himself to flattery (thus justifying the reading of fables, which in book II was considered pointless and pernicious).

Emile may now feel pity not as natural man does, through spontaneous identification with suffering creatures, but in a detached way, contemplating the human spectacle from on high or at a distance. Though still in certain respects a "savage," Emile brings knowledge and judgment to bear in order to put himself "in the place of others." Reflection, so harmful if allowed to operate prematurely, now enables him to feel compassion for their misery. Just as theatrical pretense loses its harmful effects when generalized to the entire population, so, too, does amour-propre cease to be harmful through generalization:

> People who never deal with any affairs other than their own are too impassioned to form healthy judgments. Seeing everything in relation to themselves alone and shaping their ideas of good and evil to suit their own interest, they fill their minds with a thousand ridiculous prejudices, and in anything that is in the slightest degree inimical to their own advantage they see a threat to the whole universe.
>
> *If we extend amour-propre to other individuals, we transform it into a virtue*, and there is not a single human heart in which this virtue has no root. The less the object of our attention has to do directly with us, the less the illusion of self-interest is to be feared, the more that interest is generalized, the more equitable it becomes.[35]

The transmutation of poison into antidote, of what was a source of vice and conflict into a "virtue," is accomplished by changing the point of application; the sentiment of amour-propre is the same, but its structure and distribution are different.

The poison/disease metaphor when applied to the sociopolitical sphere implies, as in the medical model, that the antidote/remedy must be administered at the proper moment. It must comfort and strengthen *(conforter)* the suffering body at the moment of truth, when the disease, having attained its natural limit, is *judged* in its evolution toward death or recovery: the power of a medicine manifests itself at the *critical* moment in the combat between nature and disease. A crisis is always an alternative: recovery is simply the more favorable of two possible outcomes. Lexicographically and semantically the concepts of *crisis* and *revolution* are of course similar and sometimes linked.[36]

In discussing the rise of inequality Rousseau describes how societies develop until they reach a "terminal point" at which "further revolutions either dissolve the government entirely or move it closer to the legitimate institution." This alternative is a crisis, analogous to the ones described in the *Social Contract*, where the two similar terms are explicitly linked:

> Just as certain diseases confuse the mind and obliterate all memory of the past, in the lives of states there are sometimes violent epochs in which revolutions do to peoples what certain crises do to individuals, in which horror of the past is tantamount to loss of memory, and in which the state, inflamed by civil war, is in a manner of speaking reborn from its ashes and, escaping from the arms of death, regains the vigor of youth.[37]

The same idea can be found in *Judgment on Polysynody*, where Rousseau speaks of the "moment of anarchy and crisis that necessarily precedes a new establishment."[38] In the ninth of the *Letters from the Mountain* he compares the legitimate government of Geneva with the arbitrary rule of a patrician oligarchy:

> But compare, and you will find on the one hand definite ills, terrible evils, unlimited and endless, and on the other hand difficulty even with mere abuse, so that if the abuse is great it will be brief and when it occurs it always brings its own remedy with it . . . There will always be this difference between the one and the other, that abuse of liberty will harm the community guilty of it and, punishing it for its wrong, will force it to seek a remedy; so that in this case the affliction is never anything other than a crisis; it cannot be a permanent condition.[39]

As terrible as the ills of arbitrary government may be (and Rousseau envisions the worst case), there is still reason for hope in the very severity of the ailment: "The worst of conditions has but one advantage: things can only get better. This is the sole resource of extreme afflictions."[40] (At the end of his life Rousseau would describe his own situation in the very same terms.) The following passage from the *Considerations on the Government of Poland* attests to the persistence of this type of argument: "Extreme afflictions call for violent remedies; one must try to heal them whatever the cost . . . Any free state that fails to foresee great crises stands in peril of death at every storm. Only the Poles have deduced from the crises themselves a new way of preserving the Constitution."[41]

Even Oriental despotism contains the remedy for its own failings:

"Oriental despotism subsists because it is harder on the grandees than on the people: it thus takes from itself its own remedy."[42] Striking as such assertions are, they are not Rousseau's final word. They merely temper the pessimistic vision of human social evolution that predominates in his work. Crises and revolutions are themselves fraught with fatal danger. Thinking to administer a remedy for disorder, one only hastens disaster: "When will men learn that there is no disorder so harmful as the arbitrary power by which they attempt to administer a remedy? This power is itself the worst of all disorders. To prevent them by such means is to kill people in order to cure their fever."[43] Here Rousseau is harking back to antimedical tradition, which he frequently invokes: the use of remedies is the worst of all maladies. The remedy in the disease is provided either by nature or by *perfected* art. Imperfect art can only do harm if it resorts to drugs.

IMAGINARY CURES

Emile and the *Social Contract* are grand theories based on the principle of using poison against itself. This same principle also governs Rousseau's affective imagination and even his behavior. It is therefore worth digressing a moment to examine some of his favorite fictions.

Valère is a fop who spends too much time in front of a mirror. On his wedding day his sister attempts to "cure him of a weakness that exposed him to ridicule."[44] She therefore orders a portrait of her brother dressed in female finery and made to look like a woman. He falls in love with the unknown woman in the portrait and tries to delay his marriage. His affliction thus attains its paroxysm. Disabused of his error, Valère, alias Narcissus, claims to be "cured of a silly affectation that was the shame of his youth."[45]

The Village Soothsayer is, taken in the broadest sense, also a story of healing. Following a traditional formula of comedy, the soothsayer advises Colette to feign infidelity and claim to love "a gentleman from town" so as to arouse the jealousy of her fickle lover Colin, whereupon he will leave "the lady of the castle" and beg her forgiveness. Colette grasps the point of the advice at once: "I will pretend to imitate the example he has set." Equal but opposite, the two infidelities will cancel each other out, and everyone will live happily ever after.

A well-meaning fairy tells the Phoenix King how he can win back the affections of the Fairy Queen: "Your best hope of curing your wife of her extravagances is to emulate them."[46] Rousseau offers the same advice to tutors of the young: "Show your pupil your weaknesses in order to cure him of his own. Let him see in you the same battles that are raging within himself."[47]

La Nouvelle Héloïse, a vast panorama of fantasy, is a novel whose characters, never fully cured of their afflictions, are condemned always to imagine newer and better remedies. Whenever a cure seems imminent or certain, it turns out to be illusory, incomplete, or temporary. Julie informs Saint-Preux that she is pregnant in these mysterious terms: "The love that caused our ills must give us the remedy for them" (part 1, letter 33). Ultimately this hope too will vanish. Otherwise the healing—marriage—would have come too easily. Rousseau's imagination requires greater sacrifices and reinforces the image of prohibition.

Of the various characters in the book, M. de Wolmar stands for self-assured rationality. He is the one character capable of manipulating the others for their own good, the clairvoyant therapist in all realms except the religious. His role is that of the demanding superego. After marrying Julie, he invites the man she had loved passionately a few years earlier to come to Clarens. His plan is to complete the cure of the former lovers. Convinced that they "are more in love than ever" yet "fully cured,"[48] he intends to eliminate the contradiction in this situation by rooting out what remains of their love. To the perspicacious Wolmar it is obvious that Saint-Preux loves Julie "in the past." In his words: "Their highly stimulated imaginations continually portrayed each to the other as they were during their separation." Present reality must therefore be substituted for the illusions that hold them in thrall. (This is the reverse of Rousseau's usual method, which is to invent an imaginary world to compensate for the inadequacy of real objects. Only after his imaginative powers dry up does he seek to moor his mind to the objective details of the plant world.[49] Then, however, the purpose of the reconciliation with reality is to preserve a sphere of activity, to perpetuate what is intended to be an innocent intellectual occupation, and not to exorcise a guilty imagination.) Saint-Preux allows himself to be persuaded: "M. de Wolmar's explanations fully reassured me as to the true state of my heart. Though all too weak, that heart was as fully cured as it could be . . . My heart is as filled with peace as is the room in which I am living . . . Although I do not enjoy all the authority of a master, I experience even greater pleasure in looking upon myself as the child of the house" (V, 2). Wolmar has apparently been able to dupe (in French: *donner le change à*) Saint-Preux's imagination by substituting one object for another: "Instead of his mistress I force him always to see the wife of a respectable man and the mother of my children; I erase one portrait with another, and cover the past with the present." Wolmar, by staying away, proposes to remove himself as an obstacle standing between the two former lovers: "The more they see each other alone, the more readily they will understand their error as they compare what they feel with what they would once have felt in a similar situation." The danger is heightened, the better to overcome it. If the malady (in the eyes of conventional morality) was previously the "meeting" of Julie and Saint-Preux, the remedy chosen by Wolmar is to bring them together again so as to root out the effects of passion: Wolmar removes himself from the scene so that the former lovers can internalize his image and accept the reality of a present in which they no longer belong to each other.

We are, however, in the realm of passionate love, and it would be to step outside love's magic circle to assume that this attempt at a rational cure is entirely successful. In love it is the incurable that is fascinating. To the end of the novel Julie remains "virtuous" but not "cured."[50] On the brink of death she confesses the continued existence of her love, for it is too late to do any harm: "For a long time I remained under an illusion. That illusion was good for me. Now that I longer need it, it has destroyed itself. You believed that I was cured, and so did I. Let us give thanks to the one who caused that error to last as long as it was useful."[51] Thus the imminence of death reveals that passion remains unhealed, that the deliberate struggle to subdue it has failed, but it also reveals a higher order in which the law of sublimated passion reigns supreme and in which another ill—the lovers' *separation*—will be definitively cured. Thus the non-healing of illegitimate love (according to the laws of reason and society) corresponds to the healing of separation (according to the law of passion). And virtue, which in this world was the handmaiden of social taboo, in the other world accomplishes the couple's eternal union: "The virtue that separated us on earth will reunite us in our eternal abode."[52] Wolmar's half-successful cure allowed the disease (in this case guilty passion, repressed but not eliminated by virtue) to persist, but in the end the tables are turned: once an ontological divide is crossed, the sickness of love becomes the supreme good. In the complex game that Rousseau's imagination is playing, forces of frustration are transformed into curative powers. Virtue and death are no longer the negation of pleasure but its preconditions. The worst misfortune that can befall desire can take on new value as an antidote. In Rousseau, one might even say, faith in the other world is not so much an act of disinterested belief as the hollowing out of a space in which the transmutation of sickness into remedy can take place. The crucial thing is the will to consolation: it demands an afterlife.

An Epistolary Therapy

Henriette, one of many total strangers who corresponded with Rousseau, wrote to tell him of her suffering and to ask for his advice. After the success of his major works, Rousseau accepted the role of confessor and spiritual guide. He did his best to live up to the expectations of the countless readers who wrote because they had not found happiness in their lives.[53] Not without irritation, and at times with suspicion, Rousseau took on the role of master of happiness, healer of souls, and dispenser of useful remedies. To judge from his responses, this therapist's role did not displease him. Instinctively, one might say, he alluded to his own ills, both to protect himself from correspondents who wanted too much from him and to heighten his charismatic powers. He was aware of his precursors in myth and religion and knew the prestige that attached to the figure of the suffering healer. A healer who had been touched by an affliction himself was more apt to dispense a useful remedy than one who had never suffered. In other words, Rousseau was qualified to serve as a guide because he himself had gone astray.

Henriette began her letter with a feminist protest against Rousseau's sarcastic remarks on the subject of educated women. Elderly, impoverished, afflicted with many ills, she viewed literary studies as her only solace, her best hope for fleeing her woes. One cannot doubt the reality of her (depressive) suffering after hearing her describe the ordeal of waking up (in a style that has no precedent):

It is a long time since I have known the happiness of waking up with the sweet tranquillity that makes one glad to exist with the prospect of a quiet and pleasant day in store. The moment of awakening is the most terrifying moment of my life. A sharp twinge in my heart snatches me from sleep, a piercing arrow of pain rouses my senses from their stupor, and the fear and terror of awakening finishes the job.

After being awakened and returned to life by such painful feelings, I find myself all alone in nature. A thousand sad and confused ideas gather and form a thick cloud that seems to envelop me. I try to get away, I struggle, I look around, I gaze upon the things around me, I see nothing to console me, I call upon reason, I see it, I hear it, but nothing speaks to my heart. Regret at not being able to sleep through the rest of my sad existence only adds to my woes. What an effort it is, Sir, to finish with any greater sense of security days begun amid such shadows! . . . What I try is to put [my heart] to sleep by fixing my mind on objects apt to hold its attention. At first there may not be much interest in them, but with time habit, reawakened curiosity, and a tincture of vanity can sometimes conspire to form a passion that is not without effect. I would be so happy if only I could find some peace, even at the cost of looking foolish.

The opportunity to write all these things down on paper is already the source of some relief:

Since I gave in to the desire to write to you and took up my unfamiliar pen, I feel that I have passed some quieter hours. Preoccupied with what I wanted to write to you, wanting to say enough and fearing to say too much, anxious about the impression that my writing would make on you, torn between the fear of looking foolish and the hope of finding a reliable and indulgent guide, daring and not daring, constant only in the feelings of esteem and admiration that the reading of your works has inspired in me, my imagination wraps you in a variety of forms. When it allows me to see only the philosopher, I am frightened; I tear everything up and burn it. When it endows you with all the kindly traits of goodness and humanity, I regain my confidence, I feel comfortable again, and I write. In the end, all of this has given me something to occupy my mind, something lively enough and strong enough to distract me from my usual thoughts and from that inner feeling that I would be so glad to lose.[54]

Rousseau's response is singular. He could hardly have failed to recognize the tone of melancholy suffering in the letter, but oddly enough he is convinced that his correspondent has disguised her true identity and that the letter is really from Suzanne Curchod (a *belle penseuse*, "a woman who courts notoriety"[55]—Gibbon wanted to marry her, Necker did so, and she became the hostess of a Paris salon). Accordingly, his response takes the tone of a man who refuses to be taken in, who will not rise to the bait. He castigates amour-propre, vanity, and wit. His suspicions are ill founded, yet despite his error about the identity of his correspondent, Rousseau's rude tone may not have been entirely out of place. In a manner reminiscent of a fairly common psychoanalytic technique, he looks beyond the explicit message to its implicit intention: "Above each of your lines I read these words in large characters: *Let us see if you will have the audacity to condemn a person who thinks and writes in this way not to think or read any more.* This interpretation is assuredly not a criticism, and I can only feel gratitude that you count me among those whose judgment matters to you." More to the point, Rousseau, in an attempt at individual guidance, rehearses arguments from his philosophy of history:

> One can no more regain simplicity than one can regain childhood. The mind, once in effervescence, remains so forever, and anyone who has thought will think for the rest of his life. Therein lies the greatest misfortune of the reflective state: the more one is aware of its ills, the more one increases them, and all our efforts to escape from this condition only serve to bog us down that much more deeply.
>   Let us speak not of changing our condition but of what benefit you may derive from yours. That condition is unhappy and must always remain so. Your ills are serious and without remedies . . . And to make them bearable you are looking for at least a palliative. Is that not the purpose of your study plans and occupations?

Rousseau begins by stating that the woman's present illness is incurable: there is no turning back. He makes her condition sound even bleaker than she does and offers not the slightest reason for hope, as if he knew by instinct that it is wise to be rude to people in depression and that merely *answering* her plea is already enough of a gift. He attempts to trace the illness back to its source (but blindly, since he believes that the woman at the other end is Suzanne Curchod): "But what is this vaunted sensibility? Do you want to know, Henriette? In the final analysis it is a form of amour-propre, which makes comparisons. I have put my finger on the seat of the disease." Rousseau adopts the same tactic he used in the first discourse: Henriette's chosen remedy, he says initially, is nothing but a more acute form of her affliction: "On the pretext of working for independence, you work for domination. Hence far from alleviating the burden of opinion that makes you so unhappy, you increase its weight. That is not the way to make your waking up more serene." Later, however, Rousseau offers, as he has hinted he would, his approval of Henriette's decision. Study, which is her affliction, can also cure it, but on one condition: that it is not a distraction or a diversion but a means of self-reconciliation:

> Although my ideas in this respect differ greatly from yours, we are almost in agreement as to what you must do. For you, study is now the Achilles' spear that must heal the wound it made. But you want merely to nullify the pain, and I would like to remove its cause. You want to distract your attention from yourself by means of philosophy. I would like philosophy to detach you from everything and return you to yourself. . . . Then, content with yourself yet incapable of being discontent with others, you will sleep peacefully and awake with pleasure.

Telephus and the Spear of Achilles

At the beginning of the *Remedia Amoris* Ovid plays with the same allusion to Achilles: "I have already taught you the art of love. Now learn the art of how to love no longer. The hand that wounded you can also heal you. The same soil often produces both healthy and harmful herbs. The rose grows close to the nettle, and Achilles' spear itself closed the wound it inflicted on Hercules' son."[56]

In the *Metamorphoses* Ovid has Achilles say: "Telephus twice felt the power of my spear."[57] And in the *Tristia* he mentions Telephus again: "Telephus would have died of an incurable wound if the hand that wounded him had not also healed him."[58] In the ancient world the name of Telephus, healed by the spear that wounded him, symbolized "healing by the weapon that inflicted the wound." The erotic uses of this concept are not difficult to imagine: the object of desire inflicts a wound that cannot be healed except by possession of that same object. Consider the following two epigrams from the *Greek Anthology:*

I carry my love as a wound. Instead of blood tears flow from my wound, which never runs dry. My affliction leaves me helpless, and Machaon himself has no balm to soothe my distress. I am Telephus, young lady. And you, you be my loyal Achilles: may your beauty slake my desire, just as it smote me.[59]

If your present to me [a pair of apples] is a symbol of your breasts, I greatly appreciate the favor. But if you stop there, how wicked of you, having touched off such a violent conflagration, to refuse to put it out. The man who wounded Telephus also healed him. Do not treat me, little girl, more cruelly than one would treat an enemy.[60]

Even more striking, however, was the use of this myth element to denote the ambiguity of literary language. Ovid, as we have seen, used it to evoke the double power of his poetry—erotic and anti-erotic. In a more edifying context, Plutarch uses the image of Telephus to describe the effects of philosophical language:

When some wise dictum has bitten you and made you suffer, why not take advantage of what is useful in it? Telephus's wound, healed according to Euripides by "rust scraped from the spear," is not the only wound to be cured in that way. The wounds that the incisive words of the philosophers inflict on the souls of well-born youths are to be cured by the very same words that caused them. One must accept this suffering, these nips, without being crushed or discouraged by the criticism . . . Let us bear with these early purifications, these first disruptions, in the hope that such torments and trials will bring us compensations as sweet as they are glorious.[61]

The legend of Telephus is known to us through the mythographers as well as through surviving fragments of the tragedy Euripides devoted to him. It is worth pausing a moment to examine it in greater detail. Telephus's childhood can be read as a variant of the Oedipus myth (Rank includes it in his collection[62]) in which the incestuous marriage of son and mother is prevented in the nick of time by divine intervention. The story can be summarized as follows:

Telephus, the son of Hercules and Auge, was exposed immediately after his birth and raised by a doe . . . When the boy grew up, he obeyed the oracle's orders and went to the court of Mysia to look for his parents. Teuthras, the king of Mysia, was at that time involved in a foreign war that was going badly for him. He announced that he would give his adoptive daughter Auge and his crown to anyone who could deliver him from his enemies. Telephus took command of the Mysian troops and after leading them to total victory was recognized as heir to the Mysian kingdom.[63] Teuthras awarded him Auge's hand in marriage, but when he entered her bedroom she threatened to kill him unless he left at once. As Telephus was prepared to use force, the gods sent a dragon, which separated the two and frightened Auge so badly that she threw down the sword she was holding. Telephus again insisted on his rights. Auge called for help to her lover, Hercules, and they then recognized one another.[64]

It is hard to be sure that there is any necessary connection between the legend of Telephus's childhood and the story of the adult hero, but one can obviously let one's imagination play freely with the intervention of the dragon and the appearance of the strong father prior to the infliction of a wound that will take some time to heal.

The story, as reconstructed from available sources by the compiler Chompré, continues as follows:

> The Greeks on their way to Troy wished to land in Telephus's territory, but he opposed them with armed force, resulting in a fierce battle . . . Telephus was wounded in the hip by Achilles . . . The oracle he consulted told him that he could be healed only by the same hand that had inflicted the wound. Since it did not seem likely that his enemy Achilles would want to help him, Clytemnestra (according to Hyginus) advised him to abduct Orestes in order to force Agamemnon to make Achilles agree to take part in the healing. But the hero could not be moved, so Ulysses said that the meaning of the oracle was that the spear that had caused the wound must serve as the remedy. He therefore removed some rust from the tip of the spear and used it to make a poultice, which he sent to Telephus, who was soon healed.[65]

Pliny the Elder interpreted this use of rust quite literally as a demonstration of the hemostatic and scar-inducing qualities of certain metallic filings. He might have meditated more allegorically on the fact that the medicinal substance was not the same as the substance that caused the injury. Between the wound and the healing the metal had been altered. Time had done its work. When applied the second time, the iron was nothing but a powder. The repetition was remedial only because the spear had in the meantime suffered its own affliction, as it were.

More generally, one might think of coining the word *telephism* to refer to a heightening of the ambivalence or ambiguity of the sado-masochistic personality structure. Briefly, using Freud's description of sado-masochism,[66] I would distinguish three variants of telephism:

a. An active, sadistic (Achillean) variant: first inflict a wound, then agree to heal it. Or invest an intense libidinal charge in the care lavished on an object that one has previously injured. Beat, then cajole; set a fire, then (to borrow Rousseau's expression) "set the pumps to working." The Kleinian notion of *reparation* captures this sequence of attitudes.

b. A moderate, reflexive variant: subject oneself to suffering in order to participate later in a gratifying exercise of self-consolation, of narcissistic reintegration of the wounded ego. Here, obsessionality can manifest itself doubly, first in the search for suffering, then in the labor of reparation.

c. A passive variant: to expose oneself to injury so as to be comforted later, if possible by those responsible for the injury. Subject oneself to beating in order to attract the active compassion of one's persecutor. Provoke the hatred of others and ask that it be turned into love.

The myth of Telephus is important, I think, because one can derive from it a psychological structure homologous to certain theological and cosmological themes (Gnostic, Christian, and revolutionary): the alleged cause of evil can be reinterpreted as the cause of a future good, and violence inflicted (or endured) is presented as a harbinger of future healing. *Felix culpa!* It is a fortunate malady that leads to a healing of all ills.[67] The blood of the Grail, which flows from the spear of Longinus that pierces Christ's flank, will heal the ailing King. The words of the oracle to Telephus, that the wounder shall be the healer *(ho trosas iassetai),* can be invoked by the most diverse theodicies. Of course Rousseau offers the most fully developed example of a Telephian philosophy of history and a Telephian existentialism, which are at once spontaneously experienced and clearly spelled out. That is what is so interesting about the exchange of letters between Rousseau and Henriette. The philosophy of Rousseau can be seen offering healing to the unknown correspondent, but Rousseau speaks to the distant letter-writer as he would later speak to himself in the *Reveries*. His method is the very one that will later oblige him to forsake philosophical writing for autobiography. Remember that Rousseau came to think of his philosophical works as an evil he had been induced to inflict upon the world, an evil whose consequences he would continue to suffer until the end of his days but that he would attempt to repair by new writing.

Henriette wrote twice, and Rousseau answered both letters. With this abundant source material we can make out two forms of Telephism: an intellectual form, having to do with the dangers and healing powers of study, and another, much more profound version.

When Rousseau wrote Henriette that "anyone who has thought will think for the rest of his life" and that, for her, "study is now Achilles' spear," he was applying to the destiny of an individual what he had already asserted about human history and proper social institutions, namely, that they are "most apt to denature man in a favorable way."[68] Culture, itself a malady, if developed to perfection becomes the new good, the agent of healing.

Something else that Rousseau says is more directly relevant to the sphere of the emotions. Henriette must be willing to give up other people, to break her ties with them, to forgo her "need of them." She must become "sufficient unto herself": "You say that you have enjoyed hours of calm while writing to me and telling me about yourself. It is surprising that this experience has not shown you the way and taught you where you must look to find, if not happiness, then at least peace."[69]

For Rousseau, the saving resource is thus the monologue of the soul, which, having broken all its ties, converses inwardly with itself. This is not what Henriette had in mind: she had not renounced communication with others, had not abandoned that hope. Hence in the second letter she resists Rousseau's interpretation: she wrote to him not to observe and console herself but to arouse his interest, to be heard. Why, she asks, were the hours spent in writing so precious? "Not, as you believe, because I was telling you about myself, but because I was speaking to you and preoccupied with what I was saying."[70] The desire for a meeting of the minds could hardly be better expressed. Henriette was successful in her aim in any case, because Rousseau ended his first letter by saying: "The most important thing was to make you aware of how much you interest me."[71] Later he also said: "What I promise you, and it is a promise I shall keep, is to think about you always and never to forget you."[72] But Henriette expressed her desire for communication as a desire to flee herself, to forget herself, and thus opened herself up to Rousseau's reproach. She hoped to "distract herself from that deep and painful feeling that follows her everywhere." She was afraid of anything that brought her "too close to herself." She would have liked to "wrest herself free" of her self, to "lose herself in this inward feeling," to "distract herself there." Rousseau answered that she must not seek to wrest herself free of her self but hold on to her self by wresting herself free of people and things. Against the centrifugal impulses of a soul that seeks escape into the world he offers the traditional (Stoic and Christian) lesson: *redi in te ipsum* (go back into yourself). Note his tactics. First he alludes to a feeling of impasse, of failure of the therapeutic relation, of incurability:

> I thought I glimpsed a plan for rescuing you from the anxieties you describe without recourse to the distractions that according to you are the only possible remedy and that according to me are not even a palliative. You tell me that I am wrong and that what I thought I saw was not the case. How could I possibly find a remedy for your condition when that condition is inconceivable to me? To me you are a distressing and humiliating enigma. I thought I knew the human heart, and I know nothing of yours. You are suffering, and I cannot give you solace.[73]

This further refusal of treatment (which can be interpreted as aggressive, as indicating a desire to wound) is followed by a discussion, initially in a questioning mode, of the remedy approved by Rousseau. As comparison with other, similar examples would show, Rousseau's therapeutic practice was first to wound or frustrate so as to be in a position to follow up with a caress or with salutary advice. Furthermore, the remedy, when he finally agrees to administer it, turns out to involve the neutral (or partially passive) form of Telephism: break with others or accept the distressing reality of their "insensitivity" in order to savor in oneself, and starting with oneself, the pleasure of *compensation:*

What? Because nothing outside yourself satisfies you, you want to flee yourself, and because you have reason to complain of others, because you despise them, because they have given you the right to do so, because you feel in yourself a soul worthy of esteem, you do not wish to console yourself with it for the contempt inspired in you by other souls that do not resemble yours? No, I cannot understand anything so bizarre, it passes me by.

This sensitivity that makes everything so unsatisfactory to you—should it not retreat into itself, should it not fill your heart with a sublime and delicious feeling of amour-propre, and haven't you always in it a resource against injustice and a compensation for insensitivity? It is so rare, you say, to encounter a soul. That is true, but how is it that you can have one and not be satisfied with it? If one were to probe people of a narrow and constricted sort, one would recoil from them, push them away, but after feeling so uncomfortable visiting others, what a pleasure it is to return home. I know how much the need for attachment makes it distressing to sensitive hearts that attachments are impossible to form. I know how sad that state is, but I also know that it is not without its pleasures. It causes rivulets of tears to be shed; it produces a melancholy that bears witness about ourselves that we should not wish to forgo. It causes us to seek solitude as the only refuge, where we find ourselves alone with all that we have reason to love. I cannot state this too strongly: I know neither happiness nor rest in estrangement from my self. On the contrary, I am every day more certain that one cannot be happy on earth except insofar as one shuns things and explores the self.[74]

For the edification of his correspondent Rousseau preaches by example, as he would later preach, in the *Reveries,* for the edification of posterity. The answer to one question remains unclear, however. Is Rousseau suggesting that we are wounded by the insensitivity of others or that we wound ourselves by shunning "things"? This is a point about which he needs to maintain confusion. Once I suffer such a loss, however, it is clear that my only recourse is to fasten amorously on my self, to labor long and hard on consolations drawn from my inner resources, to invest the bulk of my passionate energy in closing a wound that I simultaneously work to keep open. If the remedy lies in the exercise of my sensibility, its calming virtue stems from the fact that I can *interpret* suffering as a consequence of the characteristic superiority of the sensitive soul. To be sure, the malady arises out of other people's incomprehension and even hostility, but it is easy to give consoling and flattering reasons for those hateful sentiments. The victim thus has direct proof of his worth. Illness becomes a distinction that guarantees his superiority. The extravagance of the affliction is a necessary condition for the subject to take full pleasure in himself as the one exception from an otherwise universal malady. Rousseau of course prefers to ignore that he may himself have been an agent of the disease, may have lent it a helping hand. In the reflexive mode Telephus wounds himself so as to "compensate" himself later on. But for one who is fond of deep wounds, the trick is to persuade oneself that the injury was caused by Achilles' shaft. Recall that Rousseau invariably needs to construct an external, exculpatory genealogy of evil.[75] That is why he needs to convince himself that the reparative effect of reverie is the complete *opposite* of the ill. Even if the mind of the dreamer is aware that it depends on evil and its "shadows" to produce certainty of its own transparency, it does not consider itself to be implicated in the evil to which it responds. The projective mechanism ensures that it believes itself to be wounded by *others* and healed by itself. The wound is indicted for coming from outside, and healing is praised as coming from within. How could it be otherwise? The full power of compensation cannot be brought to bear without the conviction of facing up to an unknown power. If it were too clear that the subject was the cause of his own wound, the reparative effort would be hobbled at its very source. Now we can understand Rousseau's endlessly repeated assertions that he is "happy in spite of his enemies," assertions intended to convince himself that, in elaborating the compensation, the "supplement," the substitute activity, he is fully successful in his aims.

FURTHER EVIDENCE

Rousseau uses the same phrase on two separate, and noteworthy, occasions in the *Confessions:* "What might have ruined me saved me" (or "preserved me"). The first use is in connection with the spanking administered by Mademoiselle Lambercier and Jean-Jacques's concomitant discovery of masochistic pleasure: "But when the passing of the years had finally made me a man, it came to pass that *what might have ruined me preserved me.* Instead of disappearing, my former childish taste became so strongly associated with the other that I could never separate it from the desires kindled by my senses."[76] An earlier version of this passage reads: "*What might have ruined me saved me* for a long time from myself. At the age of puberty the object with which I was occupied diverted me from the one I had to fear. One idea, substituted for the other, stirred me without corrupting me."[77]

The same phrase occurs again almost verbatim when Rousseau describes the beginning of his stay at the home of Mme de Warens and his recourse to the "dangerous supplement that deceives nature": "What stimulants! The reader who imagines them must look upon me as if I were already half dead. On the contrary: *what might have ruined me saved me,* at least for a time."[78]

In other words, evil (perversity, autoeroticism) turns out to have saving graces: "vice" turns out to contain its own antidote—according to an interpretation dictated by the conscience, which stigmatizes carnal commerce as the supreme evil, compared with which any diversion or perversion reflected onto the self is beneficial.

The memory of Mademoiselle Lambercier is closely connected with the idea I have been developing in this essay. The episode of the broken comb completes the "salutary" effect that Rousseau ascribes to the spanking: "Who would believe, for example, that one of my soul's most vigorous resources was tempered in the same spring where lust and weakness flowed in my blood?" And in speaking of the "execution" administered by Uncle Bernard, Rousseau adds: "It was terrible. If, seeking the remedy in the disease itself, he had wished to deaden my depraved senses forever, he could not have found a better way to go about it."

At times Rousseau compares the effervescence of love to a disease and paradoxically attributes curative value to the misfortunes that stem from it. Consider, for example, the curious relation between misfortune and healing implicit in these lines on the origin of *La Nouvelle Héloïse:* "The intoxication that took hold of me, though lively and wild, was so durable and powerful that to recover from it took nothing less than the unforeseen and dreadful crisis of the misfortunes into which it plunged me."[79]

Consider these lines of youthful verse, composed at Chambéry:

Et le mal dont mon corps se sent presque abattu
N'est pour moi qu'un sujet d'affermir ma vertu.[80]

[And the disease that has all but overwhelmed my body
is but an occasion for me to bolster my virtue.]

At first sight these lines seem to express a commonplace idea: the soul, by resisting a disease, can derive spiritual benefit from it. A psychoanalyst would speak of "secondary gain." When Jean-Jacques, afflicted with fever, seeks refuge in Madame de Warens's bedroom, the pleasure of his tears yields the same therapeutic benefit: "As if tears were my nourishment and remedy, I fortified myself on those which I shed in her presence, with her, seated on her bed and holding her hands in mine."[81]

Consider now the account in book VI of the *Confessions* in which Rousseau describes his extenuated and anxious state, which ends with a sudden, violent auditory disturbance:

Imagine my surprise and my fright. I thought I was dead. I crawled into bed. The doctor was called. Trembling, I described my case, assuming there was no remedy for it . . . This accident, which might have killed my body, killed only my passions, and I thank heaven every day for the beneficial effects it had on my soul. I can truly say that I did not begin to live until I looked upon myself as a dead man . . . Finally, in spite or rather because of my condition I felt irresistibly impelled toward study, and though I continued to look upon each day as my last I studied with as much ardor as if I were supposed to live forever. People said that it did me harm; I believe that it did me good.[82]

Significantly, Rousseau is not sure whether to say he took to study "in spite of" or "because of" his condition: the benefits of study are first considered to be an antidote to his disease, but he corrects himself immediately and presents them instead as a direct, if paradoxical, benefit of his affliction. Note, moreover, the indication of passivity: "I felt irresistibly impelled," implying that the passion for study was as much an involuntary affliction as the illness that preceded it. Immediately thereafter, however, we encounter the verb *to study* in an active, intransitive form: "I studied." Here we have a perfect example of a reversal of the kind pointed out by J.-B. Pontalis, in which Rousseau responds with voluntary action to a situation of abandonment or rejection. Rousseau's attitude toward what he believes to be his imminent death is reminiscent, moreover, of his attitude on the night of his flight from Geneva, when the gates of the city close behind him: "The turnabout occurs at once: *he* is leaving, as if anticipating and dismissing in advance any possibility of rejection."[83] For evidence, consider this striking sentence in which death, the expulsion from life as the drawbridges of earthly existence are raised behind, is described as if it were a journey: "Whether it seemed good to go on learning right up to my final hour, or whether a glimmer of hope that I might go on living remained hidden in the depths of my heart, my anticipation of death, so far from diminishing my zeal for study, seemed to stimulate it, and I hastened to amass a few goods for the other world, as if I believed that all I would have there was what I brought with me."[84] A sense of impending death triggered an intense effort of narcissistic enrichment in a desexualized and therefore less anxiety-ridden domain.

The service that this conviction of impending death rendered to Jean-Jacques's intellectual apprenticeship will later find its counterpart in the service that a conviction of universal conspiracy renders to therapeutic reverie. Once again, extreme affliction becomes an occasion for happy "working through" *(perlaboration)*. Rousseau's unhappiness is so severe that his condition cannot possibly worsen, and therefore he can devote himself entirely to an effort of compensation. The word appears on virtually every page of the *Reveries,* not in the religious sense in which it was used in *Emile* (compensation awarded by God) but in the sense of a substitute or "supplement" that the ego produces from its own substance. Rousseau was often conscious of, and admitted his predilection for, seeking desperate situations. In the preface to *La Nouvelle Héloïse* he wrote: "I have already accused myself of worse things, perhaps, than anyone else will accuse me of."[85] In a letter to his editor he admitted: "I am well aware that my constant inclination is to put things in the worst possible light" (13 September 1758).

In the *Dialogues* he has "the Frenchman" say the worst possible things that can be said about him. He plunges the sharpest of weapons deep into his own flesh. He explains why in his introduction: "I took the only course available to explain myself: among the various possible suppositions, I chose the worst for myself and the best for my adversaries . . . To say everything that could be said in their favor was my only way of finding out what they were actually saying."[86] In this relatively little-known text Rousseau tortures himself in order to reproduce as accurately as possible accusations he has not heard directly but has mysteriously divined from the signs on people's faces. He wants to demonstrate as quickly as possible that things could not possibly be any worse and therefore that he has nothing more to fear or to lose. The consequence that he does not fail to draw from this is of course once again double-edged: his persecutors, thinking to do him harm, have actually done him good. The dialogue form makes it possible to alternate between the injurious discourse of the Frenchman and the compensatory discourse of Rousseau.

At times Rousseau simply modifies his interpretation of an event, to which he gives first one meaning, then another. On the day he tried unsuccessfully to leave the manuscript of the *Dialogues* on the altar of Notre-Dame he thought he saw "heaven itself conspire in the iniquity of men."[87] Later, however, he ascribes a diametrically opposite meaning to the event:

> Gradually overcoming my initial shock, I began to reflect more calmly on what had happened to me, and, my cast of mind being such that I am as quick to console myself for a past misfortune as to take fright at an anticipated one, it did not take long before I began to look at the failure of my attempt in a new light . . . In the end, the miscarriage of my plan, which had affected me so profoundly, upon reflection came to seem a boon from heaven, which had prevented me from carrying out a design so contrary to my interests.[88]

Rousseau usually accepts the affliction as irrevocable so that he may enumerate the resulting benefits: he was "delivered from the anxiety of hope";[89] he was reduced to relying on himself, which was all he asked; consigned to solitude, he found that nothing could disturb his tranquillity, and he was free "to forge consolations" to his heart's content.[90] He put the finishing touches on the exclusion to which he found himself subjected and thus put himself in a position to take his revenge in the most narcissistic way possible. Were he not surrounded by an "edifice of shadows," he would not be able to claim for himself "the transparency of crystal." His exclusion by wicked men becomes irrefutable proof of the persistence of his innate goodness:

> What have I still to fear, since all is done? Now that they can no longer make my condition any worse, they can no longer cause me any alarm. Anxiety and fear are evils from which they have delivered me once and for all . . . Such is the good that my persecutors have done me by using up all the arrows of their animosity. They have deprived themselves of any further hold on me, and now I can mock them.[91]

> Let us learn, therefore, to seize these advantages in compensation for the wrong they have done me. By inuring me to adversity they have done me more good than if they had spared me its afflictions . . . Instinctively surrendering to the emotions that attract me, my heart still feeds on the feelings for which it was born, and I rejoice along with the imaginary beings that produce and share them as if those beings really existed.[92]

In the introduction to the *Dialogues* Rousseau decided to say "all that could be said" in favor of his persecutors. Now he says that *they* have "used up all the arrows of their animosity." Those hostile arrows are tantamount to the initial thrust of Achilles' spear. But the Rousseau of the *Reveries* ignores, or pretends to ignore, what the Rousseau of the *Dialogues* knew: that he himself forged and launched the arrows that rain down upon him, that he imagined the accusatory discourse as a way of uncovering a plausible cause for the signs of hostility he detected all around him. "Tell me what crimes I have committed and how and by whom I was judged!"[93] These words appear in a pamphlet that Rousseau attempted to distribute in the streets after completing the *Dialogues,* as if he had completely forgotten that it was he himself who reconstructed and mimicked the imagined discourse of his accusers. This paranoid forgetfulness, which transforms a self-inflicted wound into a wound inflicted by others, is no doubt part of the healing process. It opens up a space in the writing where the text can believe that it is working purely to heal the wound, when in reality it was the same text that inflicted the wound in the first place by striking a blow that is now carefully concealed.

In Book II of *Emile* Rousseau alludes to his childhood fear of the dark. He wants his fictional pupil Emile to overcome this fear through training and habit. "The cause of the affliction, once discovered, indicates the remedy . . . So do not argue with a boy whose fear of the dark you want to cure. Take him there often, and rest assured that no philosophical argument can do as much good as this habituation."[94] Rousseau dealt with the darkness of conspiracy in the same way, though without ever familiarizing himself with the thing he feared.

In the tenth reverie the description of the encounter with Mme de Warens is scarcely begun when it is interrupted by a Telephus who has healed his self-inflicted wound. The final, purely elegiac image is of "the one short period" in his life when he was "loved by a woman full of tenderness and sweetness." A key idea in this passage is *plenitude*— of a finite kind, to be sure, threatened by inadequacy and soon troubled by anxiety but still intact in memory.

The reverie of Easter 1778, in which the presence of *maman* predominates, no longer speaks of affliction or celebrates compensation. Rousseau would die a few weeks later. Rousseau said of himself: "I was born almost dead." One is tempted to reverse the formula and say: he died almost cured, in the resurrection of his first great happiness. Is there a connection between the tranquillity of this final reverie (which differs from the earlier ones in that it does not speak of regaining peace as a goal) and the imminence of Rousseau's death? The point, if there is one, is this: when the malady disappears along with the concomitant need to search for a remedy, it is because vital energy has all but run dry. This serenity, this peace, this apparent healing are premonitory signs of death.

II. The Social Aspects of Music

To Jacek Wozniakowski

"All matter is colored, but sounds reveal movement and the voice reveals a sentient being. Only animate bodies sing." In the context of other remarks, this statement is revealing. The distinction among colors, sounds, and voices, which is found in chapter 16 of the *Essay on the Origin of Languages,* shows clearly that Rousseau regarded music as an art of vital expression and communication. The implications of this are considerable: music theory becomes a vast subject, which includes such other modes of communication as speech and the organization of families, peoples, and governments. The comprehensive theory that can be deduced from Rousseau's writings establishes a close relation among music, politics, and the history of language. The development of that theory can be followed by tracing the images of human togetherness (French: *rassemblement*) that Rousseau propounds in his work.

The basic outlines of the subject are to be found in the *Discourse on Equality*. Everything begins, in the protective bosom of nature, in solitude and silence. The initial dispersion that Rousseau envisions is the exact opposite of congregation. But natural man is not condemned to absolute solitude: occasionally he meets another person for brief bouts of combat or sex. These momentary encounters are accompanied by an equally fleeting vocal sign, the cry, which intermittently disrupts the primordial silence. Rousseau points out the usefulness of the cry in the time before articulate speech became necessary to the functioning of a society that did not yet exist:

> Man's first, most universal, most energetic language, and the only one he needed before it became necessary to persuade men gathered together in assemblies, was the cry of nature. Since this cry was elicited only in response to a kind of instinct on urgent occasions, to ask for help in time of great danger or for relief in time of violent ills, it was not of much use in the ordinary course of life, during which more moderate sentiments predominate.[95]

The contrast is stark between a passive and passionate prelanguage (the elicited cry) and polished speech, which manifests its power in oratory, that is, in the political act par excellence ("to persuade men gathered together in assemblies"). As Rousseau develops his argument in a series of conjectures, he considers what obstacles might have impeded the emergence of articulate speech. He hints, however, that language would over the course of the centuries become what we know it is: a system of signs possessing "a constant form" and thanks to which it becomes possible "to speak in public" and "influence society."

In the second part of the *Discourse on Inequality* Rousseau outlines the development of social life and language. He then draws attention to the importance of song in festivals, whose purpose is to celebrate the happiness of life in a "state of nascent society." But these festivals contain the seeds of future ills: they are an occasion for making comparisons and formulating preferences and thus permit the awakening of amour-propre, from which stem "repulsive and cruel" passions along with the earliest form of inequality:

> As ideas and sentiments followed one after another, and as minds and hearts exercised their powers, the human race became increasingly tame, relations expanded, and bonds grew tighter. People formed the custom of gathering in front of their huts or around a large tree: song and dance, true children of love and leisure, became the amusement or, rather, the occupation of idle men and women gathered together in groups. Each person began to look at the others and to want to be looked at himself, and public esteem was valued. The one who sang or danced the best, the handsomest, the strongest, the most adroit or eloquent became the most esteemed, and this was the first step toward inequality.[96]

In the *Essay on the Origin of Languages* the same festive scene is described but its role in Rousseau's argument has changed: the festival, he now maintains, was the "origin of societies and languages in the hot countries."[97] It was simultaneously the source of song, accent, speech, amorous feelings, and exogamic marriage. In contrast to the second discourse, no shadow mars this pastoral scene à la Claude Lorrain. Everything began when shepherds and maidens came together at watering holes, described in prose that itself rises to lyrical musicality:

> The first family bonds were formed there; the first encounters of the sexes took place there. Young maidens came looking for water for the household, and young men came to water their flocks. There, eyes accustomed to the same sights since childhood now began to see sweeter things. These stirred the heart; their unfamiliar allure made it less savage, and it felt pleasure at not being alone. Imperceptibly water became more necessary. The animals became thirsty more often. One hastened to the place and, once there, was reluctant to leave. In that happy time, when nothing marked the hours, there was no need to count them. Time had no other measure than amusement and boredom. Beneath ancient oaks, the conquerors of time, ardent youth forgot its ferocity by degrees, as little by little each tamed the other. Through striving to make themselves understood, people learned to explain themselves to others.[98]

The repetition of *there* insistently marks a place of happiness (like a dancing foot stamping on the ground), a repeated commencement. How long the prelude—a mute pantomime of arrivals, glances, departures, returns—goes on! Rousseau deliberately delays the emergence of the need to "explain oneself" to others in order to emphasize the simultaneity of the sentiments that underlie all expression, sentiments that are crowned immediately by a pleasure that does not lead, as pleasure does among the corrupt and civilized, to the death of desire. The paragraph ends with a transmutation of water into fire and work into celebration: "There the first festivals were celebrated, feet jumped for joy, and eager gestures no longer sufficed. Voices accompanied gestures with impassioned accents; pleasure and desire, merged into one, were felt at once. There, finally, was the true birthplace of nations, and from the pure crystal of the fountains sprang the first fires of love."[99]

This often cited passage could well be analyzed for its rhythmic, phonic, and accentual structure as well as for its shrewd mixing of inchoative past tenses with iterative imperfects, the result of which is to make language begin its long history in prolonged moments during which no time was kept.

Thus a model is provided of a primitive language that was at the same time a pure and original melody. "The first languages were melodious and passionate; only later did they become simple and methodical." Rousseau works variations on this theme: "One would sing rather than speak."[100] An integrated musical language composed of signs indistinguishable from the sentiments they express permitted communication in which the intended message was infallibly transmitted to its recipient: unity, emotional oneness, manifested itself at all levels.

But that unity was fragile, and it disappeared as accents faded and melody and passion subsided. Once the unity was destroyed, music and words, both degenerate, became strangers to one another. Chilled to the core, language was now useless for anything but acts of tyranny and indirect communication. As "articulations" (consonants) took on greater importance, the speech of the civilized nations grew fainter; it lost the accent and sonority that had been its only means of "persuading an assembled people." Meanwhile, music, led astray by the development of harmony, deprived of its melodic plenitude, still offered superficial pleasure to the ears but could no longer touch the heart. Thus the "moral effects" of primitive language were lost. The cooling of language was accompanied by a loss of liberty. "Noise" invaded music, thwarting all communication of emotion.

As is well known, Rousseau in his debate with Rameau honed his arguments against the primacy of harmony, which he considered a "barbarous" invention. When Rousseau's first attempt at musical composition debuted in Paris in 1744, he had been treated rather "brutally" by the composer, whom he had previously admired and whose theoretical works he had assiduously read. Rousseau definitely had grounds for resentment, and he may have indulged his hostility to Rameau by developing a theory of music at odds with the master's. He took the side of Italian proponents of opera buffa who attacked the "din" of French music and attacked Rameau in articles that Diderot commissioned for the *Encyclopedia*. He continued the attack first in *La Nouvelle Héloïse*, then in the *Essay on the Origin of Languages* (not published until after his death), and finally in the *Dictionary of Music*. Personal grievance thus played a considerable role. But why did Rousseau feel so wronged? By denying the originality and value of Rousseau's music Rameau had barred his access to Parisian society, where Rousseau had hoped to "make a name for himself." Rameau had intervened just as Rousseau was about to emerge from obscurity into the limelight, or so he believed. Jean-Jacques hoped to win the approval of connoisseurs while preserving his "independence." He staked his all on winning notoriety and esteem with his opera *The Galant Muses* in 1744: "Now that my opera was finished, the time had come to profit by it. That was a far more difficult 'opera.' No one can make it in Paris who lives in isolation. I thought of asking M. de la Poplinière to produce my work . . . M. de la Poplinière was Rameau's Maecenas."[101] It is hardly surprising, therefore, that Rousseau saw the rival responsible for his continued isolation as the apostle of an art of non-communication, a music-obstacle.

Rousseau's revenge is central to the next book of the *Confessions*, which tells the story of the staging of his opera *The Village Soothsayer* at Fontainebleau in the presence of the king and court.[102] He is fully compensated for the humiliation he had suffered at the hands of Rameau. As dramatized in the autobiographical text, this compensation comes in the form of an approving murmur that runs through the entire audience, gathering strength as it rises to the loge where Rousseau is seated. All the emotion felt by the assembled crowd is concentrated in this murmur:

> From the first scene, which is truly a scene of touching naïveté, I heard high up in the loges a murmur of surprise and applause unprecedented in performances of this genre. The growing ferment was soon perceptible throughout the hall and, as Montesquieu might put it, its effect only enhanced its effect. That effect was at its height in the scene of the two brave little lovers. Because there is no clapping in the king's presence, every note could be heard, and both the piece and its author benefited. All around me women who to me seemed as beautiful as angels spoke in half-whispers: "This is charming, this is delightful. There is not a sound in it that does not speak to the heart." The pleasure of giving emotion to so many kind people moved me to tears myself, and at the first duet, when I noticed that I was not the only person crying, I could no longer contain myself.
>
> I am nevertheless certain that at that moment the concupiscence of sex had much more to do with my feelings than did the vanity of the author, and surely if only men had been present I would not have been consumed, as I was continuously, by the desire to gather up with my lips the delicious tears that I caused to flow. I have seen works elicit deeper sighs of admiration but never have I seen a rapture so complete, so sweet, or so touching prevail throughout a performance, and especially in a first presentation at court. Those who saw it must remember it, for the effect was unique.[103]

What is happening here is nothing less than a repeat of the fusion accomplished by the primitive festival, of the exchange of glances and loving sighs in which pleasure and desire flourish freely in innocent suspense. But the pleasure is no longer that of the first encounters under ancient oaks: Rousseau savors a joy that he has deliberately shaped, that of being the indirect cause of "a rapture so complete, so sweet." The labor of art was required to make this happen. Rousseau becomes an author in order to forget—supreme reward—his literary glory and experience only the immortal desire to slake his thirst: to gather up tears with his lips, thereby stanching the primitive thirst that drew flocks, shepherds, and maidens together around the ancient watering holes.

Under certain conditions, therefore, a disease that has grown steadily worse throughout human history can find its remedy. Instead of the incomprehensible "ruckus" of the French opera, proof of the decadence of a society given to artifice, it is possible to create another kind of music, a music that flows from the heart, that is the product of a truer taste. In no less a hotbed of civilized perversion than a court theater, that music, by setting peasant lovers singing and reciting, is capable of awakening the true passion of the beginning of time, and even jaded courtiers are capable of receiving the revelation in their hearts.

Rousseau did not advocate a straightforward "return to nature" in either his philosophy of culture or his political philosophy. To be educated Emile must first be completely denatured. Rousseau was convinced that we must look to "perfected art for the cure for the ills that inchoate art *(l'art commencé)* inflicts on nature."[104] When Henriette, the mysterious letter-writer, asks Rousseau if she is to be condemned for seeking consolation in literature, he answers, as we have seen, that since the harm has already been done, literature will be her "Achilles' spear," the allusion of course being to Telephus's wound, caused but also cured by Achilles' spear.[105]

Is there perhaps a similar tendency in Rousseau's philosophy of language and music? If a malady that has afflicted generations cannot be totally cured, can't there at least be some form of reconciliation that would reestablish the lost plenitude, or a vivid image of it, without repudiating the knowledge, technology, and instrumental means developed by civilized reason? Of course music and language are now separate arts, and this division cannot be forgotten any more than the nostalgic image of primary unity. But the conflict can be mollified, and the separate realms need not remain ignorant of or hostile to each other. Rhetoric, altered by the influence of writing and the muted tone of evolved language, can be revived in both literary style and solid philosophical argument: the effect on the reader's heart is then the guarantee of a rediscovered power, a restored communication. Rousseau, of course, worked hard toward that end.

The power of music could be regenerated in a similar way. Words and song, melody and harmony need not always be in opposition, as shown by the shared pleasure and emotion of the audience at the first performance of *The Village Soothsayer*. Further evidence can be found in a well-known note to the *Letter to d'Alembert* in which Rousseau describes a festival in the Saint-Gervais district of Geneva, where the celebrating populace dances with a regiment of soldiers. The unforgettable images of collective emotion can be explained by Rousseau's music theory: simple melodies, composed to touch the heart and remind it of its true attachments, bring tears in the one case and set the crowd to dancing in the other.

It is impossible to exaggerate the importance in Rousseau's thought of symbols of regeneration, which open a breach of hope and point the way to possible repatriation. These images are all the more striking because they stand out against the disastrous present, which is radically condemned. At the end of the *Essay on the Origin of Languages* the worst apparently prevails: nothing is left of the bonds responsible for the happiness of primitive societies and virtuous republics. In chapters 19 and 20 Rousseau deplores first the death of music and then the death of eloquence:

> In this way song became, by degrees, an art entirely divorced from speech, in which it originated; the harmonics of the tones obscured the inflections of the voice; and finally, limited to the purely physical effect of the concurrence of vibrations, music was deprived of the moral effects it had produced when it was doubly the voice of nature.[106]

> Societies have assumed their final form: only cannon or cash could change them now. And since there is nothing more to say to the people other than "Give money," it is said with placards on street corners or with soldiers in homes. No one need assemble for that. On the contrary, the subjects must be kept apart: that is the first maxim of modern politics.[107]

Yet despite this definitive fall into moral dispersion and civil servitude, Rousseau's personal conviction keeps up its demands, its exhortations to search for compensation, to turn language and music, such as they are, into means of assembling men again, in a new, possibly imaginary, setting.

Let us therefore examine Rousseau's writings on music more closely. *The Village Soothsayer* is an opera. What is an opera? Rousseau gives his definition in one of the *Dictionary of Music*'s key articles: "The elements of opera are poetry, music, scenery. Poetry speaks to the mind; music, to the ear; painting, to the eyes; and all must join together to move the heart, to impress upon it one impression conveyed via several organs."[108] Moving the heart had been the central event of the first festivals, back in the time when speech and music were still unified. But these two means of expression had evolved in different ways and were now strangers to one another. The purpose of opera was precisely to reunite them and thus to achieve, in a work of late civilization, the unanimous joy that people had once experienced in the exchange of glances, in dancing, in the truthful effusion of amorous voices, in the simultaneity of pleasure and desire. According to Rousseau, Greek theater, which relied on "accented language" (unlike French), had been able to preserve something of the prior unity: "All their poetry was musical, and all their music declamatory . . . I take it for granted that Greek music was true recitative."[109] We moderns, however, must find other ways to reconcile music and words in the lyrical performance. Unity, no longer spontaneous, must be created. And it can be created by art, just as political unity can be the result of "social art." Art is nothing but the invention of substitutes or "supplements" for the privileges of the primary human associations, now forever lost. When those substitutes are imperfect, they merely aggravate the lack they are meant to compensate: "The less one is able to touch the heart, the more one must flatter the ear. We are forced to seek in sensation the pleasure that sentiment refuses. Therein lies the origin of airs, of symphony, and of that enchanting melody that so often embellishes modern music at the expense of poetry, but which, in the theater, the man of taste rejects when it flatters but does not move him."[110] Just as the opera must reconcile poetry, music, and painting, music itself must make sure that airs, choruses, symphony, and melody combine in proper proportion to find the way to the "heart." That way is filled with numerous obstacles, with "bad substitutes." In primitive festivals "joyful movement" preceded voice and called it forth, but in modern opera ballet is added after the fact. Dramatic dance and pantomime are superfluous elements in opera. Rousseau (in the article entitled "Opera") rejects them in the name of stylistic unity. The celebrations that are ingeniously introduced into opera almost invariably disrupt the unity of action. They are mere "disconnected leaps" and "pointless dances." Movement, now a separate language, ought to be reserved for additional entertainments: "A very agreeable way to end the show is to stage a ballet after the opera, just as a minor play is staged after a tragedy. The new performance has nothing to do with the one that comes before, so one can choose a different language; another nation appears on stage."[111] Nor does Rousseau have anything kind to say about the constant use of mythology in French opera from Lully to Rameau: this was but another unfortunate palliative, along with overlavish scenery and elaborate mechanical devices. Such subterfuges are necessary to hold the audience's attention when one attempts to "apply" music to languages like French, which lack sufficient accent and inflection.

In order to avoid a surfeit of artifice, language and music ought to fit together. Unfortunately this is not the case with French, which imposes intolerable constraints: "When the language has neither sweetness nor flexibility, the rough character of the poetry keeps it from serving the song, the very sweetness of the melody prevents it from aiding in proper recitation of the verse, and one senses in the forced union of the two arts a perpetual constraint that is an affront to the ear and destroys both the allure of the melody and the effect of the declamation." Carrying his condemnation of French music even further, Rousseau adds: "This defect is without remedy, and to attempt strenuously to apply music to a language that is not musical is to make that language even cruder than it would have been otherwise."[112] In extraordinary circumstances, however, this situation is subject to change. Such is the privilege of genius, to which Rousseau devotes an entry in his *Dictionary of Music*. Here Italian opera is held up as a model that the French musician might imitate, as if it were possible—with the aid of genius—to transfer to French the virtues of a more sonorous language, a language more suitable for melodic invention. Rousseau avails himself of the opportunity to summarize his theory of the mimetic, expressive, and communicative effects of music. If conceived by genius, music has the power to represent and translate all external objects and to transmute all internal events by raising them to the highest degree of emotive incandescence. Although it is in the very nature of music to depend on chronological succession, its "moral effect" is to annihilate time, almost to eternalize momentary emotions—an oxymoron as surprising as the "heat" bestowed on "frost":

The genius of the musician subjects the whole world to his art. He paints all pictures with his sounds. He makes even silence speak. He renders ideas by feelings, feelings by accents, and the passion he expresses he stirs in the depths of the heart. Desire, through him, takes on new charms. The pain he sets moaning calls forth cries. He burns always and is never consumed. He expresses frost and ice with heat. Even in painting the horrors of death he carries in his soul that feeling for life that never leaves him and that he communicates to hearts made to feel it. But, alas, he can say nothing to those where its seed does not exist, and his prodigies are scarcely perceptible to those incapable of imitating them. Do you therefore wish to know whether some spark of this devouring flame animates you? Run, fly to Naples to hear the masterpieces of Leo, Durante, Jomelli, and Pergolesi. If your eyes fill with tears, if you feel your heart palpitate, if shudders run through you, if emotion takes your breath away, take Metastasio and work. His genius will kindle yours, you will create after his example. That is how genius is made, and other eyes will soon yield up the tears that the masters have made you shed.[113]

The privilege of genius is to reawaken the primitive cry, but now wrested from the spectator by a perfectly imitated moan. Here again is the communion in tears that Rousseau made the climax, almost the epiphany, of the first performance of the *The Village Soothsayer* as recounted in the *Confessions*. Here, however, the communion is even broader, embracing first the disciple and his model and then extending to the public at large. The criterion of genius is not so much originality as it is capacity to feel emotion, frenzy, and rapture, which—from Paris to Naples, from admired master to inspired pupil, from Italian to French—cross all boundaries to ensure the union of hearts and to fashion the invisible society composed of those who rise above the "vulgar herd."

Such communion is possible solely because of the unifying intuition typical of the production of works of genius. To designate this power Rousseau employs an Italian expression, which he makes an entry in his *Dictionary: prima intenzione*. I have deliberately introduced the notion of intuition, thinking of the faculty that the neo-Platonists, most notably Marsilio Ficino, attributed to the sharp tip of the soul *(mens)*. Along with the angels the soul enjoys the privilege of taking in at a single glance *(uno intuitu)* the totality of being and time *(totum simul)*. Rousseau offers a sentimental—that is, aestheticized and deintellectualized—version of this doctrine:

> An air or piece *di prima intenzione* is one that takes shape suddenly and completely and with all its parts in the mind of the composer, just as Pallas lept fully armed from the brow of Jupiter. Pieces *di prima intenzione* are among those rare strokes of genius whose ideas are so closely related that they form, as it were, a single idea, and none could have come to mind without the others. In music, pieces *di prima intenzione* are the only ones that can cause those ecstatic, rapturous, and exalted feelings that transport listeners outside themselves: one feels them, divines them instantly. Connoisseurs never mistake them.[114]

This entry echoes the one on "the unity of melody," one of Rousseau's most important theoretical texts. On this score Rousseau is dissatisfied with an aesthetic assumption widely shared by his contemporaries, which he characterizes in these terms: "There is in music a successive unity that relates to the subject and by which all the duly linked parts compose a single whole, which we perceive in its entirety and in all its relations." This first kind of unity concerns the global composition of the work. Later, however, Rousseau reflects on another kind of unity: "A unity of more subtle, more simultaneous substances, which imperceptibly gives music its energy and force of expression." This unity involves the components of "modern" music, namely, melody and harmony, which Rousseau elsewhere criticizes for having become antagonistic. Here, however, he asserts that this opposition, in which he has hitherto taken the part of melody, is only temporary. Genius can reconcile the superficial *(de sensation)* and fleeting pleasure of harmony with the more profound *(de sentiment)* pleasure of melody, which constantly demands a new kind of attention. By effecting a happy fusion of both genius can avoid the overly simplistic unison quality that is nevertheless so touching in popular tunes as well as the surfeit of polyphony that Rousseau rejects:

> Music, therefore, must necessarily sing in order to touch, to please, to sustain interest and attention. But how, in our systems of chords and harmony, is music to go about singing? If each part has its own

melody, all those melodies heard at once will cancel one another out, leaving no melody at all. And if all the parts use the same melody, one no longer has harmony, and the concert will be all in unison.

The manner in which a musical instinct, a certain unspoken sentiment of genius, unwittingly overcame this difficulty and even profited by it is quite remarkable. Harmony, which might have stifled melody, animates it, reinforces it, determines it: the diverse parts, without merging with one another, contribute to a single effect, and though each one seems to have its own melody, one hears only a single melody emerging from the assembled parts. That is what I call *unity of melody.*[115]

Rousseau clearly credits himself with superior knowledge, capable of discerning processes that proceed unbeknownst to us and unbeknownst even to genius. Expressions such as "unaware" and "unwittingly" allude rhetorically to unsuspected feelings, to intuitive apperceptions. These unnoticed processes—detected only by Rousseau—are good: they lead toward a salvation of sorts. Of course in that respect the advantage remains with the Italians: "It is in this principle of the unity of melody, which the Italians sensed and obeyed without understanding it but which the French neither obeyed nor understood—it is, I was saying, in this great principle that the essential difference between the two musics lies."[116] Once again Rousseau presents himself as an exceptional individual: the principle that went unobeyed in one case and unobserved though instinctively obeyed in the other did not escape his scrutiny; he alone perceived it clearly. Later in the same text he says that, having "discovered" this principle, he immediately attempted an "application" in *The Village Soothsayer* (1752) and shortly thereafter formulated the theory in his *Letter on French Music* (1753). The series of events follows an empirical order: first the illuminating intuition, then the practical proof with the success of the *Soothsayer,* and finally the theoretical statement, formulated only after the fact and supported by irrefutable evidence. In the *Letter on French Music* Rousseau states that unity of melody is, in his view, an "indispensable rule, no less important in music than unity of action in a tragedy, because it is based on the same principle and aimed at the same objective."[117]

Another invention that Rousseau claims as his own, in French music at least, and which he says he tried out in *The Village Soothsayer,* is that of the obbligato recitative. Recitative is first defined as "the means of unifying song and speech."[118] Thanks to recitative, accent, which was paramount in primitive language, again assumes its proper place in more highly developed musical forms. If the recitative is obbligato, that is, intimately associated with an instrumental part, its power may be even greater. It can then be a unifying factor in the piece, ensuring that the declamation, shared by the actor who speaks the lines and the orchestra that plays the melody, serves a single goal. Because the actor overcome by emotion cannot express himself fully, the orchestra helps out by substituting music for the ineffable message. It then becomes possible to "tell all," as the halting voice is backed up by the instruments:

> *Obbligato recitative:* A recitative combined with ritornellos and symphonic devices which, as it were, oblige both actor and orchestra so that each must be attentive to and wait for the other.
> These passages, alternating recitative with melody embellished by all the splendor of the orchestra, are the most touching, most ravishing, most energetic in all modern music. The actor, agitated, carried away by a passion that does not allow him to tell all, interrupts himself, halts, holds back, and during these pauses the orchestra speaks for him. Silences filled in this way affect the listener infinitely more than if the actor himself were to say all that the music suggests. Until now French music has made no use of the obbligato recitative. An attempt was made to give some idea of the technique in one scene of *The Village Soothsayer.*

Although unity of melody might create a more "simultaneous order," the obbligato recitative, based on the mutual obligation of the reciting voice and the orchestral melody, ensured that the recitative would have a coherent temporal structure by filling in the silences that extreme passion imposed on the spoken voice. In both cases art introduces a complement, an adjunct: harmony "adds" to the expressiveness of the melody, and the orchestra "fills" the silent moments. (In the "melodrama" *Pygmalion* the complementarity of the *spoken* voice and the orchestral music stems from the same principle, once again meeting the demand for full emotional expression.)

To formulate principles, define bonds and "obligations" capable of assuring the unity of the work, and thereby to establish communion among composer, performers, and public: this program irresistibly calls to mind the program that Rousseau would later formulate in his "principles of political justice," the *Social Contract*.

Musical rules and political structures had of course long been seen as analogues, and a metaphorical system had been created as the repository of this "kinship": the happiness or internal peace of a society might be referred to as symmetry, harmony, accord, concert, and so on. Rousseau made use of this metaphorical system, which can be traced back to Plato and the Pythagoreans, but in a flexible fashion and without explicitly reflecting on its significance. More significantly, Rousseau presents both his musical beliefs and his political ideas as the result of a conversion or illumination. According to the account in the *Confessions*, it was in Venice that Rousseau had the "first idea for [his] *Institutions Politiques*." Then, on the road to Vincennes, in a famous moment of "bedazzlement," he had a vision of his "sad and grand system" in its entirety. Now, it so happens, he also dates his conversion to Italian music from the time of his stay in Venice. According to the *Confessions*, this change of opinion came about in a short period of time owing to the extraordinary consequences of several revealing events: "I had brought with me from Paris the Parisian prejudice against Italian music, but I had also received from nature a sensibility against which prejudices cannot stand. I soon felt for that music all the passion it inspires in those made to judge it. As I listened to the barcaroles I discovered that I had never heard singing before."[119]

In the fictional account given in *La Nouvelle Héloïse*, however, the conversion is the effect of a single evening of music. Saint-Preux listens to the castrato Reggianino, and, immediately won over by the truth, renounces all his earlier illusions:

> How mistaken I have been until now about the products of this charming art. I felt that they had little effect and blamed this on the weakness of the music. I told myself that music was nothing but empty sound, which can only flatter the ear and which affects the soul only slightly and indirectly. The impression of chords is purely mechanical and physical. What does it have to do with feeling, and why should I hope to be more moved by a beautiful harmony than by a beautiful accord of colors? I did not perceive, in the accents of melody applied to those of language, the powerful and secret link between passions and sounds. I did not see that the imitation of the various tones with which the emotions animate the speaking voice

gives the singing voice the power to stir the heart, and that the energetic portrait that the person performing gives of the movements of his soul is what charms his listeners.[120]

The decisive experience is a series of surprises and discoveries:

I soon felt, in the emotions this art caused in me, that it possessed greater power than I had imagined. I scarcely know what delightful sensation imperceptibly took hold of me. The music was no longer a pointless series of sounds, as in our recitals. With each phrase some image entered my mind or some sentiment entered my heart. The pleasure did not stop at the ear but penetrated to the soul. The performance flowed effortlessly, with charming ease. All the performers seemed animated by the same spirit.[121]

The alert reader will notice a parallel: the "same spirit" that animates the performers is a variant of the general will, the key concept of the *Social Contract*. To be sure, the spirit of the musicians is a general will of brief duration, limited to a single night and to a small circle of performers. Still, one can hardly escape the comparison with the celebrated formulation of the social contract and its consequences:

If we exclude all that is not essential from the social pact, it can be reduced to the following terms: each of us jointly subjects his person and capabilities to the supreme direction of the general will, and we receive, as a body, each member an indivisible part of the whole.
Instantly, in place of the individual person of each party to the contract, this act of association produces a moral and collective body composed of as many members as the assembly has voices *(voix)*, and that body receives from the selfsame act its unity, its common *ego*, its life, and its will.[122]

Note that the word *voix*, which can mean either voices or votes and which here alludes to universal suffrage, is one of those multivalent terms that can be understood either in a "literal" (linguistic, musical) sense or a "figurative" (political) sense. The use of the word in the political vocabulary is sufficiently unequivocal that there is no need to add to what has been said thus far about the social aspects of music a discussion of the musicalization of society. Still, it is impossible to avoid the conclusion that the notion of unity, whose emergence we have just examined, establishes a link between Rousseau's aesthetics and his politics: each one in its own sphere provides an answer to the fundamental question of how individuals communicate. Thus the history of societies can be looked at as a history of voices.

In the *Essay on the Origin of Languages* Rousseau maintains that the effect of the "first voices" was to "bring men together." Among the peoples of the south it was passion, working through inarticulate, musical voices, that established the first human convention. Celebration around the watering hole was, as we have seen, the "birthplace of nations." In the north, by contrast, need was paramount: there, articulate voices (harsher and more broken up by consonants) called for help, uttered the formula of the contract, and exhibited the will of the political "body." Contractual *concertation* brought remedies and substitutes: it produced civil liberty in place of natural independence; it put an end to the war of all against all, which pitted individuals now unequal against one another; and it thus reestablished, in the form of a voluntary organization, the unity primitive men and women had known when they gathered in spontaneous, festive assemblies.

Consider, in this connection, a key passage from the *Social Contract:* "The more *concert* prevails in the assemblies, or, in other words, the closer opinions are to unanimity, the more the general will predominates; but lengthy debates, dissent, and tumult presage the ascendancy of particular interests and the decline of the State."[123] There is danger in the multiplicity of voices, each of which expresses a particular interest instead of the general interest. The desired unanimity is compromised when factions proliferate and "small societies influence the larger society." Then, Rousseau adds, "the general will becomes mute."[124]

It is striking that Rousseau characterizes what is wrong in terms very similar to those he uses to criticize the deleterious effects of making harmony and polyphony preeminent in music. "Any music in which one can make out more than one melody at once is bad, and . . . the effect is the same as that of two or more speeches delivered at once in the same tone. There are no exceptions to this rule, hence there is no question what one ought to think about those marvelous musical forms in which one tune serves as accompaniment to another."[125] The danger, analogous to the danger of factions within a state, is one of destruction: "If each part has its own melody, so many melodies heard simultaneously will destroy one another."[126] When Rousseau hears "four-part psalms" sung in the Protestant churches of his native land, he at first feels rapture, but this is soon followed by a very different feeling: "Little by little the noise numbs me."[127] Noise, analogous to the tumult that Rousseau fears in the city, is what he allegedly dislikes in Rameau's operas and in French music generally: such music does not "speak" to the heart. In other words, it becomes "mute," like the general will in a state riven by particular interests. Rousseau claimed to feel greater affection for the unison structure of popular songs. Such songs, he says, are not without harmony, because each note calls forth its harmonics. Clearly, there is a parallel between these unison songs and the unanimity of peoples in the grip of an overwhelming patriotic fervor.

One further remark needs to be made. Genius, the product of a powerful instinct, should be employed in blending melody with harmony, that is, in assuring the unity of melody, the composition *di prima intenzione*. The function of genius in music is therefore not without analogy to the role that Rousseau, in the *Social Contract*, ascribes to the legislator, whose "great soul" is constantly employed in persuading individuals to sacrifice their particular interest to the general interest; his mission is to assemble men so as to obtain from them "the union of understanding and will."[128]

In the historical situation in which Rousseau found himself, political unity could be achieved only by transforming the system or by resisting the forces corrupting society. What was needed was a "mechanic to invent the machine."[129] Just as the musical genius is alone capable of composing a great work, a body politic, at its inception, needs a man who feels "capable of changing human nature, as it were, a man capable of transforming each individual and who by himself is a perfect and solitary whole yet part of a greater whole from which he somehow receives his life and his being."[130]

As we saw earlier, *The Village Soothsayer* proved to Rousseau's satisfaction the usefulness of his musical principles. But proof of his legislative principles was less easy to come by. Rousseau did not become the lawgiver of the Corsicans or the Poles. He never got beyond the stage of consultant to "peoples in need of institutions." Primitive festivals and regenerated societies would remain postulates of speculative reason or goals to the imagination.

If he could not unify a nation, it was within Rousseau's powers as a musician to unite the members of a "small society." He had enjoyed that privilege in his youth at Annecy in Mme de Warens's soirées. In such a setting it was not necessary to compose an entire opera. With an intimate group of friends it was enough to compose a tune or a song to fill everyone's heart with joy and bring the group closer together. These days of happiness, which Rousseau described so well, almost always ended with an evening song. Take, for example, the day on the Isle of Saint-Pierre that is described in the fifth reverie: "After supper, if the evening was fair, we would all go together for a walk around the grounds to breathe the cool lake air. We would rest in the pavilion, laugh, converse, or sing some old song easily as good as your modern ditties, and finally we would go to bed content with the day and desiring nothing but the same for the morrow."[131]

To breathe "the lake air": again, water, which Rousseau says he always loved passionately. In the *Essay on the Origin of Languages* he made watering holes the place where couples met and primitive festivals were held. But this lakeside sojourn is a final moment, almost an end to a story that Rousseau is enjoying for his own personal benefit. The ardor of amorous youth has given way to tranquillity. The evening song, laden with memory (it is an "old song"), substitutes for the great event of language's inception. A quiet walk with friends takes the place of primitive dances. Yet once again, the spirit of music infuses the communal life, the life of "all together." It attests to the unity of a small community that hopes to go on living in just the same way: "After a nice tune one feels satisfied. The ear desires nothing more. The tune remains in the imagination. You take it with you and repeat it at will . . . The true music-lover never forgets the beautiful tunes he hears during his lifetime."[132] And so Rousseau suggests that time has come to a halt in a paradise regained of plenitude and repetition, which, standing at the end of history and through the power of art, echoes the uncounted hours beneath clear skies and "ancient oaks, the conquerors of time," when pleasure and desire were, by nature, one.

6

⁓

FABLE AND MYTHOLOGY
IN THE SEVENTEENTH AND
EIGHTEENTH CENTURIES

Defining the status of ancient myths in the seventeenth and eighteenth centuries involves consideration of two quite dissimilar domains: one embraces all cultural products (poetry, theater, ballet, painting, sculpture, decorative art) in which mythological themes have a place; the other comprises historical, critical, and speculative texts that attempt to elaborate a *knowledge* or science of myth. At the time this distinction was clearly expressed by terms that indicated the sharp difference that contemporaries saw between the use of mythological themes and the scholarly understanding of myth, namely, *fable* and *mythology*.

The Function of Fable in Classical Culture

La fable [we retain the French term, whose meaning is not captured by the English "fable"] encompassed all traditional ideas concerning pagan deities. Largely based on Hesiod, Ovid, Apollodorus, and more recent vulgarizers such as Natale Conti, *la fable* was a compendium of genealogies, adventures, metamorphoses, and allegorical correspondences. Since mythical themes were ubiquitous—in the ancient authors one read at school, in the tragedies one saw in the theater, in historical paintings, in monuments erected on public squares, in residential decor—*la fable* was an essential part of a gentleman's education. A circle was thus established: one had to know *la fable* in order to understand works of ancient and more recent culture; and, because people were taught *la fable* and the ancient model remained alive, new works would frequently borrow from it their subject matter or certain ornamental accessories—figures, emblems, locutions.

Rollin, in book 6 (part 4) of his *Traité des études* (1726), which remained authoritative for more than a century, mentions *la fable* and offers a subtle justification for studying it: "There is scarcely any subject having to do with belles-lettres that is of greater use than the one I speak of here, nor is there one better suited to profound erudition." Without knowledge of *la fable* knowledge of literature was impossible:

> It is [an advantage] of very great extent . . . to know authors, whether Greek or Latin or even French, in whose reading one is stopped short if one is not to some degree saturated in *la fable*. I am not speaking only of poets, for whom *la fable* is of course almost a natural language. It is also frequently employed by orators and, if felicitously applied, can make for some very powerful thrusts . . . Books of other kinds are exposed to the eyes of all the world: paintings, engravings, tapestries, statues. These are enigmas to those who ignore *la fable,* which often provides the explanation and meaning of the work. These subjects come up in conversation fairly often. It is not, so it seems to me, a pleasant thing to remain mute and appear stupid in company because one has failed in youth to master a discipline that costs so little to learn.

Knowledge of *la fable* is even necessary for understanding the world of culture in general. It is therefore one of the prerequisites for participating in those "conversations" in which educated men are called upon to play their role. For Rollin, *la fable* is indispensable for anyone who wishes to understand cultivated society and to be accepted in select "company." Its function, therefore, is twofold: it is a figurative language that offers access to a certain discursive structure, and it is a social recognition signal that allows individuals capable of deciphering mythic fictions in a similar way to identify one another.

Jaucourt says much the same thing in his article "La Fable" in the *Encyclopedia:*

> That is why knowledge, at least superficial knowledge, of *la fable* is so widespread. Our theater, our lyrical and dramatic plays, and our poetry of all genres allude to it constantly; the engravings, paintings, and statues that decorate our offices, galleries, ceilings, and gardens are almost always derived from *la fable;* and finally, it is so widely

used in all our writings, novels, brochures, and even ordinary speeches that beyond a certain point it is impossible to be ignorant of it without blushing at such want of education.

La fable is the patrimony of the arts. It is a source of ingenious ideas, humorous images, interesting subjects, allegories, and emblems, which can be used felicitously or not so felicitously depending on the artist's taste and genius. Everything acts, everything breathes in this enchanted world, where intellectual beings have bodies, where material beings are animate, where fields, forests, and rivers have their own private deities. These characters are chimerical, I know, but the role they play in the writings of the ancient poets and the frequent allusions of the modern poets have made them almost real for us. Our eyes are so familiar with them that we find it difficult to look upon them as imaginary beings.

The anonymous author of the *Encyclopédie élémentaire,* which was published in 1775, expresses irritation with *la fable* yet considers it a necessity. The terms in which he recommends Chompré's *Dictionnaire de la fable* (previously hailed by Rollin) clearly indicate that this work, which was both an allegorical iconology and a catalogue of mythical heroes, was intended not so much to delve into the substance of myth as to make it possible to decipher the artists' use of attributes. In a sense, we are dealing with a semiological code for expressing "intention" in a consecrated language:

> This is a collection of puerile tales devoid of all verisimilitude, which would deserve contempt if these chimeras were not absolutely necessary for understanding the ancient authors, perceiving the beauties of poetry, painting, and allegory, and even for using countless traditional expressions, as when we say that a person is a Megaera, a Fury, or a Muse . . . I urge my readers to acquire M. Chompré's handy pocket *Dictionary.* It is highly useful for young people and indeed for everyone. If one is looking, say, for the subject of a tapestry, a painting, or an allegorical piece, one will certainly find it in this work.
>
> If there is an eagle, look up the word, and it will refer you to Jupiter, to Periphas, to Ganymede. If there is a scythe, you will find Saturn and Time. If a figure holds a trumpet, the word trumpet will send you to Renown . . . From the attributes you will become familiar with the subjects, and with a little judgment you will guess the draftsman's intention.[1]

The dictionary was thus useful for going from one language to another. It was a translation tool that enabled artists and poets to find appropriate "figures" and that also allowed readers to work backward from the figure to the original idea. Use of the dictionary assumes that there is a disparity between appearance and meaning, but this disparity is immediately eliminated by the establishment of a system of fixed correlations, which does away with anything that might be strange about the allegory. As a result, the use of mythical figures becomes nothing more than a stylistic flourish. The reader or viewer must translate the image *trumpet* into the concept *Renown*. While the image of the trumpet may divert us for a moment owing to its elegant form or copper sheen, the *knowing* reader will not linger over such a literal perception, which is supposed to be only a temporary intermediary, an index to the "higher" or "noble" register of expression.

Reduced to a lexicon of this type, *la fable* becomes in a sense ahistorical, even though it refers to a fictive past located in the geography of antiquity: everything in it is simultaneous, even the genealogies. Its interconnections develop synchronically, as if it were the vocabulary of a single, invariant state of language. Its internal chronology is not part of historical time. Once the gods and their denominations, cults, relations with places and peoples, and so on become an object of historical research, *la fable* becomes an object of erudition and ceases to be the closed, self-sufficient system I have described. It becomes the business on the one hand of "antiquarians," who content themselves with cataloguing and comparing the archaeological evidence such as statues, altars, and coins, with such written sources as inscriptions and literary texts, and on the other hand of "mythologists," who formulate hypotheses as to the origin of particular myths, the differences and similarities between the religious beliefs of different peoples, and so on. This is a difficult and treacherous field, and Rollin advises educators to stay out of it: "It is a good idea, in my view, to avoid what pertains only to erudition, which might make study of *la fable* more difficult and less agreeable, or at least to relegate reflections of this kind to brief notes."

Jaucourt concludes his *Encyclopedia* article on "La Fable" with a program of mythological learning that goes beyond mere familiarity with the figures of *la fable*:

To extend one's curiosity to the point of attempting to penetrate the various meanings or mysteries of *la fable,* to understand the various systems of theology, to become familiar with the cults of the pagan divinities—this is a science reserved for a small number of scholars; and this science, which covers a vast segment of belles-lettres, and which is absolutely necessary for comprehending the monuments of antiquity, is known as *Mythology.*

Mythology, then, involves interpreting the figures of *la fable* in such a way as to meet the demands of historical, genetic, and philosophical understanding. While *la fable* itself, in its easy, vulgarized form, is a universally valid way of "poeticizing" anything, mythology inquires about its origins, its intellectual significance, its value as revelation, and its links with institutions and customs. In other words, the semantic difference between *la fable* and mythology can be formulated as the difference between a generalized and stabilized interpretive system and a rational investigation of that interpretive system according to other standards of validity.

The revival of myth at the end of the eighteenth century would come from this scholarly reflection, which aimed to understand mythical invention in a different way, whereas the stereotyped figures of *la fable* proved sterile and tiresome. But before I embark on a survey of new mythological theories, I want to give a clearer description of the way in which *la fable* functioned in "classical" European, and especially French, culture in the seventeenth and eighteenth centuries.

In a culture that tolerated the coexistence of sacred and profane spheres, *la fable* obviously belonged on the profane side: it was the stuff of high-society entertainment. I would even go so far as to say that *la fable*'s avowed absence of truth value was the sign par excellence of the frivolousness of the high-society life. *La fable* was meant to be nothing but fiction, but ornament. At best it was erudite memory. Its authority was immediately declared to be nil as against that of the religious authorities. Aestheticized paganism, its pretensions confined to the graceful and beautiful, was not a dangerous rival to the Christian orthodoxies—unless souls allowed themselves to be captivated to an unusual degree and the impure examples of the pagan pantheon began to inspire passion.

Listen once more to Rollin, the perfect spokesman for the religious institution of the early eighteenth century. In including *la fable* in his program of education his intention was not only to foster better understanding of literature and art. *La fable* was also to stand as a warning, a proof by counterexample of the truth of Christianity:

> This study, when carried out with the precautions and wisdom required and inspired by religion, can be of great utility to young people. First, it teaches them what they owe to Jesus Christ, their liberator, who wrested them from the powers of darkness and brought them into the admirable light of the Gospel. Before him, what were men like? . . . *La fable* teaches us. They were blind worshipers of the demon and bowed down before gold, silver, and marble; they gave money to deaf and dumb statues; they accepted animals, reptiles, even plants as gods . . . Each story in *la fable,* each circumstance in the life of the gods, ought to make us feel confusion, admiration, and gratitude all at once . . . A second advantage of *la fable* is that by revealing the absurd ceremonies and impious maxims of paganism, it ought to inspire in us a new respect for the august majesty of the Christian religion and for the sanctity of its morality.

Belief is thus reserved for revealed dogma, for the one legitimate authority, while scorn is to be poured on the very same pagan figures that Rollin himself admits are ubiquitous in everyday life. Despite *la fable*'s many seductions, its unreal quality leaves no doubt as to the vanity of life in this world. Its very presence is a sure indicator that profane desire strays toward "false" objects. The need to guide love toward its true object—God, Christ—only becomes more imperious.

But the demarcation between the sacred and the profane has its own legitimacy: it is postulated by religious authority itself. In determining the limits of its strict jurisdiction, religious authority tolerates a more relaxed realm, which is kept under surveillance but not subjected to the strictest regulation. So long as the connection with the sacred order is not broken, a part of human life is allowed to unfold in profane space and time. Figures inherited from an outdated and discredited form of the sacred, namely, paganism, can innocently serve as ornament for the part of human life not directly governed by the truths of religion. Of course, the products of the imagination are dangerous, and figures of desire subject human souls to grave peril. But for that very reason orthodoxy is willing to tolerate a pantheon no longer capable of attracting serious belief; superficial survival is granted to what Christian morality otherwise rejects and represses. Thus, in an almost equitable compromise, Christianity (especially Counter-Reformation Catholicism) allowed to subsist alongside it, but in the form of gratuitous imagery and innocuous fiction, the whole spectrum of polytheistic instincts that it had historically supplanted and that true believers were exhorted to reject and transcend. This compromise authorized a certain duplicity: the *worldly* (including the king himself) could enjoy secular amusements, surround themselves with pagan scenery, and even perform in mythological ballets yet heed their preachers and receive the sacraments.

Love and ambition—the two broad areas in which worldly desire *(libido sentiendi, libido dominandi)* is exercised—celebrate their triumphs in mythical guise. The recourse to the mythical code in love poetry was part of a system of distancing, which, by placing emotion in a heroic or pastoral fictional setting, made it possible to show desire in a purified, glorified form divorced from trivial contingencies. All elements of discourse were transposed into a new key, at once more playful and "polite"—these being the defining characteristics of the *galant* attitude. The chief source of myth, Ovid's *Metamorphoses,* was itself highly playful, and in order to satisfy the widespread taste in cultivated circles for novelty and "spice" artists and poets felt called upon to outdo their model in this regard. The result is particularly clear in rococo art, with its penchant for decorative profusion, supple sinuosity, and miniaturization. But the element of intellectual play, at times combined with more authentically felt ingredients, is already clearly present in mannerism and concettism (Marini's *Adone,* for example). It can also be found in seventeenth-century preciosity and was still present in late-eighteenth-century badinage. Benserade's *Métamorphoses d'Ovide mises en rondeaux* (Ovid's Metamorphoses Set in Rondeaus) is an example of excessive preciosity: by paraphrasing Ovid in a regular minor verse form, by abridging and reworking a Latin text whose mythical content had already been playfully lightened, the author added zest to a familiar text. The playful element of the text was intensified. Compared with the original the rondeau yielded a mythology in miniature, compressed into a twelve-line stanza whose first four syllables were repeated twice, the second time to conclude the poem. At the end of the Ancien Régime, in C. A. Demoustier's *Letters to Emily on Mythology,* the mythological narrative is reduced to a farrago of badinage and verse. Some episodes are in verse, as are some commentaries on the narrative along with gallantries addressed to "Emily," the recipient of the letters. Inherited from the seventeenth century, this form shed so much of its former ballast that it was reduced to insignificance. The mythological content dwindled to the point where it served chiefly as backdrop for a series of adventures and pretext for a leisurely didacticism that aimed primarily to please. A work composed under the patronage of Mme de Genlis went one step further: nothing remained of the gods but their names, in calligraphic characters that formed a kind of emblem.

The mythical repertoire, useful for transposing contemporary events and feelings into a fictional key, could also be used in a triumphal sense, to magnify and celebrate. Miniaturization was only one penchant of the playful imagination, a means of achieving innocent frivolity. But when the intent was to glorify, reality was no constraint. Mythological fiction permitted hyperbolic praise that Christian discipline would have ruled out. The Christian celebration of victory in battle culminated in adoration of the armies' God: *Te Deum laudamus.* But the Christian celebration was accompanied by a secular, hence mythological, celebration, which exalted the prince himself: he might, for example, be compared to Mars or Hercules or be declared Bellona's favorite. When a prince was born, his Christian baptism would be celebrated in myth-inspired ceremonies or poems heralding nothing less than the imminent return of Astraea and the golden age. The apotheosis of the prince could be legitimately represented provided that the divine images used for the purpose were understood to be obsolete and purely for show. This sham divinization was an occasion for an outpouring of celebratory energies. Captives of their Greek and Latin originals, those energies could be extravagant because they claimed to be nothing more than a simulacrum. The Sun King could dance in the costume of Apollo. Jupiter could descend from the heavens in an operatic machine to announce to future centuries an illustrious lineage of sovereigns.

Although the conventions of Greek and Latin mythology encouraged a purifying or glorifying transmutation, the system was vulnerable because its only authority derived from aesthetic habit. Nothing protected it from parody or from the deflating tendency to abandon mythic embellishment in favor of the ordinary reality of desire.

The thrust of satire and comedy in the seventeenth century was to strip away masks, to reverse attempts at purification (preciosity) or glorification (the aristocratic ideal), and to literalize what the mythological code treated metaphorically. Spurning canvases in which desire was exalted and divinized, satire returned to earth and to the reality of raw instinct. An excellent example can be found in the "Discours sur le voyage de Saint-Germain-en-Laye" from the *Cabinet satyrique* (1618). The mythical background is *read* as an erotic stimulant:

> Mais faisons, je vous pry, pour saouler nostre veuë,
> Dans la chambre du Roy encore une reveuë.
> Voyez, en cest endroit, comme Mars et Venus
> Se tiennent embrassez, languissans et tous nuds;
> Voyez les à ce coing, en une autre posture:
> Avez-vous jamais veu si lascive peinture?
> Haussez un peu les yeux, et voyez les encor
> En une autre façon, dessus ce plancher d'or;
> Voyez les icy pres, tous deux encor aux prises.
> Quoy! tout est plain d'Amours et de flames éprises,
> Dans ceste belle chambre! Allons, fuyons ces lieux:
> Sortons-en, je vous prie, ou bien faisons comme eux!

[But I beg you, let us feast our eyes once more on the king's chamber. See, in that place, how Mars and Venus embrace, languishing and naked. See them, in that corner, in another posture: have you ever seen such lascivious painting? Raise your eyes a little and see them again in another position above that golden floor. See them here, nearby, again embracing. Look! Everything in this beautiful chamber is full of Cupids and consumed by flame. Let's flee this place, let's get out, I beg you, or else let's do as they do!]

Toward the pseudo-sacred one can be sacrilegious with impunity. The burlesque makes free play with this license. The great mythical images used to ennoble the circumstances of public and private life are means of transmutation and disguise. By distorting and caricaturing them one effects a return to trivial reality: to disguise what was a means of disguise is to negate the purity of the figurative glory and to rediscover the texture and odor of the world as it is for a witness without illusions. Dassoucy's *Ovide en belle humeur,* Scarron's *Virgile travesti,* the young Marivaux's *Homère travesti,* and Blumauer's late *Vergils Aeneis travestirt* (Vienna, 1782–1794) are not merely assaults on the most respected literary models. They also use those models to attack the *virtues* whose exaltation was accomplished by the epico-mythical tradition: martial exploits and the sacrifice of one's life for glory and the fatherland.

Mockery, in attacking the heroes and gods of antiquity, aims more generally at the heroic ideal. The merely happy life is to be valued more. Immortality is denounced as an illusion, a fool's bargain offered the hero, a counterfeit currency in which mythological celebration pays those who shed their blood on the battlefield. In the aftermath of the wars of Louis XIV, parody as practiced by Marivaux attacked not only the ancients and their proponents but even more the illusions of military glory. Verses like these, spoken by Andromache to Hector, tend to dampen martial ardor. They "demystify" the commonplace of imperishable memory:

> Ah! grands dieux! lorsque j'envisage
> L'affligeant état du veuvage,
> Je sens qu'un lit est bien affreux,
> Quand, dans ce lit, on n'est plus deux!
> Jadis, le sanguinaire Achille
> Tua mon père en une ville . . .
> Eh bien! comment la nomme-t-on?
> Je ne me souviens plus du nom.
> Il l'enterra, dit-on, lui-même,
> D'une magnificence extrême:
> Mais quand un corps est enterré,
> A quoi lui sert d'être honoré?
> Avec quelque éclat qu'on enterre,
> On n'a de gîte que la terre.

[O! Great gods! When I envisage the distressing state of widowhood, I know what an awful place a bed is when it is no longer shared by two people. Once upon a time, bloody Achilles killed my father in a city . . . So, then, what was that city called? I no longer recall the name. He buried him, they say, himself, in extreme magnificence. But when a body is buried, what good does it derive from being honored? No matter how splendid the burial, one's resting place is still the earth.]

This resolutely terrestrial profession of faith (which depicts death as nothing more than burial) rejects the "pagan"[2] image of immortality but suggests skepticism about Christian immortality. More generally, the destructive effects of burlesque parody of myths or of pastoral or military fables extend beyond the aesthetic sphere and the hierarchy of "official" values to attack indirectly the highest authority. Although the world of *la fable* is fictitious, it contains images of sovereignty comparable to the highest contemporary forms. An attack on Jupiter or other mythical gods is tantamount to an attack "in effigy" and without risk on, for example, the king, the nobility, the sanctity of God, or the authority of the pope. Since the mythical world is, by decree of the spiritual authorities, a profane world without genuine sacred content, there is no blasphemy or lèse-majesté in distorting it. Libertine criticism of religion and of centralized monarchy can thus proceed in roundabout fashion, without (seeming) to attack powers other than those continually condemned by the most orthodox Christian tradition. The duality of the (Christian) sacred and the (mythologically embellished) profane was thus arranged in such a way that writers could make free now with the distinctness or reciprocal exclusion of the two spheres, now with their parallelism or isomorphism. By highlighting the formal similarities between pagan and Christian sovereignty (regarding, for example, the structural function of the supreme deity or the role of miracles), one could, without risk, launch a polemic against Christianity (or its superstitious aspects) by pretending to attack only the pagan gods (as Bayle does, for example, in the article "Jupiter" of his *Dictionary*). By contrast, emphasizing the incompatibility of Christianity and paganism could lead to a more dangerous form of hostility toward Christianity: an outright choice in favor of the world of myth. Using as cover the aesthetic tradition that acclimatized mythological fiction and gave it its patent of nobility, rebellious thought proclaimed its preference for pagan myth over Church-imposed doctrine, which it alleged to be no less mythical and misleading but far less amusing. Anti-Christian feeling now revealed its true face: we see this at several points in the post-Renaissance period but above all in the eighteenth century. In Voltaire, the approval of paganism in

Apologie de la fable attests not so much to an authentic admiration of
the world of myth as to a sharp eye for a propaganda opportunity:

> Savante antiquité, beauté toujours nouvelle,
> Monument du génie, heureuses fictions,
>   Environnez-moi des rayons
>   De votre lumière immortelle:
> Vous savez animer l'air, la terre, et les mers;
>   Vous embellissez l'univers.
> Cet arbre à tête longue, aux rameaux toujours verts,
>   C'est Atys, aimé de Cybèle;
> La précoce hyacinthe est le tendre mignon
> Que sur ces prés fleuris caressait Apollon.

[Learned antiquity, beauty always new, monument of genius,
happy fictions, wreathe me in the rays of your immortal light. You
know how to animate the air, the land, and the seas; you embellish
the universe. That high-topped tree with evergreen limbs is Atys,
beloved of Cybele. The precocious hyacinth is the tender youth
that Apollo caressed on these flowery meadows.]

Other examples follow. Voltaire then continues:

> Tout l'Olympe est peuplé de héros amoureux.
> Admirables tableaux! séduisante magie!
> Qu'Hésiode me plaît dans sa théologie
> Quand il me peint l'Amour débrouillant le chaos,
> S'élançant dans les airs, et planant sur les flots!
> Vantez-nous maintenant, bienheureux légendaires,
> Le porc de saint Antoine, et le chien de saint Roch,
>   Vos reliques, vos scapulaires,
> Et la guimpe d'Ursule, et la crasse du froc;
> Mettez la Fleur des saints à côté d'un Homère:
> Il ment, mais en grand homme, il ment, mais il sait plaire;
>   Sottement vous avez menti:
>   Par lui l'esprit humain s'éclaire.

[All Olympus is filled with amorous heroes. Admirable pictures!
Delightful magic! How Hesiod pleases me when, in his theology,
he portrays Cupid bringing order to chaos, leaping into the air and
hovering over the waves! Speak praise to us now, legendary saints,
of Saint Anthony's pig and Saint Roch's dog and Ursula's wimple

and the filth on the frock. Put the Flower of the saints alongside a Homer: he lies, but as a great man, he lies, but he knows how to please. You have lied foolishly, whereas he has illuminated the human spirit.]

Here Voltaire seems inclined not so much to enter the world of myth as to enlist it as an ally in his struggle for Enlightenment and for a civilization of earthly happiness. His "apology for myth" does not require him to venture onto the bewildering ground of the past. It merely confirms his choice, already announced in the celebrated poem *Le Mondain* (The Worldling), in favor of urban civilization and the pleasure to be had from the arts. Voltaire's Homer, who "illuminates the human spirit," is in no sense a "primitive." Myth, as extolled by Voltaire, is nothing more than a profane modern amusement sharply opposed to religious practice. The dichotomy of the sacred and the profane is nowhere more evident than in the final lines of the poem, which establish an equality between the terms they distinguish:

Si nos peuples nouveaux sont chrétiens à la messe,
  Ils sont païens à l'Opéra.
L'almanach est païen, nous comptons nos journées
Par le seul nom des dieux que Rome avait connus;
C'est Mars et Jupiter, c'est Saturne et Vénus,
Qui président au temps, qui font nos destinées.
Ce mélange est impur, on a tort; mais enfin
Nous ressemblons assez à l'abbé Pellegrin,
"Le matin catholique, et le soir idolâtre,
Déjeûnant de l'autel, et soupant du théâtre."

[If our new peoples are Christian at mass, they are pagan at the Opera. The almanac is pagan, we count our days by the names of the Gods that Rome once knew. Mars and Jupiter, Saturn and Venus preside over time and seal our fates. This mixture is impure; we are wrong. But in the end we are rather like abbé Pellegrin, "Catholic in the morning, idolatrous at night, lunching at the altar, supping at the theater."]

This "impure mixture" would find its belated apotheosis in Parny's *La Guerre des Dieux* (The War of the Gods, 1799), a licentious poem in which the gods of Olympus subject the "modern deities" to the most unspeakable outrages.

Thus far I have looked at myth only in its most general formal aspect: as the agent of an aesthetic transformation in the profane sphere, assuming that the point of departure was usually some circumstance of life that one wished to celebrate, purify, or magnify. But the mythological code, with its many variables and branches, also exists for itself, independent of any embellishments for which it might serve as medium. It offers a vast "canvas" full of passions, extreme situations, and monstrous acts. By making choices and selections within this body of preexisting material desire and imagination are able to project their truest energies. Certain works of the seventeenth and eighteenth centuries can be regarded as reinterpretations of the great mythical themes, though with the reservation that the artists' purpose was not so much to alter the signification of myths as to use them to permit full expression of their talents. Of course a myth, in its traditional form, imposes a constraint in the form of a "subject" that must be respected. But in an aesthetic that, unlike our own, attached no higher value to "originality" capable of producing form, subject, and style, indeed all the components of a work of art, *ex nihilo,* the stylistic freedom the artist was allowed in the treatment of a well-known myth was sufficient in some cases to unleash very deep forces. Even what might seem gratuitous in a myth or tragedy could exercise intense powers of attraction, on the order of a hidden meaning. With its free and playful form the story of Psyche as recounted by La Fontaine is fraught with symbols superimposed on the basic plot and having to do with the theme of secrecy and the strategy of the gaze. *Andromaque, Iphigénie,* and *Phèdre* are plays in which the psychologized mythological element allows Racine to express the dark powers of passion. Abandoned, Ariane and Dido provide, in many operas, an opportunity for melodious musical laments, for tearful songs. More generally, under the cover and with the warrant of a traditional myth, desire could *impersonally* achieve imaginary gratification: the traditional mythical structures would not be seen as obstacles until insistence on *personal* expression became paramount.

The role of the mythical universe as a basis of and screen for projective desire went hand in hand with a more intellectual function: an elaborate pedagogical, political, and moral edifice could be erected around the epico-mythical framework, which made it possible to embellish, enlarge, and "detemporalize" the moral instruction of young princes. Fénelon's *Télémaque* is simultaneously a prose poem, an "educational romance," and a description of a political utopia. The Odyssean setting with its tumultuous seas and apparitions of Amphitrite, with its nymphs and lush islands, ensured the harmonious fusion of disparate components. Mentor, who is Minerva, gives instruction couched in the form of profane myth but containing the most rigorous precepts of Christian doctrine in a distilled, universalized, and readily assimilable form.

When, moreover, one examines the choices that seventeenth- and eighteenth-century writers made within the available body of mythical material, it becomes clear that in each period certain themes crop up again and again, attesting to certain shared anxieties. Frequently these anxieties reflect a particular moment in the history of sensibility. It is not a very audacious claim to say that the baroque, obsessed with the fluidity of appearances, was fond of myths of metamorphosis (of which Bernini's *Daphne* is one example among many). If *Pygmalions* were commonplace in the eighteenth century, it was not only because that century raised the question of how matter is infused with life but also because the artists of that time dreamed of perfecting their mimetic powers to the point where they might indeed be rewarded by the loving embrace of a work suddenly come to life. It is not without interest that Rousseau's only text on a mythological subject is none other than a *Pygmalion,* in which the writer's fundamental narcissism is given free rein: his desire is rewarded by a creation modeled after his ideal. But here we touch on an extreme case. The Pygmalion myth represented, in a language that was *still* mythical, the imperative of self-expression, whose next manifestation would be the refusal of all mythical mediation, of any recourse to a preexisting body of material. Somewhat later (around 1800), certain great heroic myths (Prometheus, Hercules, Ganymede) would be invoked to express hope and rebellion: the apotheosis of the human hero hinted at a future in which the ancient gods would reign no more, having been replaced by man. Here again mythical language tends toward its own abolition, since the vanishing of the gods' authority inevitably means the decadence of the traditional imagery associated with them. One might then trace the idea of total myth through Wagner's *Götterdämmerung,* ending in the collapse of the mythical universe—a universe conceived as the expression of an ancient *law* of the world now become obsolete. But this tendency was by no means the only one at work. Indeed, it was balanced by a precisely opposite tendency, as we shall see next.

The Flourishing of Mythological Theories

Thus *la fable,* a stable body of well-known stories and symbols capable of being repeated indefinitely, could, in proper circumstances, be brought back to life, reinvigorated, and reanimated by a lively imagination with the faculty of projecting its dreams onto preexisting imagery. Eighteenth-century musicans and painters (more often than poets) were sometimes capable of breathing new life, passionate emotion, and even some of the strangeness of invention into old mythical themes.

But the renaissance of myth came about in a more circuitous fashion. Paradoxically, it was the result of scholarly investigation, which seemed at first sight to lead to the death of myth, to its permanent disqualification. Mythology—learned discourse about myths—destroyed the mythical universe of *la fable* yet at the same time laid the foundation for myth to flourish once more in an expanded and rejuvenated form. The process was a gradual one, and it is not difficult to reconstruct its stages.

The mythology of the seventeenth century was a combination of varying degrees of "antiquarian" knowledge (concerning the attributes of the gods, the location of cults, the written sources, ancient coinage, and so on) with the conjectures of theologians. The most convenient hypothesis, which goes back to Clement of Alexandria, was that the pagan gods were a degenerate, pluralized reflection either of the true God of Genesis or of the kings mentioned in the Bible. Infidel and sinful peoples gradually ceased to comprehend the universal revelation in its original clarity. After the dispersion at Babel, they forgot the first God, the only God, so that nothing now stood in the way of their making deities of their princes, rivers, and beasts. But just as the languages of these peoples were, in the eyes of etymologists, corrupt derivatives of Hebrew, their deities hinted at the holy religion of which they were a distorted image. Abbé Banier succinctly summarized this widely held view:

In primitive times men worshiped only one God. Noah's family continued to worship the creator as his fathers had done before him, but it did not take his descendants long to sully the purity of religion. The crimes in which they indulged soon weakened the idea of Divinity, and people began to attach that idea to perceptible objects. What seemed most brilliant and perfect in nature received their homage, and for that reason the sun was the first object of their superstition. From the cult of the sun men moved on to the worship of other stars and planets, and all the heavenly host . . . attracted religious cults, as did the rivers and the mountains. But that was not the end of it. Nature itself was regarded as a divinity, and under various names it was worshiped by different nations. Finally, great men, owing to their conquests or to their invention of the arts, seemed to deserve honors that were due only to the Creator of the Universe. Thus we see the origins of all the gods worshiped under paganism.

This summary treats different traditional theories of the origin of myths (euhemerism, astral symbolism, and so on) as equivalent for the purpose of explaining as well as indicting the false religions while retaining intact the authority of the original revelation, the truth of which is vested in Christianity.

But this orthodox mythology, in developing psychological explanations for the crimes and sacrileges of the infidel nations, laid the groundwork for even bolder speculation about the grounds of belief and worship in all their forms. Skeptics would later make use of these ideas to challenge the authority that orthodoxy sought to preserve and reinforce. The weapons the Church used against superstition could easily be turned against faith, and the most common ruse was to attack dogma itself by pretending to pursue the dogmatists' struggle against idolatry. The God of the Hebrews was then subjected to a *causal* interpretation similar to that which the theologians had applied exclusively to the gods of paganism. The explanation given by Lucretius— *insitus horror* (V, 1160–1239)—was now applied to all cults. Much of seventeenth-century "libertine" thought was based on this return to the teachings of Epicurus. And myth, instead of appearing to be secondary and derivative, now came to seem like man's *primary* response to the terrors of dream, to the great events of nature, and indeed to all that was *astonishing*.

Fontenelle's brief dissertation on the *Origin of Fables* gives simple causes for myths and polytheism: ignorance, amazement, terror in the face of powers sensed everywhere in nature, a propensity to explain the unknown in terms of the known. Myths offer us "the history of the errors of the human spirit." Accordingly, there is no point in wasting time learning the ins and outs of ancient myths; instead, we must practice mythology as Fontenelle does, in order to rid ourselves of our illusions: "It is not a science to fill one's head with all the extravagances of the Phoenicians and the Greeks, but it is one to know what led the Phoenicians and the Greeks to those extravagances. Men are so much alike that there is no people at whose foolishness we need not tremble."

Here we see a combination of contempt for myth with an affirmation of the epistemological value of reflection on the beginnings of man's relation to the world and on the errors committed by minds engaged in those early efforts of understanding. With the savage as with the child, it all begins with an unfortunate propensity to give incorrect explanations until the intelligence, slowly but steadily disillusioned, reaches the point where it is capable of laughing at its childish beliefs and even of knowing *why* it allowed itself to make up such myths. The cultivated mind also takes warning: these "primitive" errors, which are committed by all peoples, are also permanent, and nothing is easier than to relapse into committing them again. Men must always be on their guard if they are not to succumb to the constant temptation of mythification. The imagination remains susceptible even when reason demurs:

> Although we are incomparably more enlightened than those whose crude minds invented Fables in good faith, we easily reacquire the same turn of mind that made those Fables so attractive to them. They devoured them because they believed in them, and we devour them with just as much pleasure yet without believing in them. There is no better proof that the imagination and reason have little commerce with each other, and that things with which reason has first become disillusioned lose none of their attractiveness to the imagination.

The dichotomy of the sacred and the profane, which had allowed mythical history to subsist on the fringes of sacred history, is here replaced by the dichotomy of reason and imagination. Once again myth is considered devoid of all truth and authority, but now reason (and not revelation) is in control. But no moral reprobation attaches to the products of the imagination and their associated pleasure: they are perfectly legitimate so long as they in no way usurp reason's prerogatives. Illusion has the right to charm us, so long as we know that we are in the sphere of poetry and not of science. When we give in to the seductions of myth, we amuse ourselves by spending time in a world that we have actually transcended. The poets of the world's childhood—Homer and Hesiod—are of course admirable, but their wonderful images are merely the obverse of their ignorance. When measured against the steady progress of reason over the centuries, myth attests to the first, faltering efforts of the human spirit in a time when the soul had no resources other than metaphor to express its terrors and wonders. Moreover, this general theory of myth treats all beliefs equally: it makes no exception for the "true religion" except by precaution and with a flourish of style. The goal of education should be to free humans of all their prejudices, errors, and cults. Such disillusionment will lead to poetry that uses myth without believing in it, coldly, wittily, mockingly: this might serve as a definition of the eighteenth century's antipoetic strain.

Yet not everyone was quite so confident about the powers of cultivated reason. Hume, whose interpretation of the origin of myth was roughly the same as Fontenelle's, harbored some doubt about reason's constructs, which, he said, might prove to be no more solidly grounded than the polytheist cosmogonies. In that case our "progress" would be precarious, and the pleasure we take in ancient myths would be less childish than it seems. Uncertain as we are about the truth, myth has in its favor the advantage of beauty and yet is no more fraudulent than all that seems to have the sanction of reason. Reason disabused of itself can afford to be tolerant toward the first products of the imagination.

A full rehabilitation of myth along these lines was not long in coming. But first the spirit's primitive experiments had to overcome their aura of imperfection and be characterized instead as instances of plenitude and unity. In this reevaluation of myth it is not hard to see the return of theological thinking, which was combined with psychological explanations of the origin of man's first ideas and feelings. *Genesis* can be seen again behind (or in) the simple mental acts that constitute the first stage in the *genetic* reconstruction of the intellectual faculties of humankind. The child, the savage, the primitive human being, "stupid" though they were said to be, lived in immediate contact with the world: they were like Adam in Eden. Revelation did not come to them, as teaching does, from outside but reigned within. Their knowledge was not reflection but participation: they lived *in* familiarity with the world and its forces. In this image of primordial indivision (itself mythical) a very important role was ascribed to the powers of primitive language: it was both speech and song (as Strabo had been the first to say, and as Vossius and Vico repeated;[3] Rousseau and Herder developed the theoretical consequences). Primitive language bore within itself, Rousseau said, "the almost inevitable impression of the passion seeking communication." Word and feeling were not dissociated. Expressive fidelity was absolute. There was still no place for lies or abstraction. Man's heart and speech were not yet two. As for the gods that he imagined, whether in terror or amusement, they were simply the face that living nature turned toward him—nature to whom man was no stranger. In immediate contact with himself and with nature, man produced the first lyric poems, the first great epics, in an effusion of spirit that demonstrated both his true greatness and the limits of his mortal condition. This was the new conviction that restored a kind of ontological as well as poetic legitimacy to myth. Equal attention was paid to evidence from all primitive literatures, and as if in response to this new attention, whole mythologies emerged from obscurity, in some cases half invented: Edda, Ossian, the sacred books of the Orient, the songs of American Indians. These were seen as prefigurations of art before there was art, of poetry before there were academic rules of composition. Sometimes these "barbarities" were thought to contain a grandeur and energy that the civilized languages no longer possessed.

The result was not just an expansion of the range of mythological knowledge or a mere enlargement of the repertoire of epic or naive texts in which men of taste tired of the frivolities of their century could indulge. To those who experienced the force of these texts, the idea of a regenerated poetry, of a language restored to its primitive vigor, irresistibly inspired a desire to live and to feel in a new way that would capture the plenitude of primitive times. Nostalgic for the loss of elevated language, the mind turned toward the beginnings of society, where it hoped to find the enthusiasm from which might come songs capable of restoring lost warmth and unanimity. The modernized notion of *genius* directed attention to the voices emanating from the depths of nature and the collective consciousness. Poets, convinced that all the peoples of the world had first asserted their identity by glorifying themselves in their heroes and gods, were drawn to the past in the hope that they might unite their fellow citizens by offering them a sense of reinvented community. French poets once again turned to Greek and Roman (and to a lesser extent to Celtic and "Gallic") models. With the discovery of Nordic and Oriental antiquities, moreover, the traditional models themselves revealed a hidden face: in Homer, Aeschylus, Pindar, and even Virgil people now discovered not lapses of taste but a gigantesque, savage, and inevitably invigorating sublimity. Influenced by neo-Platonic idealism, the neoclassical system searched for Beauty's timeless forms; more than that, following Winckelmann, it affirmed that the archetypes of "beautiful nature" could not have appeared had it not been for the flourishing of political freedom in the Greek city-states. With the aid of certain displacements and condensations, statues of the Greek gods came to be seen as the ideal incarnate, fashioned by free citizens. Seen in this way, the primitive world of course shed much of its crudeness and ferocity. The serenity celebrated by Winckelmann, the reflection of an intelligible cosmos, was rather too bland to be the source of energies supposed to burst forth from the mysterious depths of living nature. For a poet like André Chénier, however, there was nothing contradictory about looking to the Hellenic past for both formal harmony *and* the heat of youthful desire, to say nothing of the most important thing of all, the powerful winds of freedom. Thus imitation of the ancients was not mere repetition of images and names; it became a reconquest of fire, a transfusion of energy: "Let us light our torches at their poetic fires." At about the same time Herder expressed the wish that the poetry of the ancients might become for the moderns not an object of servile imitation but the source of a "poetic heuristic" that would lead to the invention of an "entirely new mythology." But he immediately recognized how difficult it would be to reconcile "the spirit of reduction with the spirit of fiction," the "dismemberment of the philosopher" with the "orderly construction of the poet."

The appeal was thus addressed to the poet, who it was expected would reawaken the communal spirit by stirring men's hearts and restoring the presence of forgotten divine forces. The outcome was of interest to society, to human efforts to rekindle awareness of the ties that bound people together. The ancient gods took on political significance. They were the witnesses that the popular soul needed in order to recognize itself. They had to become once again what they used to be: the guardians, the guarantors, that the social group had conceived in its own image and in whom it discovered its truth, its inherent nature. When the poets described the return of the gods, it was primarily on the human stage that they reappeared (in the context of national or universal celebrations depending on whether their significance was particularized or generalized).

What took shape at this point was what Hans Blumenberg has called a "myth of mythology," according to which the uncertain origin of myth coincided with the origin of the nation (or of humankind) and which imposed on the inhabitants of a world in crisis the duty of rediscovering their beginnings (along with lost nature), failing which they would lose their souls and die. But no sooner had this new myth been formulated and this new duty been set out than questions arose. Could the men and women of an age of science and reason experience the same naive astonishment as youthful humankind, which populated nature with mutable divinities not subject to what K. P. Moritz called the principle of identity? In an ode entitled *The Gods of Greece* Schiller devoted a great deal of space to a description of the multiplicity of the ancient gods. Now, however, they were banished forever and would never return; nature was henceforth *entgöttert,* stripped of gods. Our poetry can live only by taking notice of their absence, by affirming that we miss them: "What is destined to live immortally in song must perish in life." Unable to adopt an attitude of *naïve* simplicity, modern poetry is doomed to *sentimental* nostalgia.

Jean Paul makes the same point in his own fashion:

The beautiful, the rich simplicity of the child enchants not another child but one who has lost it . . . The Greek gods are for us only flat images, the empty clothing of our sensations, and not living beings. Whereas then, yes, there were no false gods on earth—and every people could be received as guests in the Temple of every other people—today we know virtually nothing but false gods . . . And whereas poetry in the past was a possession of the people, just as the people were the object of poetry, today one sings only from study to study.

The impossibility of bringing ancient mythology back to life (not because it is no longer admired but because it is admired too much and because the present-day world is no longer ripe to receive it) only accentuated the dangerous wish to establish a *new mythology.* The idea can be found at the conclusion of a text (copied in Hegel's hand in 1796 but perhaps originally by Schelling and certainly inspired by Hölderlin) known under the title "Oldest Systematic Program of German Idealism":

> We need a new mythology, but that mythology must be in the service of ideas, it must become a mythology of *reason.* Ideas not presented in aesthetic, that is, mythological, form hold no interest for *the people,* and conversely a mythology that is not reasonable is an object of shame for the philosopher. In the end, therefore, the enlightened and the unenlightened will help each other out: mythology must become philosophical so as to make the people reasonable, and philosophy must become mythological so as to make the philosophers accessible. Eternal unity will then be established among us.

Hölderlin, in *Bread and Wine, The Archipelago,* and numerous other texts, chooses to speak from the intermediate moment, the interval of anxious anticipation between the irreparable disappearance of the ancient gods and the emergence of a new deity, a Dionysus or a Christ of the last hour. In 1800 Friedrich Schlegel also called for a new mythology, one that would emerge not like the old one from contact with the perceptible universe but rather "from the deepest depths of the spirit," much as harmonious order emerged "when chaos was touched by love."

Disappointed though it might be, this expectation of a new flourishing of myth (of a myth that would *again* imply the sovereignty of the unifying imagination but that would also be a triumph of sensuous reason and would no longer assume the mask of the ancient gods) attributes to the future, to history yet to come, a function whose equivalent can be found only in religious or gnostic eschatologies. Even though that myth still seems to be lacking, human time and man-made history are deeply mythified by this hope: in awaiting the advent of a new mythology as if it were a veritable second coming, this way of thinking already defines the present *mythically* as the hidden gestation of a new Adam, as a nocturnal search for the point at which the new universal dawn will break: it is a time of labor and of trial, of forward marches and obligatory halts, of efforts to begin anew. Human history, the object of this new mythopoesis, reveals an intelligible meaning. It is a reconquest, in a still unknown form, of lost plenitude, a communal restoration of unity, a return to an earlier truth, to be obtained by the birth of an entirely new world. Conceived in this way, myth, which at the beginning of the eighteenth century was pure *profane* ornament, becomes the quintessence of the *sacred,* the ultimate authority that imposes its law in advance and decides on human values "in the last instance." Although it has not yet come to pass, it is the criterion of all that does come to pass. This change is only the corollary of another change: what was *sacred* at the beginning of the eighteenth century— written revelation, tradition, dogma—has been subjected to "demystifying" critique, which has demonstrated that it is nothing but a human creation, a work of the mythmaking imagination. The sacred is thus reduced to a psychological function, but by the same token certain human faculties (emotions, consciousness, imagination) and certain collective acts (the general will) are granted a sacred function. In the intellectual history of the nineteenth century, the sacralization of myth played an important part in the humanization of the sacred. It is not enough to note, as many have done, the existence of a "secularizing" process in enlightenment philosophy, a process in which man claims for reason prerogatives that had belonged to the divine *logos.* An opposite tendency also existed: myth, at first excluded and declared to be absurd, was now endowed with full and profound meaning and prized as revealed truth (Schelling). Owing to this dual transformation the opposition of sacred and profane was restructured. The old sacred was transformed, and the profane order was invested with a mythic hope of liberating progress. In anticipation of the sovereign myth that the man of the future would invent, old myths were revived as prefigurations of revolt, desire, and the hope that man might become the master of his own destiny: Prometheus, Hercules, Psyche, the Titans. The myth of the future, whose outlines are shaped even now by a diffuse anticipation, will not only be a product of man's imagination (of the prophet-poet, the people's poet, or of humankind at work) but will also have man as its hero. The awaited Myth, which will emerge neither from the truth of history nor from the truth of the poem, is not theogony but anthropogony: were it real, it would rally nations by singing of the Man-God who produces himself by his own song or his own handiwork. All the mythologies of the modern world are but the aftermath, the debris, of this unrealized Myth.[4]

Epilogue

"As I Detest Hades' Gates"

Why Read the Ancients?

Far be it from me to suggest that the ancients spoke the truth and that we, armed with new exegetical methods, must return to their texts to discover the enduring secrets of the "human heart," of "human nature," and of "being-in-the-world." Ancient language, in which the first—simpler, more vigorous—system of representation was couched, enjoys no privilege, in my view, other than that of having come first and of having forced later ages to retain it in memory (consciously or unconsciously)—to repeat, transform, or contradict it. Of course the ancient languages can legitimately be studied as etymological sources, but that implies only a relation of derivation. In order to ascribe higher authority to the ancients, it would have to be laid down as a principle that what is said at the beginning continues to possess the highest possible validity. But just because something was done, imagined, or recounted in the most remote past to which we have access, it does not follow that it belongs to the "deepest" bedrock of the individual. Whether applied to historical time or to emotional life, spatial metaphors have only *approximate* validity.

Nevertheless, the idea that the past is preserved *within us* is an attractive one, one that has never ceased to exercise a certain charm. To justify it, the notion of phylogenetic heritage is often borrowed from biology. Freud's use of this in, among other places, the idea of the "primal fantasy" is well known. Myths and archetypes lay claim to similar status: their priority, their genetic antecedence, seemingly guarantees them a central position and function in the structural order. They are accorded a certain respect, as if, because they belong to the species' past, they must also constitute the inner space, the innards, of the individual. If that is so, then anyone who studies ancient texts is also embarking on an inward journey, a quest toward that kernel of the self where the origin persists and perdures.

The attractiveness of this idea is related to an assumption that cannot be proven: that ancient texts (or events) are universal and psychologically inescapable. Otherwise there is no reason why the legacy of the ancients should be part of the heritage of all individuals. (Usually one begins with a psychological disposition presumed to be present in all human beings and looks for mythical prefigurations, which are supposed to prove that the disposition in question is an objective and permanent part of human character. The myths of the past reflect an image of ourselves in the present. A logician would call such reasoning circular.)

To say that the remote past corresponds to our innermost selves is to deny difference, loss, or mutation and to subsume time in a continuous history, a history without gaps. The very image of a continuous passage through time suggests that the past produces the present, that the individual is the sum total of his prior experiences. To say that the individual is constructed by history is to say that history is cumulatively present and that as events recede into the past they become part of an interior structure. All self-knowledge is therefore a process of overcoming amnesia, of remembering. Conversely, all remembering is equivalent to discovering deeper layers of the personality (often compared to geological layers). A comforting corollary of some versions of this view is that the history of the species is implicit in the history of the individual: nothing in the past of the human race is alien; everything in the past is of concern to me and may enlighten me. Nothing is external, nothing human is foreign to me. All history is a mirror in which I see myself.

But what if we abandon the metaphor of an evolutionary process that preserves obsolete experiences? Doubt immediately creeps in, and that doubt is reinforced when a single, all-encompassing view of history is replaced by a pluralist view, which does not lend itself to interpretation in terms of organic growth.

There is, however, no reason why our interest in culture's past should be any less keen if that past consists not of part of ourselves but of what other men accomplished with the aid of a philosophy that is not and never will be ours and a language in which we recognize nothing of ourselves. Some cultures had nothing to do with making us what we are, and even those cultures that have influenced us may have been as much rejected as assimilated. According to Goldstein's model, which opposes the positive notion of the emergence of "new structures"[1] to the psychoanalytic model of "repression and unconscious preservation," it is legitimate to see in archaic language and myth a mode of expression that has been supplanted by other types of discourse, though the possibility of regression still exists.[2] Priority in time does not imply hidden permanence. We have emerged from the prior state and observe it from *outside*. Archaic language belongs to the past. Our task is to measure our distance from it, to gauge the difference that sustains our curiosity.

Even if history consists of a series of exclusions, our interest in a remote and unusual external object makes it a part of our present discourse. It becomes ours; in one way or another we *internalize* it. And even if the exploration of memory involves a reality that is foreign to us, any overcoming of amnesia, any "archaeology," by creating a dimension of the past outside of us, stakes out an area beyond the self without which we would be devoid of interiority. If the notion of interiority has any meaning, it is to be conceived not as a receptacle of treasures, monstrosities, or mysterious traces springing from within but as the result of our always mutable relations with the other, of our relations with the exterior, with what we have never been, with what we have ceased to be, or with words exchanged before we existed.

Here I shall consider only a few ancient texts, from Homer and the Bible. I do not claim that these texts formulate an ever-present truth in metaphorical terms. With careful reading, however, it is possible, as we shall see, to notice certain things in these texts that are of great topical relevance. I prefer to regard them initially as evidence of a remote system of thought based on a fairly simple and obvious set of images, whose implications it is up to us to decipher. I want the texts to retain all their strangeness, all their exteriority.

Why take all these precautions? These texts concern the opposition of words and thoughts, of lips and heart, of outside and inside. We will apprehend them better if we remain keenly aware of the opposition between them and us.

A Homeric Image

When Achilles declines Agamemnon's offers, conveyed to him by Ulysses, he exclaims: "For as I detest the doorways of Death [literally: the gates of Hades], I detest that man, who hides one thing in the depths of his heart, and speaks forth another" (*Iliad,* IX, 312–313, trans. Richmond Lattimore).[3] This is one of the first poetic documents in which the denunciation of duplicity is expressed in a complete and powerful way. The first words of the accusation are unparalleled in their clarity. Nothing is more striking than the opposition between what is *said* and what remains *hidden* in the depths of the self (the Greek here is not easily translated: ἐνὶ φρεσὶν). The "poetic" evocation of the gates of Hades (or "doorways of Death," even if it is no more than a stylistic flourish, a hyperbole for the most detestable thing imaginable) adds a singular analogical dimension to the statement.

Achilles' reproach is aimed at the division, the schism, that leaves *one thing* hidden while *another* is spoken. The disjunction ἕτερον–ἄλλο, which expresses this alternative, governs the structure of the statement. The alternative is not stated simply as the difference between the spoken and the unspoken. A spatial figure is used: what is not spoken is actively *hidden* in the heart. Inner space—the interior of the body—is where the cunning man dissimulates (κεύθη) what he does not say. This simple image ascribes an actual, albeit invisible and forbidden, *place* to the unspoken alternative. Thoughts? Words? The neutral ἄλλο–ἕτερον establishes equality between the spoken thing and the hidden thing: to be opposed in this way, they must be of the same essence. Their difference results from the distance between open speech and the act of hiding.

The meaning here is produced not by the nominalized adjectives, which remain enveloped in the generality of the neuter (whereas elsewhere in Homer the nouns are specific: ἔπεα, words; νόος, intention, thought, etc.), but by the opposition of the verbs: to say, to hide. Hiding is made possible by the availability of an inaccessible space and the possibility of an interposition. Physically, the interior of the body is that space, denoted by φρενες in its organic, carnal sense (diaphragm, *praecordia*).[4] But the act of hiding a thought, an intention, or a discourse, by constituting the dimension of the unspoken, simultaneously constitutes an "interiority," an abstract mental region, which superimposes itself on the image of the physical interior of the body: thus φρενεσ also comes to mean mind, intelligence, the "depths of the heart." The prerequisite for this to happen is the existence of an organic *interior* that the trope of hiding can develop. Conversely, because the act of hiding separates the spoken from the unspoken and buries the unspoken within the body, a secret place of intentionality, of unavowed thoughts, is hollowed out—the inwardness of the concealed design. Interiority is the result of an *act* of separation.

Achilles looks to the past for justification of his suspicion. Today's generous promises hide an appetite for possession and ownership, an insatiable self-interest that Agamemnon, the supreme commander of the Greeks, has always exhibited: "He, waiting back beside the swift ships, would take [the spoils of war], and distribute them little by little, and keep many" (*Iliad*, IX, 332–333).[5] The secret, hidden and retained in the "heart," is nothing other than retention itself: the refusal to give, stubborn greed. None of the prizes that Agamemnon promised through Ulysses had ever been given. Convinced that Agamemnon will not change, Achilles is no longer willing to take him at his word: "He cheated me and he did me hurt. Let him not beguile me with words again" (*Iliad*, IX, 375–376). Achilles' bitterness and stubbornness are those of a disillusioned man, a man who knows in advance that he will never receive any of what he has been promised. His complaint lingers because, according to Achilles, nothing can change the conduct of "the leader of nations." All that can change is his language, and that is deceptive. Thus the opposition between "hiding one thing in the heart" and "saying something else" becomes more explicit: it concerns the substantiality of the *gift*. Agamemnon's words merely list splendid objects and privileges, but none of them has actually been given, and none ever will be given. His words are nothing but the simulacrum of a gift: to one who has had the beautiful Briseis taken from him, this is bitter mockery.

Under suspicious scrutiny, then, the man who makes eloquent promises hides an inside, a "depth," that is not merely something hidden from view, a refusal to speak openly, but a deliberate act of frustration, a self-serving act of concealment, of refusal to award each man his fair share.

The being that hides behind flattering appearances in the heart of the other is therefore defined by stubborn greed. The accuser thinks: the interiority of the other deprives me of that which is rightfully mine. It threatens my possessions; it monopolizes them. When the other cannot be taken at his word, the rhetoric of suspicion represents the evil in a double trope; it divides the presumed enemy into two distinct "regions": idle words outside, wicked heart within. This schema underlies the whole tradition of images of evil in our culture. The modern denunciation of "ideologies" is no different: it attacks the deceptive discourses that mask private interests and selfish appetites—the refusal, once again, to *share*.

The comparison with the "doorways of Death" is wonderfully effective poetry: it reiterates and amplifies; it inscribes the hidden in a cosmic space. The gates of Hades, the most detestable of all things, not only mark the entry to another world, a forbidden space, but also define a greedy power that forever keeps what it takes, the retentive power par excellence. The man who hides his secret desire, the man whose secret is the passion to possess by barring others from access to his heart, becomes an image of the other world: to the suspicious gaze hidden inwardness is a trope for the kingdom of the dead.

But is the phrase "hidden inwardness" accurate? What if that inwardness were in fact an intensified exteriority? The gates of Hades mark the frontier of the extreme outside: they enclose a nether space inaccessible to the person who fears and curses them. The "inside" to which they bar Achilles' access takes its meaning from his own vulnerability, from his possible humiliation, from the definitive absence of those whom he has laid to rest beneath the surface of the earth. This inside contains all that he has lost, all that he can lose. The gates of Hades retain that which is no more, which is no longer entitled to the light of the sun. They also mark a boundary that living beings are powerless to cross. What the secretive man hides in his heart is just the same: the heart is what remains hidden from the gaze that wishes to dominate its surroundings. It is a second "outside" that cannot be entered by force, and whose essence, as suspicion fears and imagines it, is constituted by the will to give up nothing—to impoverish me, to annihilate me. Let us risk a generalization: the *inside* that Achilles suspiciously denounces is a space constructed of his possible failures, of his continually threatened dispossession, of his mortality: the enemy that reigns in this other world aims to exploit his strength, to make him waste his energy, without offering the slightest palpable gain or pleasure in return. What my enemy hides within is the destruction of my own inwardness.

A Biblical Image

The author of Proverbs warns the youth: "For the lips of a strange woman drop as an honeycomb, and her mouth is smoother than oil. But her end is bitter as wormwood, sharp as a two-edged sword. Her feet go down to death; her steps take hold on hell" (Proverbs 5:3–5).[6] Proverbs 7 illustrates this precept at length, almost in the form of a romance: "With her much fair speech she caused him to yield, with the flattering of her lips she forced him . . . For she hath cast down many wounded. Yea, many strong men have been slain by her. Her house is the way to hell, going down to the chambers of death" (Proverbs 7:21, 26–27). Here, again, accusatory thought is at work: it decries a difference. Initially it is the exterior that is denounced: the sweetness of the lips, the smoothness of her words. Then, inside the house, the feet move along the path that leads to death. The difference is the same as the one we found in Homer, but here we have the overtly sexualized version. The lips of the strange woman promise pleasure: "I have decked my bed with coverings of tapestry, with carved works, with fine linen of Egypt. I have perfumed my bed with myrrh, aloes, and cinnamon. Come, let us take our fill of love until the morning. Let us solace ourselves with love" (Proverbs 8:16–19). At once truthful and misleading, this is the description of an interior in which all desires might be satisfied, in which all pleasures might be experienced. The passerby is thus confronted with an image of an unsuspected place, off the "straight and narrow," suddenly made available for the comfort of the body and the pleasure of the senses, but which leads irrevocably to death. The chamber of love becomes the chamber of death. Accusatory thought sees carnal seduction turning into murder (7:23), as the steps toward the bed culminate in the subterranean world. Descended from the serpent, the destructive woman (7:26: "she hath cast down many wounded") promises rapture but delivers her victim to "the dart [that] strike[s] through his liver" (7:23). In the father's warning to his son (7:1: "My son, keep my words") the finger of accusation is pointed at exteriority, otherness, the outside world: an *other* world, *other* gods threaten the young man the moment he listens at *night* to the *strange woman*'s words. The seductive interior toward which he hastens his step is in reality that feared exterior from which no traveler returns. The unhinged youth leaps from the street, the first exterior, into a place that is outside life: death is the reward of him who "goes her ways," who "strays" (7:25), who forgets the warnings of accusatory thought. But the youth who writes his father's teachings "upon the table" of his heart (7:3), who *retains* his father's teaching, will of course not meet the same fate. Paternal law will protect him.

The Teeth's Barrier and the Surveillance of the Lips

Once the danger has been denounced, what else is to be done? How is it to be guarded against? One can refuse to heed the voice of deception, shun mendacious seduction, safeguard one's life.

Achilles' response is to reject offers he regards as insincere and to refuse to exert himself or risk his life. Threatened, he clutches fast what he does not wish to lose. To thwart the supreme commander's greed he dreams of retaining what is most precious to him: his life. "Of possessions cattle and fat sheep are things to be had for the lifting, and tripods can be won, and the tawny high heads of horses, but a man's life cannot come back again, it cannot be lifted nor captured again by force, once it has crossed the teeth's barrier" (*Iliad*, IX, 406–409). The project of a prudent retention of life (or of the soul: ψυχή) is put forward in response to a deceptive voice that offers splendid gifts and dissimulates stubborn greed: a sly invitation is met with a blunt refusal. Achilles wants to hold on to his breath, to prevent it from fleeing forever beyond the teeth's barrier: an elementary—but extremely important—form of control exercised at the boundary where a person's interior and exterior meet. Endangered by the hidden design he suspects before him, the individual seeks to protect his own frontiers; he sees to it that the barriers under his control are closed—barriers within which his life remains safe.

But having resolved not to leave his tent, not to risk his life in battle, and determined (for the time being) to hold on to life inside his "teeth's barrier," Achilles, in expressing his will, is unable to contain his wrath or restrain his anger. Ulysses had earlier reminded him of his father's advice: "Dear friend, surely thus your father Peleus advised you that day when he sent you away to Agamemnon from Phthia: 'My child, for the matter of strength, Athene and Hera will give it if it be their will, but be it yours to hold fast in your bosom the anger of the proud heart, for consideration is better'" (*Iliad*, IX, 252–256). Wisdom—and note that it comes from a *paternal* source—recommends self-control not only over life's precious substance (ψυχή) but also over proud anger (μεγαλήτορα θυμὸν). To hold (ἴσχειν) such anger within the breast (εν στήθεσσι) can be seen as the archetypal image of repression. What makes it possible to retain anger within the breast, as previously to hide secret thoughts within the heart, is the reality of a visceral interior, which the individual can treat as the receptacle of the "breath" that he refuses actively to externalize: by preventing "pride" from finding an exterior issue, the act that bars the way requires an organic interior (the breast and its organs) to serve as the "space" of the repressed discourse: thus the economy of the will that regulates, evaluates, and limits the quantity of passion that can be displayed externally gives rise to wisdom and establishes an inner dimension, a subjectivity. The self-control that Peleus recommended to Achilles does not simulate or deceive. It silences or restrains passion but does not substitute another discourse in its place. This is the virtue known as discretion or restraint, and it consists in sparing others, in refraining indefinitely from words or actions likely to wound. Similar advice can be found in Proverbs:

> In the multitude of words there wanteth not sin, but he that refraineth his lips is wise. (Proverbs 10:19)

> A fool's wrath is presently known, but a prudent man covereth shame. (Proverbs 12:16)

> Whoso keepeth his mouth and his tongue keepeth his soul from troubles. (Proverbs 21:23)

The lesson is the same: guard the doors, watch the lips, make discretion an act of will in order to demonstrate (or create) the virtue of prudence, which protects the "soul." Was it necessary to go back to such ancient texts? Universal wisdom, common sense, makes the same recommendation: keep the mouth shut, buttoned up. *Loqui ignorabit, qui tacere nesciet* (Ausonius: He who cannot hold his tongue does not know how to speak). *Qui garde bouche, si garde s'âme. En close bouche n'entre mouche* (He who keeps his mouth shut keeps his soul. A closed mouth collects no flies).

A Mytho-Biological Digression

Biologists have reaffirmed what philosophers were the first to say: an outside begins where the expansion of a structuring force ends. Or, to put it another way: an inside is constituted when a form asserts itself by defining its own boundaries. A living thing cannot exist without defining a line of demarcation (dictated by the species, by the genetic code) whereby, as it individualizes itself, it determines its limits, defines what is self and not-self: boundaries, finitude, individuality, and struggle with the outside are correlative. Hence no inside is conceivable without the complicity of an outside, on which it depends. This complicity is invariably associated with antagonism: a hostile environment forces the membrane to deploy itself in such a way as to contain and protect the constancy of the "internal environment" against the irregularities of the *Umwelt.* No outside is conceivable without an inside that holds it back and resists it, an inside that "reacts."

Between the outside and the inside, the surface of contact—membrane, film, skin, what have you—is a locus of exchange, of adjustment, of sensory signals, as well as of conflict and injury. Reciprocal dependencies are also transitions: my skin already belongs to the outside, but the horizon I take in with my gaze, the space in which I move, are in some sense mine. The outside holds me in its grip, but I take possession of my surroundings. Air and food enter my body, but the body retains what it needs.

In evoking this membrane, this sensitive boundary between outside and inside, I am simply borrowing the biological myth that Freud used in *Beyond the Pleasure Principle.* The *ball* of living protoplasm is an ideal point of departure—how can it fail to beguile? Freud, it seems, wanted to split Bichat's celebrated (and oversimplified) formula, "Life is the collection of functions that resist death," into two parts: "Life is the collection of forces that (1) tend toward the death of the individual and (2) oppose the destruction of the species." But the protoplasmic sphere with its enveloping membrane is a schematic model, useful for expressing a metapsychology in terms of general biology. As Freud knew perfectly well, the multicellular organism undergoing ontogenesis soon ceases to be enveloped in a homogeneous membrane: the morula becomes the gastrula, the sphere hollows out, tubes and orifices form, and so on. Exchanges with the environment cease to be uniform over the entire surface. Specialized organs take responsibility for various types of exchange: absorption, excretion, perception, emission of signals. Another myth, which predates Freud but can be found in his work, is evident here: human development is not simply a matter of increasing differentiation and functional specialization but also involves an increased capacity for regulation, which is accomplished through various inhibitory mechanisms. The control centers that govern this capacity for inhibition determine what can be achieved and not achieved, what can happen and what cannot—yes and no. Only an animal endowed with self-inhibitory powers can create codes and languages and defer natural responses in order to create first tools, then instrumental symbols. Now, the primordial loci of self-inhibition are the orificial organs: "freedom" and "creative power" are learned through modulation of the exchange with the outside world. Freud's attentiveness to the phenomena of orality and sphincter control was one of his strokes of genius. One can extend this to all the activities whereby individuals shape or modify the "physiological" relation between inside and outside: glottal, lingual, and labial articulations associated with the mechanism of inspiration and expiration; alimentary taboos; rituals of purification; the singular use of cosmetics, primarily on the lips and eyelids, that is, on the edges of the movable, governable orifices; body painting and tattoos. All these things define the humanity of man in various ways: the absence of fur, of natural protection, means that of all animals humans have the most tenuous, the most sensitive relation to the outside world and therefore require greater control. The effort of control is directed not only at all that is ingested or eliminated but at parts of the body vulnerable to aggression by external agents, including not only physical agents but also the gaze of the dead and the living. Humans must cover up and protect themselves: paintings, masks, and clothing superimpose an outer surface over the natural surface of the body and strengthen the defense of face and body parts previously in direct contact with the outside world.

Recall one classical definition of man: man (the perfectible animal, the sick animal) is the only natural being that also lives in large part outside the natural order. He is the only natural being that must work in order to survive: he must use his activity, his technology, against the hostility of the outside world. The converse is also true: since man has acquired technology, he can confront the severest of environments, he can inhabit the outside world. Forced to endure *expulsion* from nature, man conquered powers that made him the *invader* par excellence.

The language of myth says all this equally well. The Garden of Eden was the place where the human body and external nature were in spontaneous harmony. Violating the taboo and eating the forbidden fruit made the surface of the body more sensitive ("they knew that they were naked"). From the moment they became aware of the surface of their bodies Adam and Eve were outside the Garden. The guilt attached to the original act of eating spread to all aspects of life. From then on, eating, the enjoyment of food of any kind, became inseparable from punishment ("In the sweat of thy face shalt thou eat bread"). The orifical act of giving birth would also be painful ("in sorrow shalt thou bring forth children"). Man was not only expelled from the Garden; he also learned that his life would unfold *out* of the earth from which his body was taken and *into* which it was destined to return (Genesis 3:19). In other words, the fall was more than just a passage from inside to outside. It marked the point at which human beings were condemned to unremitting, painful, and conscious awareness of the points of contact or transition between the interior of the body and the perilous external world. The (sometimes obsessional) control exerted over these points of transition is the principal palliative that humans have for their condition as expellees. Having been placed outside, they must keep a careful eye on their relations with their new environment, in which they can no longer place their trust. In Judaism, rules regarding what words can be spoken or not spoken, dietary laws, circumcision, rituals of purification, the custom of affixing the text of the Law to the doorpost of dwellings, and the enforced interruption of work (hence of the struggle with the outside world)—all these things reveal the extreme importance attached to controlling what passes from inside to outside and vice versa.

Consider, more generally, the various images of human achievement proposed by different cultures. The heroic ideal invariably includes the virtue of discretion: reasoned words are preferable to violent acts, opportune silence is preferable to imprudent speech, and in some cases cunning deception is preferable to dangerous truth. The hero must know how to speak, hold his tongue, and even make things up. The fully human person is one who knows the proper use of all available resources, who knows how to strike, to speak, to remain silent. Wisdom in each case consists in restraining unreasonable impulses, in not allowing potentially disastrous words or gestures to find a way *out*, thus giving an advantage to the external enemy.[7] Civilization is built on this artifice.

The Proof in the Olive Tree

> *What is given to the interior is also given to the exterior, and vice versa. The phenomenon reveals nothing that is not in the essence, and there is nothing in the essence that is not made manifest.*
>
> Hegel, *Encyclopedia*, Sec. 139.

When Patroclus dies, Achilles can no longer contain himself. He goes out impetuously and falls into a warlike frenzy. He knows (from a prophecy that remains vivid in his memory) that he is condemning himself to death but that his glory will outlive him. His huge investment has no future but its own end: he will never know the happiness of homecoming.

It is Ulysses who is completely in control of himself and able to modulate perfectly his relations with both enemies and friends. Skilled in speech, able in combat, fertile in ruse, he keeps a close eye on the "teeth's barrier" and protects his soul by restraining his words. When necessary he can cunningly disguise his violent intentions. But above all he knows how to repress his anger, to defer the moment of action: πολυμήχανος (which can be translated approximately as "artful, resourceful") is one of his epithets. If, in the tradition of moralizing interpretation, he appears to be the quintessential rational hero, it is because he always knows how to choose, from among the various resources that ensure his mastery of speech, silence, and fabulation, the one appropriate to the circumstance: simulation, dissimulation, frank avowal, supplication. The virtuosity with which he governs his language, sometimes to hide his thought, at other times to contain his passion, qualifies him to confront the worst the outside world has to offer. No matter how many adventures and voyages Homer sends him on, Ulysses' inexhaustible powers are equal to his countless trials. Under close scrutiny it becomes clear that those powers nearly all involve the art of separating what must be kept to oneself (held within, in the breast, in the depths of the heart) from what can advantageously be let out. Should he hide or confess his desire to return to Ithaca? Should he travel under a false identity or use his true name? Should he assume an invented past or tell the true story? Ulysses' mastery is to know, in an almost universally hostile world, how much can be externalized: the danger is everywhere so urgent that it is better to adopt the name Nobody. To test the intentions of others it is better to approach them under a borrowed identity. Athena helps out with this strategy by changing her protégé's appearance, and on at least one occasion she is paid back when Ulysses, failing to recognize her, spins out a tall tale and speaks "the opposite of the truth" (*Odyssey,* XIII, 250–331). Thus it is danger, omnipresent on foreign soil, that gives rise to a voluntary cleavage between *outside* and *inside,* between what *may* be said and what *must* be kept secret. At times prudence counsels not taking in anything that comes from outside: Circe's brews, the Sirens' songs. In the Siren episode, the hero, who takes the greatest risk (only he does not stop his ears with wax), also sees to it that he is most forcefully restrained: he has himself bound to the mast so as not to be seduced by the devouring external world. Ulysses drinks Circe's brew but only after rendering it harmless with the "herb of life." The hero can absorb dangerous substances with less risk than others because he knows the antidotes on his own or because a god has revealed them to him. He is a master at controlling what can cross the "teeth's barrier" or penetrate the ear to enter the inside of his body. Our interest in the hero is heightened when the narrative shows him most completely exposed to the exterior, most *open,* in appearance, to the external danger but also more ingenious and able to respond more quickly than other men.

While visiting Eumaeus, Ulysses speaks the same words as Achilles: "I hate as I hate Hell's own gate that weakness that makes a poor man into a flatterer."[8] His wrath, like Achilles', is directed at men who do not speak the truth. But here the words of outraged righteousness are used by the hero almost parodically as a means of deception. His words are a half-truth, ambiguous at best, because Ulysses, disguised as a beggar clad in skins and rags, is announcing the imminent arrival of one Ulysses. He is lying, and he is also telling the truth. He lies in order to bring the truth hidden in people's hearts out into the open, in order to find out who has remained loyal: an excellent example of what seventeenth-century Italian moralists would call "honest dissimulation." (In the frightful labyrinth of court intrigue, it was best to remain under cover until you could be sure of being served or betrayed; to reveal a secret was to surrender power.)

Nothing is more useful to maintaining a false exterior than to protest hatred of false exteriors. Ulysses, for us, is the prime example of the infinite facility of speech: one can say anything, invent anything, cause anything to be believed. He is allowed to invent as many fictions as he wishes. His invention merely conceals what remains immutable in his heart: the desire to return home, to recover what belongs to him: his house, his wife, his children. The inner constancy, the unyielding intention to regain possession of palace, throne, and bed, excuses all his external inventions. His tall tales are merely ruses to deceive his enemies until the true Ulysses can regain his permanent home. The fictions have free rein while the hero remains discreetly outside, aloof. Ulysses' homecoming signifies the end of his lies and therefore of the narrative that traces his quest to regain his lost possessions.

The man who, to protect his enduring project, resorted to temporary fictions ultimately found himself faced with the difficult task of proving to others what his real name and legitimate rights were. Because he was believed when he lied, because he had convinced people with his disguise, he must provide the most irrefutable of proof to win recognition of the truth. Given Penelope's suspicion ("I armed myself long ago against the frauds of men, impostors who might come," *Odyssey*, XXIII, 215–217),[9] would pure inner conviction, simple subjective certainty of a preserved identity be enough? How should the real Ulysses, whom lies had hidden and protected, reveal himself? Mere words will not suffice. Inner certainty cannot manifest itself directly in the declaration "I am."

The end of *The Odyssey* teaches an important lesson: that the hidden portion of the self, its dissimulated identity, can manifest itself only with help from outside. While visiting Eumaeus, Ulysses, with Athena's assistance, is suddenly transformed from a beggar into something like a god, and to the son who wants to welcome him as a god he says simply: "I am your father" (*Odyssey*, XVI, 188). In the palace, however, certain definitive *signs* are also required. Some of these signs attest to present virtues, such as Ulysses' strength in drawing his bowstring. But this sign is only an indicator of strength: it does not prove that the strength is actually that of Ulysses. It contains no guarantee of *sameness*, no assurance of identity, which is to say, of a link with the past. The old dog Argos's instinctive recognition remains shrouded in the animal's agitation and is immediately obscured by death. The irrefutable proof will be furnished by the durable traces of past acts: traces inscribed in the body and traces imprinted on places and things.

First there is the "great scar." This "sign of truth" (σῆμα ἀριφρ-αδες, *Odyssey*, XXI, 217) is the result of an encounter with animal violence, with the tusks of a boar. Ulysses' identity, which inner conviction alone is insufficient to establish after an absence of twenty years, is validated by an external mark, the vestige of a wound inflicted by a defensive blow that "ripped out flesh above the knee" (*Odyssey*, XIX, 450). (Erich Auerbach studied this episode at length in an admirable chapter of his *Mimesis*.) When Ulysses later attempts to prove who he is to Penelope, he succeeds only when he tells the story of how he built their marriage bed. To test the man she is still unwilling to acknowledge as her husband, Penelope orders that the bed be set up *outside* the bedchamber:

> "Make up his bed for him, Eurykleia.
> Place it outside the bedchamber my lord
> built with his own hands. Pile the big bed
> with fleeces, rugs, and sheets of purest linen."

> With this she tried him to the breaking point,
> and he turned on her in a flash raging:

> "Woman, by heaven you've stung me now!
> Who dared to move my bed?
> No builder had the skill for that—unless
> a god came down to turn the trick. No mortal
> in his best days could budge it with a crowbar.
> There is our pact and pledge, our secret sign,
> built into that bed—my handiwork
> and no one else's!
> An old trunk of olive

grew like a pillar on the building plot,
and I laid out our bedroom round that tree,
lined up the stone walls, built the walls and roof,
gave it a doorway and smooth-fitting doors.
Then I lopped off the silvery leaves and branches,
hewed and shaped that stump from the roots up
into a bedpost, drilled it, let it serve
as model for the rest. I planed them all,
inlaid them all with silver, gold and ivory,
and stretched a bed between—a pliant web
of oxhide thongs dyed crimson.
There's our sign!
I know no more. Could someone else's hand
have sawn that trunk and dragged the frame away?"

Their secret! as she heard it told, her knees
grew tremulous and weak, her heart failed her.

(Odyssey, XXIII, 177–206)

The word σῆμα (sign) occurs four times in this episode (XXIII, 188; 202; 206; 225). Literally translated, lines 188–189 would read: "a great sign is built into (τετύκται) into this elaborate bed (ἐν λέχει ἀσκητῷ) ." Only husband and wife (and faithful chambermaid) understand the symbolic significance of this sign, which involves a private "code" used only by the couple. It is Ulysses' permanent possession of this code that ensures the permanence of his identity. But what is the signifier here? An object built by Ulysses himself, with his own hands. His description of the construction of a room and a piece of furniture is validated by a durable object, the bed, of which the poet makes an immutable "referent" possessing the evidence that inner conviction cannot achieve. The "I made" and the object resulting from that act are more convincing than "I am" could have been. Thus the proof of Ulysses' personal identity lies outside himself, in the bed and bedchamber he built with his own hands—the confirmation of his true essence.

In writing of Homer's epic Erich Auerbach emphasized the beautiful and smooth externality of the narrative: "The basic impulse of the Homeric style [is] to represent phenomena in a fully externalized form, visible and palpable in all their parts, and completely fixed in their spatial and temporal relations."[10] Concerning the passage we are reading, only one thing needs to be added: the narration of external activity *takes the place* of expression of personal identity (and in the full sense of the term: it develops in space, it is situated in space). That narration offers an adequate equivalent of personal identity—adequate in the sense that it is enough to overcome Penelope's last remaining doubts. When an individual is capable of producing such powerful signs outside himself, his *being* is effectively realized externally and need not be sought anywhere else.

There is no need to allegorize; it is enough to read, attaching full value to each term. Here interpretation is not out to uncover something that is hidden. What it confronts is an *open* narrative in which the final shadow of doubt is overcome in Penelope. For the person listening to the poem, who was never in doubt about the hero's identity, this story, like that of the wound and the scar, is simply an unknown piece of the past that is brought back into the foreground: everything is fully illuminated. What Ulysses must do (it is his final ordeal) is to describe the unusual way in which he built the marriage chamber. The Return is then complete; the end recovers the beginning, or, more precisely, the end—the repossession of wife and marriage bed—is achieved by means of narrative repetition of the act that created the nuptial chamber. The deed of ownership, in the absence of written documents (unknown to Homer), lies in the shared secret of the labor that brought the marriage bed into being. Thus "inner" identity is revealed by that quintessential act of externalization, labor. The story of the making of the bed dispels any suspicion of *fiction* and ensures that the hero will fully regain rights that he never relinquished. It is not Hegel who tells us this: it is the succession of crystal-clear words and images in the Homeric epic.

If the proof of identity enters the narrative by way of an external act, note that the purpose of that act is to construct a physical *interior*: well-fitted doors and roof and carefully hewn stones ensure that the nuptial chamber will be well sealed. Ulysses is building an enclosure within an enclosure: the image he draws is that of a concentric structure, an enclosed space, a protected *inside*. Here, to use a word analyzed at the beginning of this book, we should recognize one of the founding acts of *civilization*.

The center of this space is marked by the olive tree—at first straight and alive, then shaped by human hands. It had sprung up (ἔφυ) majestically long before the chamber was built. Its presence spurred

Ulysses to begin construction. The tree dominated the space that labor organized around it. It was a natural presence, suffused with the force that gave it its abundant foliage and its voluminous and powerful trunk. Even after being cut and hewn, it still struck roots deep into the earth. Through a community of substance its vital energy was conveyed to the bed supported by its wood. The "cultural" labor of decoration and luxury was implanted, or mortised, into the massive natural presence. This sumptuously finished piece of furniture was built to be immovable.

The tree in the wedding chamber, rooted in the earth, is presumably a symbol of "external" nature. We see it as the pure *outside*, which the "cultural" act of building captures and places at the center of its artifice. But one might turn this around and say that the earth in which the tree's roots grow is a living *inside*, which nourishes and sustains the tree's growth. The unbreakable bond with the soil establishes a continuity that allows the primitive vegetal power, the *physis*, to subsist in the work of culture. By not ordering the olive trunk to be cut down, the faithful wife has preserved the natural sign of the center, the powerful, hewn trunk that, by remaining the same, makes possible the husband's homecoming and the repetition of the happy past.

In this reading the relative position of inside and outside may therefore change at any moment. When Ulysses prunes, squares, and drills the olive tree, it is surely in the outside world that his labor does violence to the beautiful natural presence of the tree. But this violence is the application of knowledge (Ulysses works "well and with know-how") in which man's inner aptitude is developed through the exercise of mastery over an object—on external material. And this labor, recounted in the past, evoked as a remote externality, becomes the very heart of the present in the scene of recognition. As a kind of vertigo effaces the distinction between outside and inside, the moment is ripe for an embrace: Penelope throws her arms around Ulysses' neck.

NOTES

INDEX

NOTES

1. The Word *Civilization*

1. The essential works on this subject are Lucien Febvre et al., *Civilisation. Le mot et l'idée* (Paris: Centre International de Synthèse, 1930); Joachim Moras, *Ursprung und Entwicklung des Begriffs der Zivilisation in Frankreich (1756–1830)* (Hamburg, 1930); R. A. Lochore, *History of the Idea of Civilization in France (1830–1870)* (Bonn, 1935); Emile Benveniste, "Civilisation—Contribution à l'histoire du mot," in *Hommage à Lucien Febvre* (Paris, 1954), rpt. in *Problèmes de linguistique générale* (Paris, 1966) [in English: *Problems in General Linguistics*, trans. Mary Elizabeth Meek (Coral Gables: University of Florida Press, 1971]; E. de Dampierre, "Note sur 'culture' et 'civilisation,'" *Comparative Studies in Society and History* 3 (1961):328–340. The third volume of *Europäische Schlüsselwörter*, published in Munich in 1967, is devoted to *Kultur und Zivilisation;* this collaborative work provides abundant linguistic information based on French, German, English, and Italian examples. I am greatly indebted to it. See also André Banuls, "Les mots *culture* et *civilisation* en français et en allemand," *Etudes germaniques* (April-June 1969):171–180; Georges Gusdorf, *Les Principes de la pensée au siècle des Lumières* (Paris, 1971), pp. 310–348; Philippe Béneton, *Histoire de mots: culture et civilisation* (Paris: Presses de la Fondation Nationale des Sciences Politiques, 1975).

2. Based on E. Huguet, *Dictionnaire de la langue française du XVIe siècle* (Paris, 1925).

3. One wonders if the juridical definition of *civilisation* did not delay acceptance of the second, more modern definition. It is difficult to say for certain, but earlier definitions, particularly when they have a precise technical meaning, generally tend to fend off challengers.

4. The Mirabeau in question is Victor de Riquetti, marquis de Mirabeau (1715–1789), author of *L'Ami des hommes ou Traité de la population* (1756) and the father of the revolutionary orator (Honoré-Gabriel de Riquetti).

5. Moras, *Ursprung,* pp. 8–9; compare Febvre, *Civilisation,* p. 47, n. 17.

6. M. Frey, *Les Transformations du vocabulaire français à l'époque de la Révolution* (Paris, 1925).

7. Louis Sébastien Mercier, *Néologie* (Paris, 1801), 2 vols. The word *civilisation* is not included.

8. Emile Benveniste speculates that the word was used earlier in English by Adam Ferguson somewhere in his lectures or private manuscripts, but this has yet to be proven. Moras did not find the word *civilization* in the work of the econo-

mists Melon and Cantillon or in the writings of Mandeville and Montesquieu, which Mirabeau knew well.

9. Turgot's manuscripts, published (1913–1923) by G. Schelle, do not contain the word *civilization*, which was probably added by Dupont de Nemours to his edition of Turgot's works. See Febvre, *Civilisation*, pp. 4–5. Catherine Larrère tells me that the word does appear in d'Argenson, *Considérations sur le gouvernement ancien et moderne de la France* (1765, rpt. 1784), which was written sometime between 1740 and 1750. The manuscript was widely read. D'Argenson saw a great deal of and admired the abbé de Saint-Pierre.

10. "Sur la civilisation de Russie," in Denis Diderot, *Mélanges et morceaux divers. Contributions à l'Histoire des deux Indes*, ed. Gianluigi Goggi, 2 vols. (Siena, 1977), vol. 2, pp. 375–389. In the 1781 edition of Raynal's work, Diderot's contribution appears in vol. 10, book 19, p. 27.

11. François Guizot, *Histoire de la civilisation en Europe* (Paris, 1828), 1846 ed., p. 16.

12. Benveniste, "Civilisation," p. 340.

13. See Ronald L. Meek, *Social Science and the Ignoble Savage* (Cambridge: Cambridge University Press, 1976); Pasquale Salvucci, *Adam Ferguson: Sociologia e folosofia politica* (Urbino: Argalia, 1972).

14. On Rousseau and Comte, see the article by Henri Gouhier in *Le Temps de la réflexion IV* (Paris: Gallimard, 1983), p. 127.

15. Adam Ferguson, *An Essay on the History of Civil Society*, 3rd ed. (London, 1768), p. 203. English writers refer to this as the "law of unintended consequences." I have used the term *conséquence non maîtrisée* to describe a narrative and explanatory pattern that Rousseau applies both to his own life and to history. See my "Le dîner de Turin," *La Relation critique* (Paris: Gallimard, 1970), p. 144. Although the word *civilisation* was widely used in France, the English preferred the term *refinement*. In 1797 Pierre Prevost translated Ferguson's "On Refinement" under the title "Traité de la civilisation."

16. Quoted in Moras, *Ursprung*, p. 38.

17. Ibid., p. 43.

18. Ibid., p. 41. Compare Chateaubriand, *Mémoires d'outre-tombe* (Paris: Flammarion, 1948), vol. 1, p. 226: "Cynicism in human relations, by annihilating moral sense, brings a kind of barbarism back into society. The barbarians of civilization possess the Goths' powers of destruction but not their powers of creation."

19. François Hartog, *Le Miroir d'Hérodote* (Paris, 1980), p. 329. See Emile Benveniste, *Vocabulaire des institutions indo-européennes* (Paris, 1969), vol. 1, pp. 363–367.

20. Fontenelle, "Discours sur la nature de l'églogue," *Oeuvres* (1742), vol. 4, pp. 135–136, 140. On polite conversation and the rules that governed it, see Carlo Ossola, "L'homme accompli. La civilisation des cours et l'art de la conversation," in *Le Temps de la réflexion* (Paris: Gallimard, 1983).

21. Ibid., p. 128.

22. *De la poésie dramatique*, chap. 18, in Diderot, *Oeuvres esthétiques*, ed. P. Vernière (Paris: Garnier, 1959), p. 261.

23. Quoted in [Guizot], *Dictionnaire universel des synonymes de la langue française* (Paris, n.d.), p. 166.

24. Ibid., p. 166.

25. Ibid., pp. 166–167.

26. Ibid., p. 167.

27. Ibid., p. 191.

28. Charles P. Duclos, *Considérations sur les moeurs de ce siècle* (1750), in *Oeuvres complètes* (1820), vol. 1, p. 12.

29. Ibid., pp. 35–36.

30. Condorcet, *Esquisse d'un tableau historique des progrès de l'esprit humain* (Paris, 1794), pp. 334–338. In the *Dictionnaire de la conversation*, 2nd ed. (Paris, 1870), the physician and writer J.-J. Virey held that civilization is incompatible with tyranny and asserted that "no true civilization is possible without some degree of freedom for both thought and action." But he was convinced that different races had different aptitudes: "Without pretending to disinherit any human race from its rights to any sort of development it is capable of attaining, one is nevertheless obliged to point out, in light of the facts of history and physiological constitution, that some are more inclined than others to the exercise of intellectual faculties and civilization . . . The most ardent defenders of freedom for the Negroes (of whom we, like all friends of humanity, are of course supporters) cannot explain the eternal inferiority, the constant barbarity, that afflict obscure tribes throughout Africa." A half a century later Jules Ferry would speak of the "educational and civilizing mission of the superior race," while deploring that awareness of that mission was not sufficiently widespread among the colonists (quoted by H. Schilgers-Scheele and Putt in *Kultur und Zivilisation*, p. 35).

31. Edward Gibbon, *The History of the Decline and Fall of the Roman Empire*, chap. 38.

32. Proclamation to troops embarking for Egypt. After his fall Napoleon said: "England and France held in their hands the fate of the earth, and above all that of European civilization. What harm we have done ourselves!" Quoted by Moras, *Ursprung*, p. 61.

33. *Kultur und Zivilisation*, p. 24.

34. Ibid.

35. Ibid.

36. Ibid.

37. Victor Hugo, *Oeuvres politiques complètes*, ed. Francis Bouvet (Paris: Pauvert, 1964), pp. 694–695.

38. Especially during World War I, when the French contrasted the idea of civilization with the German idea of *Kultur*. See E. R. Curtius, *L'Idée de civilisation dans la conscience française*, trans. H. Jourdan (Paris, 1929).

39. Edmund Burke, *Reflections on the Revolution in France* (London: J. Dodsley, 1790), p. 117.

40. Ibid., p. 118.

41. Mallet du Pan, *Considérations sur la nature de la révolution de France* (London: Brussels, 1793), p. 27. Mallet du Pan is here quoting from a text he wrote in 1791. See Bronislaw Baczko, "Le complot vandale," in *Le Temps de la réflexion* (Paris: Gallimard, 1983), p. 195, from which I take this citation.

42. As an example, consider these words of Vautrin to Rastignac in *Le Père Goriot*: "Paris, you see, is like a forest of the New World, home to twenty savage tribes, to Illinois and Hurons, that live on what the various social classes produce." The *arriviste* dandy and the common murderer differ, Vautrin says, only in their

choice of means. Sade expresses the same idea of a savagery preserved beneath a facade of civilization. In *Aline et Valcour* Zamé, lawgiver of the utopian city Tamoé, reproaches the Frenchman Sainville for having preserved the barbarian practice of human sacrifice. The only difference is in the choice of victim: the modern Celts immolate criminals rather than prisoners of war. "In completing your civilization, the motive changed, but you preserved the habit. You continue to sacrifice victims not to gods thirsty for human blood but to laws that you characterize as wise because you find in them a specious reason for indulging in your old customs, and the appearance of a justice that was fundamentally nothing other than a desire to preserve horrible customs you could not forswear." See *Oeuvres complètes* (Paris, 1976), vol. 4, pp. 307–308.

43. In Cesare Lombroso, *L'Homme criminel* (translated 1876) and Emile Zola, *La Bête humaine,* criminal tendencies are an archaic element that persist by atavism. See Jean-Michel Labadie, "Le corps criminel: un aujourd'hui dépassé," in *Nouvelle Revue de Psychanalyse* 26 (Autumn 1982):121–134.

44. Moras, *Ursprung,* gives a good sense of the ideas of Joseph de Maistre, Louis de Bonald, and Ballanche concerning "Christian civilization."

45. This was Mme de Staël's conviction in 1800. For her, as Moras points out, civilization was the meaning of history: "One of the principal final causes of the great events we have been through is the civilization of the world" *(De la littérature).*

46. Benjamin Constant, *De la religion,* 5 vols. (Paris, 1824–1831), vol. 1, pp. xxxviii–XL.

47. Ibid., pp. xliii–XLIV.

48. Ibid., pp. xli–XLII.

49. Enthusiasm, a word that has today lost its power to mobilize, was the rallying cry of Mme de Staël and the "Coppet group." It made possible a synthesis of classical remembrances with the idea of a new literature of Christian and Nordic inspiration.

50. J. H. Jacobi, *Woldemar* (1779), trans. Vandelbourg, 2 vols. (Paris, 1796), vol. 1, pp. 154–155.

51. Claude Lefort, *L'Invention démocratique* (Paris, 1981), p. 173.

52. Charles Baudelaire, "Edgar Poe, sa vie et ses oeuvres," in *Oeuvres complètes,* ed. C. Pichois, 2 vols. (Paris: Pléiade, 1975–1976), vol. 2, p. 297.

53. Charles Baudelaire, "Notes nouvelles sur Edgar Poe," in *Oeuvres complètes,* vol. 2, pp. 325–326.

54. Charles Baudelaire, "Pauvre Belgique," in *Oeuvres complètes,* vol. 2, p. 820.

55. Friedrich Engels, *Der Ursprung der Familie, des Privateigentums und des Staats* (1884); in English: *The Origin of Family, Private Property, and the State.*

56. In Italian the opposition is based on the contrast between the old word *civiltà* and *civilizzazione,* whose more recent formation and French origins made its use distinctive, as in Leopardi's notes to *Zibaldone.* The word *cultura,* like *culture* in French, introduced a third resource, in which the influence of the German concepts *Kultur* and *Bildung* was often discernible. On the history of the debate in Germany, see texts and bibliography in *Kultur und Zivilisation.* See also note 1 above. John Stuart Mill and Matthew Arnold are valuable informants about the English scene. See also Fernand Braudel, *Ecrits sur l'histoire* (Paris: Gallimard, 1969), pp. 255–314.

57. Friedrich Nietzsche, "Aus dem Nachlass der Acthzigerjahre," in *Werke*, ed. Schlechta, 4 vols. (Munich, 1956), vol. 3, p. 837. In 1914 Thomas Mann wrote: "The German soul is too deep for *civilization* to be for it a superior, or perhaps even the highest, notion. It is horrified at the spectacle of corruption and disorder and *embourgeoisement*." And this: "Politics is a thing of reason, democracy, and civilization; morality, on the other hand, is a thing of culture and soul." See "Gedanken im Kriege," in *Die neue Rundschau* 25 (1914), fasc. 2, pp. 1478, 1474. In 1929 Curtius (see note 38) would try to bury this dispute, while Heidegger of course would revive it after his own fashion. The culture-civilization antithesis plays a cucial role in Oswald Spengler's *Decline of the West*. See Jacques Bouveresse's article in *Le Temps de la réflexion IV*, p. 369.

58. See esp. *The Future of an Illusion* (1927), chap. 1, and *Civilization and Its Discontents* (whose German title is *Das Unbehagen in der Kultur;* 1930). Freud's views on the instinctual sacrifices required by civilization have been widely commented on. See especially Eugène Enriquez, *De la horde à l'Etat: essai de psychanalyse du lien social* (Paris: Gallimard, 1983).

59. See Jean Molino, "Combien de cultures?" in *Les Intermédiaires culturels,* proceedings of a colloquium of the Centre Méditerranéen d'Histoire Sociale, des Mentalités et des Cultures (Université de Provence and Henri Champion, 1978), pp. 631–640.

60. See, in Marcel Mauss, *Oeuvres* (Paris: Editions de Minuit, 1969), vol. 2, pp. 451–487, a 1913 paper written in collaboration with Emile Durkheim, as well as Mauss's paper "Les civilisations," in Febvre, *Civilisations*. Relativism and historicism, the consequences of this approach, form the basis for the rejection of ethnocentrism. But the rejection of ethnocentrism presupposes a value judgment and therefore a refusal of total relativism.

61. "Ruins and Poetry," *New York Review of Books* 30, no. 4 (17 March 1983):20.

62. G. W. F. Hegel, *Phänomenologie des Geistes,* VI, B (Der sich entfremdete Geist, die Bildung), I and II. On the notion of *Bildung* and *Bildungsroman,* see Antoine Berman's article in *Le Temps de la réflexion IV* (Paris: Gallimard, 1983), p. 141.

63. Eric Weil, *Essais et conférences,* 2 vols. (Paris, 1970), esp. vol. 1, chap. 12: "La science et la civilisation moderne, ou le sens de l'insensé," pp. 268–296.

64. Among various recent theories, some have stirred controversy owing to their systematic nature. The best known are Arnold Toynbee, *Civilization on Trial* (Oxford, 1948); Norbert Elias, *Uber den Prozess der Zivilisation,* 1936, 2nd ed. (Bern-Munich: Francke, 1969). Among discussions of the subject after 1945, see "Civilisation," a special issue of *Chemins du Monde* (Paris, [1947]); *La culture est-elle en péril?* Rencontres internationales de Genève (Neuchâtel: Editions La Baconnière, 1955); *Où va la civilisation?* Rencontres internationales de Genève (Neuchâtel: Editions La Baconnière, 1971); "Malaise dans la civilisation?" *Le Débat* 23 (January 1983) and 24 (March 1983).

65. Jorge Luis Borges, *Labyrinths,* ed. Donald A. Yates and James E. Irby (New York: New Directions, 1962), pp. 127–131.

2. On Flattery

1. Chevalier de Méré, "De la vraie honnêteté," *Oeuvres complètes* (Paris, 1930), vol. 3, p. 72.

2. La Bruyère, *Les Caractères:* "Des jugements," 42.

3. Méré, "De la vraie honnêteté," p. 73.

4. From the standpoint of linguistic analysis, this selection criterion is analogous to the one that defines "special languages." This selection at the verbal level corresponds closely to another at the moral level which authorizes "legitimate" passions and represses "shameful" ones. For individuals, respect for the verbal code and its aesthetic rules is a guarantee of membership in an elite. But it is a fragile guarantee, open to suspicion and always in need of confirmation.

5. Méré, *Oeuvres complètes,* vol. 3 (Paris, 1930), pp. 157–158. Méré's thought has often been compared with that of Baltasar Gracian (1601–1658). The same spirit can be found in the work of Torquato Accetto, the theorist of "honest dissimulation." See his *Della dissimulazione onesta,* ed. Salvatore S. Nigro (Genoa: Costa e Nolan, 1983).

6. An equilibrium is thus established through adoption of a common metaphorical code and effort to achieve a similar degree of variation from literality.

7. This theme would be taken up by various preachers. Bossuet, for example, had this to say in *Sur la charité fraternelle:* "Enough about the flatterers who surround us on all sides. Let us speak about a flatterer that is inside, that lends authority to all the others. All our passions are flattering; our pleasures are flatterers. Our amour-propre above all is a great flatterer, which constantly applauds us within. And so long as we listen to that flatterer, we will not fail to heed the others. For the flatterers on the outside, venal and prostituted souls, are well aware of the strength of this internal flattery. That is why they work with it and act jointly, in concert. They insinuate themselves so adroitly into the commerce of our passions, into the secret intrigue of our heart, into the complacency of our amour-propre, that they force us to agree with whatever they say."

8. The double meaning of the verb *courtiser* (to court, to ingratiate oneself with) confirms the operation of flattery in the political as well as the erotic sphere. There is no shortage of textual evidence. Consider this passage from Pierre Charron, *De la sagesse,* book 3, chap. 10: "Two sorts of people are subject to flattery, who never lack for people ready to furnish them this kind of merchandise and who are always ready to accept it: Princes, with whom ill-intentioned people seek to gain credit in this way, and women, for nothing is so apt or frequent to corrupt the chastity of women as to puff them up by feeding them with praise." The word "merchandise" makes clear that this is a transaction.

9. Aristotle, *Nicomachean Ethics,* II, VII, 13 (1108a25), in Richard McKeon, ed., *The Basic Works of Aristotle* (New York: Random House, 1941), p. 961.

10. The perfect example of this relationship can be found in Tacitus. See A. de la Houssaye, *La Morale de Tacite: de la flatterie* (Paris, 1686). The Greek tradition is no less important. Plato's *Gorgias,* for example, compares the rhetorical art of the sophists with flattery and the culinary arts.

11. *Britannicus,* act 4, scene 4. Compare La Bruyère, *Caractères,* Du souverain, 28. The same maxims are attributed to Mathan in *Athalie,* act 3, scene 3.

12. *Fables,* 8, 14.

13. A. Ernout and A. Meillet, *Dictionnaire étymologique de la langue latine* (Paris, 1939), p. 15.

14. [Guizot], *Dictionnaire universel des synonymes* (Paris: Penard, n.d.), p. 138.

15. O. Bloch and W. von Wartburg, *Dictionnaire étymologique de la langue française* (Paris, 1968), p. 265. See also W. von Wartburg, *Französiches Etymologisches Wörterbuch*, XV, 2, pp. 139–141.

16. Note how Corneille *disciplined* his language: in correcting the line, "Nous aurons tout loisir de *baiser* nos maîtresses" (We will have all the time in the world to *kiss* our mistresses, *L'Illusion comique*, IV, 9), sometime after 1660 he replaced *baiser* with *flatter* in order to tone down what might seem "base" in the notion of physical contact. *Flatter* indicates the least possible contact or perhaps even the absence of contact altogether, the verbal sublimation of the caress.

17. Theophrastus's schematic portrait omits neither the caress nor the portrait. La Bruyère's translation, which develops the implicit values, might serve as evidence for the prosecution: "If by chance the wind blows bits of straw into your beard or hair, he is careful to remove them . . . He buys fruits . . . he gives them to the children [of the citizen]; he kisses them, he caresses them . . . and if he sees a flattering portrait of the master somewhere, he is touched by the resemblance and admires it as a masterpiece." More recently, Paul Valéry astutely sums up an age-old lesson in *Rhumbs*: "The human plant seems to flourish with praise. As you watch, the obscene flower opens up and the leaves quiver. It is a deep tickle, which some people practice lightly . . . The experienced man rebels against being manipulated and refuses to obey this pleasure as the body does under the slow strokes of a knowing courtesan. But that revolt itself is a mild protest of pride that arises from the feeling of always deserving more praise than is given. In such a gesture self-love attains its supreme degree." Valéry, *Oeuvres*, vol. 2 (Paris: Pléiade, 1960), p. 648.

18. Boileau, *Satires*, VIII.

19. Here is the full text:

> Maître corbeau, sur un arbre perché
> Tenait en son bec un fromage.
> Maître renard, par l'odeur alléché
> Lui tint à peu près ce langage:
> "Et bonjour, Monsieur du Corbeau.
> Que vous êtes joli! que vous me semblez beau!
> Sans mentir, si votre ramage
> Se rapporte à votre plumage,
> Vous êtes le phénix des hôtes de ces bois."
> A ces mots, le corbeau ne se sent pas de joie;
> Et pour montrer sa belle voix,
> Il ouvre un large bec, laisse tomber sa proie.
> Le renard s'en saisit, et dit: "Mon bon monsieur,
> Apprenez que tout flatteur
> Vit aux dépens de celui qui l'écoute.
> Cette leçon vaut bien un fromage sans doute."
> Le corbeau honteux et confus,
> Jura, mais un peu tard, qu'on ne l'y prendrait plus.

And here is Norman Spector's translation, from *The Complete Fables of Jean de la Fontaine*, ed. and trans. Norman Spector (Evanston: Northwestern University Press, 1988), pp. 5–7:

> At the top of a tree perched Master Crow;
> In his beak he was holding a cheese.
> Drawn by the smell, Master Fox spoke, below.
> The words, more or less, were these:
> "Hey, now, Sir Crow! Good day, good day!
> How very handsome you do look, how grandly *distingué!*
> No lie, if these songs you sing
> Match the plumage of your wing,
> You're the phoenix of these woods, our choice."
> Hearing this, the crow was all rapture and wonder.
> To show off his handsome voice,
> He opened beak wide and let go of his plunder.
> The Fox snapped it up and then said, "My Good Sir,
> Learn that each flatterer
> Lives at the cost of those who heed.
> This lesson is well worth a cheese, indeed."
> The Crow, ashamed and sick,
> Swore, a bit late, not to fall again for that trick.

20. La Fontaine denounces both the dangerous pretension of one who wishes to be what he is not ("the frog who wants to be as big an ox") and everyone's overestimation of his own beauty: "My portrait has thus far had nothing to say against me" (*Fables*, I, 7: "La besace"). Ostentation remains the common denominator.

21. La Bruyère, *Les Caractères*, "Des grands," 49.

22. Ibid., "Des jugements," 90.

23. This fable can be taken as an ironic commentary on chap. 23 of Machiavelli's *Prince*.

24. La Bruyère, *Les Caractères*, "De l'homme," 78.

25. Ibid., "Du souverain," 20.

26. "Nothing is beautiful but the truth; only the truth is likeable" (*Epitres*, IX).

27. Boileau, *Discours au roi*.

28. "My thought is available and open to the light of day everywhere" (*Epitres*, IX).

29. *Epitres*, IX.

30. Ibid.

31. Ibid.

32. Ibid. See, in *Aesthetics*, the remarkable passage in which Hegel defines satire as a transitional form between classical art and romantic art characterized by infinite subjectivity.

33. *Epitres*, VIII.

34. *Satires*, XI.

35. This point is made by Jacques Guicharnaud, *Molière* (Paris: Gallimard, 1963), pp. 510–517, and Jacques Lacan, *Ecrits* (Paris: Gallimard, 1966), pp. 173–175.

36. *Le Misanthrope*, I, 1.

37. Boileau, *Epitres*, VIII. Horace, Juvenal, Boileau, and Alceste share the same regrets for a virtuous age in the remote past.

38. *Satires*, II to Molière.

39. It should come as no surprise that during the Revolution Fabre d'Eglantine blackened the character of Philinte. This essay is limited to a survey of seventeenth-century French "classics." It could be extended to include other periods and literatures. I shall merely mention Diderot's *Neveu de Rameau* and Hegel's remarkable commentary in the *Phenomenology of Spirit*. After *Le Neveu de Rameau* I see no major text on flattery even though rich men and poor men, powerful men and ambitious men still exist in all societies. What has changed is surely the conditions of exchange, the rules of the transaction. The flatterer at court could expect generosity or employment in return for the "narcissistic gratification" he provided. The modern world calculates differently and attaches a different exchange value to money and the perquisites of power. Note, however, that during the French Revolution critics attacked demagogues as "flatterers of the people." Since the people had taken the place of the sovereign, it was taken for granted that they were similarly vulnerable to verbal deception. Since then flattery has come to seem somewhat old-fashioned. The flatterer, as one who apparently belongs to an outmoded way of life, has ceded his place to a very active successor: the seducer.

3. EXILE, SATIRE, TYRANNY: MONTESQUIEU'S *PERSIAN LETTERS*

1. Aram Vartanian, "Eroticism and Politics in the Lettres Persanes," *Romantic Review* 50, no. 1 (1969):23–33.

4. VOLTAIRE'S DOUBLE-BARRELED MUSKET

1. *Candide ou l'Optimisme*, critical ed. by André Morize (Paris, 1913), p. 79. For an English translation, see Donald Frame, trans., *Candide, Zadig and Selected Stories* (New York: New American Library, 1961).

2. On passivity, see Christopher Thacker's remarks in the introduction of his critical edition of *Candide* (Geneva, 1968), pp. 10ff.

3. I have dealt with some literary and artistic aspects of this theme in *Portrait de l'artiste en saltimbanque* (Geneva, 1970; rpt. Paris: Flammarion, 1983).

4. On fabulation see Geoffrey Murray, *Voltaire's Candide: The Protean Gardener, 1755–1762*, Studies on Voltaire and the Eighteenth Century, vol. 59 (Geneva, 1970).

5. THE ANTIDOTE IN THE POISON: THE THOUGHT OF JEAN-JACQUES ROUSSEAU

1. Jean-Jacques Rousseau, *Oeuvres complètes* (Paris: Pléiade, 1959–1969), vol. I, p. 7. Hereafter referred to as *O.C.*

2. *O.C.*, I, pp. 7–8.

3. *O.C.*, III, p. 26.

4. Ibid.

5. See F. Baker, "Remarques sur la notion de dépôt," *Annales Jean-Jacques Rousseau* 37 (1966–1968):57–93.

6. *O.C.*, III, p. 27.

7. *O.C.*, III, p. 76.

8. *O.C.*, III, p. 95.

9. *O.C.*, III, p. 56.

10. *O.C.*, II, p. 972.

11. *O.C.*, III, p. 56.

12. *O.C.*, III, p. 39.

13. *O.C.*, II, p. 972.

14. *O.C.*, II, p. 974; compare Pliny the Elder, *Naturalis Historia* XXIX, 32. Homeopathic remedies were employed in medicine throughout the centuries. Montaigne disapproved: "I do not like to cure the disease by the disease" (*Essais*, III, 13). Hahnemann, the theorist of homeopathic medicine, developed the ancient principle. In paragraph 132 of his *Organon* (1810) we read that the first ingestion of homeopathic medicine is followed by "a homeopathic aggravation of the disease," because "the disease caused by the medication must of course be, to some degree, stronger than the disease one wants to cure in order to overcome (*überstimmen*) and extinguish it."

15. *O.C.*, III, p. 227.

16. *O.C.*, II, p. 25. Rousseau hoped to succeed where he believed Richardson had failed. In a letter to Duclos dated 19 September 1760 he wrote: "I still think that such reading is dangerous for girls. I even think that Richardson was sadly mistaken in wishing to instruct them through novels. That is like setting fire to the house in order to set the pumps to working."

17. *O.C.*, II, p. 6.

18. *O.C.*, II, p. 227.

19. *Lettre à d'Alembert* (Paris, 1967), p. 130.

20. Ibid., p. 155.

21. Ibid.

22. Ibid., p. 131.

23. Ibid., p. 139.

24. Ibid., p. 140.

25. Ibid., p. 223.

26. Ibid., p. 225.

27. Ibid., p. 227. On the history of relations between Rousseau and Voltaire, see Henri Gouhier, *Rousseau et Voltaire. Portraits dans deux miroirs* (Paris: Vrin, 1983); Jean Starobinski, "Rousseau et Voltaire," *Critique* 449 (October 1984).

28. Ibid., p. 234.

29. *O.C.*, III, pp. 288, 479.

30. *O.C.*, IV, p. 640.

31. *O.C.*, IV, p. 654. Mme de Staël in 1798 proved herself to be a good student of Rousseau: "The same creature, the same tree, that contains the poison often contains the remedy as well, and in correcting a man's character one finds in the passion that leads him astray the resources necessary to guide him. Moralists and legislators will always go wrong if they seek remedies in contraries rather than in the very principle that has been denatured by circumstance." Germaine de Staël, *Des circonstances . . .* (Geneva: Droz, 1979), p. 273.

32. *Emile*, book 4, *O.C.*, IV, p. 493.

33. Ibid., p. 523.

34. Ibid., p. 535.

35. Ibid., p. 547.

36. *Emile*, book 3, *O.C.*, IV, p. 187. The notion of *crisis* can of course be traced back to Hippocrates.

37. *Social Contract*, II, 8, *O.C.*, III, p. 385.

38. *O.C.*, III, p. 638.

39. *O.C.*, III, p. 891.

40. *O.C.*, III, p. 895.

41. *O.C.*, III, p. 998.

42. *O.C.*, III, p. 843.

43. *O.C.*, III, p. 828.

44. *O.C.*, II, p. 980.

45. *O.C.*, II, p. 1018.

46. *O.C.*, II, p. 1181.

47. *O.C.*, IV, p. 664.

48. *O.C.*, II, p. 508 (letter 14 of part 4). Etienne Gilson has commented on this letter in a detailed study, "La méthode de M. de Wolmar," in *Les idées et les lettres* (Paris, 1955), pp. 275–298.

49. "The deeper the solitude in which I live, the more I need some object to fill the void, and those that my imagination refuses to give me or that my memory rejects are provided by the spontaneous productions that the earth, unforced by men, presents to me wherever my eyes turn" (VII, *Rêverie*, *O.C.*, I, p. 1070).

50. Rousseau likes to describe incomplete cures. He was never able to "cure himself fully" from the temptation to commit petty thefts (*O.C.*, I, p. 32) or masturbation (*O.C.*, I, pp. 594–595, and variant, p. 1569). The virtuous Savoyard vicar was "not especially well disciplined" with respect to the temptations of the flesh (*O.C.*, IV, p. 563).

51. *O.C.*, II, p. 740.

52. *O.C.*, II, p. 743.

53. I touch on this subject in "Rousseau en 1764" in *Ecriture 13* (Vevey, 1977), pp. 123–131, rpt. in *Questions sur l'autorité* (Lausanne: L'Age d'Homme, 1989).

54. Letter no. 3192 in R. A. Leigh, ed., *Correspondance complète de Rousseau* (Geneva and Oxford, 1965–1989), vol. 19.

55. These are the terms Rousseau uses in his response dated 7 May 1764. See ibid., vol. 20, pp. 18–24. The editor, R. A. Leigh, points out the affinities between this letter and the argument of *The Discourse on Inequality*.

56. Ovid, *Remedia amoris*, lines 43–48; *Amores*, IX. Other Latin examples include Horace, *Epodes*, 17, 8; Propertius, II, 1, 63–64. The hero was known from tragedies of Aeschylus, Euripides, Ennius, and others, now lost. In the Renaissance the legend was part of common knowledge. The formula remained proverbial until the middle of the nineteenth century. To cite several examples at random: "The great remedy for the license of the press lies in the freedom of the press; it is Achilles' spear, which heals the wounds it has made" (Camille Desmoulins, *Le Vieux Cordelier*, no. 7, text edited and introduced by Pierre Pachet [Paris: Belin, 1987], p. 13). Did Balzac have Desmoulins's text in mind in *Les Illusions perdues* when he had Lucien de Rubempré say, "The newspaper is most definitely like Achilles' spear, which healed the wounds it made" (Balzac, *La Comédie humaine*, ed. P.-G. Castex [Paris: Gallimard-Pléiade, 1977], vol. 5, p. 462). In an 1815 article Benjamin Constant

wrote: "Violence is not like Achilles' spear; it does not heal the wounds it causes" (Benjamin Constant, *Recueil d'articles, 1795–1817,* ed. E. Harpaz [Geneva: Droz, 1978]).

57. *Metamorphoses,* XII, 112.

58. *Tristia,* V, 2, 15.

59. From Makedonios, *Greek Anthology,* V, 225. The English translation here is based on the French translation by P. Waltz ("Les Belles-Lettres").

60. From Paul the Silentiary, *Greek Anthology,* V, 291.

61. Plutarch, *How One Must Listen,* 16.

62. Otto Rank, *Der Mythus von der Geburt des Helden* (Deuticke, 1909), pp. 21–22. The essential facts can be found in Carl Robert, *Die griechische Heldensage* (Berlin, 1923), pp. 1138–1160.

63. F. Noël, *Dictionnaire de la Fable,* 3rd ed. (Paris, 1810).

64. Chompré, *Dictionnaire portatif de la Fable,* new ed. (Paris, 1801).

65. Ibid.

66. Freud, *Gesammelte Werke,* X: *Triebe und Triebschicksale,* pp. 210–232.

67. In *De doctrina christiana* Augustine sees divine wisdom as a therapeutic treatment that works sometimes by opposition and sometimes by the effect of like on like: *Morte mortuos liberavit* (I, XIV, 13). Pascal uses this as an argument in his *Prière pour le bon usage des maladies.* In a "Sermon for Ash Wednesday" Fénelon writes: "This ash . . . although it represents death . . . is a remedy that yields immortality." Baudelaire, in a translation of Thomas De Quincey's *The Opium Eaters,* adds to the English text's description of the torments of "troubled sleep": "Until, finding a remedy in the very intensity of the pain, human nature explodes in a loud cry" (chap. 2).

68. *O.C.,* IV, p. 249.

69. *Correspondance complète,* vol. 20, p. 21.

70. Ibid., p. 123.

71. Ibid., vol. 20, p. 22.

72. Ibid., vol. 22, p. 10.

73. Ibid., pp. 8–9.

74. Ibid.

75. As I showed in "Le dîner de Turin," *La Relation critique* (Paris: Gallimard, 1970); English translation: "The Dinner at Turin," in *The Living Eye,* trans. Arthur Goldhammer (Cambridge, Mass.: Harvard University Press, 1989).

76. *O.C.,* I, p. 17.

77. *O.C.,* I, pp. 1156. See Philippe Lejeune, "La punition des enfants, lecture d'un aveu de Rousseau," in *Le Pacte autobiographique* (Paris, 1975), pp. 49–85, and "Le peigne cassé," *Poétique* 25 (1976):1–30.

78. *O.C.,* I, p. 109; see Philippe Lejeune, "Le 'dangereux supplément,' lecture d'un aveu de Rousseau," *Annales Economies, Sociétés, Civilisations* 4 (1974):1009–1022; and the chapter entitled "Ce dangereux supplément," in Jacques Derrida, *De la grammatologie* (Paris, 1967), pp. 203–234.

79. *Confessions,* IX, *O.C.,* I, p. 427.

80. *O.C.,* II, p. 1129.

81. *Confessions,* V, *O.C.,* I, p. 222.

82. *O.C.,* I, pp. 227–232. On this episode and other problems touched on

above, see the excellent commentary by Pierre-Paul Clément, *Jean-Jacques Rousseau, de l'éros coupable à l'éros glorieux* (Neuchâtel, 1976), esp. pp. 188–202.

83. J.-B. Pontalis, *Entre le rêve et la douleur* (Paris, 1977), p. 150.

84. *O.C.*, I, pp. 232–233.

85. *O.C.*, II, p. 27.

86. *O.C.*, I, pp. 662–663.

87. *O.C.*, I, p. 980.

88. *O.C.*, I, p. 981.

89. *O.C.*, I, p. 986, repeated p. 997.

90. *O.C.*, I, p. 132.

91. *O.C.*, I, p. 997.

92. *O.C.*, I, p. 1081.

93. *O.C.*, I, p. 990.

94. *O.C.*, IV, p. 384.

95. *Discours de l'inégalité*, *O.C.*, III, p. 148.

96. *O.C.*, III, p. 169.

97. *Essai sur l'origine des langues*, chap. 9, new critical edition by Jean Starobinski (Paris: Gallimard, 1991), p. 106, cited hereafter as *E.O.L.* For a complete English translation, see Jean-Jacques Rousseau, *The First and Second Discourses . . . and Essay on the Origin of Languages*, edited, translated, and annotated by Victor Gourevitch (New York: Harper and Row, 1986). The languages of the north stem from a different source (chap. 10).

98. *E.O.L.*, p. 106.

99. *E.O.L.*, p. 107.

100. *E.O.L.*, p. 70.

101. *Confessions*, book VII, *O.C.*, I, p. 333.

102. Ibid., book VIII, *O.C.*, I, pp. 378–379.

103. Ibid.

104. *Fragments politiques*, *O.C.*, III, p. 479. The formula also occurs in the first version of *The Social Contract*, *O.C.*, I, p. 288.

105. See the first part of this chapter.

106. *E.O.L.*

107. *E.O.L.*

108. *Dictionnaire de musique*, article "Opéra." (The only editions of this work date from the eighteenth and nineteenth centuries. References are therefore to articles only, pagination omitted.)

109. Ibid.

110. Ibid.

111. Ibid.

112. Ibid.

113. Ibid., article "Génie."

114. Ibid., article "Prima intenzione."

115. Ibid., article "Unité de mélodie."

116. Ibid.

117. *E.O.L.*

118. *Dictionnaire de musique*, article "Récitatif." Gluck's use of the device is familiar, as, of course, is the even more ingenious use by Mozart in *Idomeneo*.

119. *Confessions*, book VII, *O.C.*, I, pp. 313–314.

120. *La Nouvelle Héloïse,* I, letter 48, *O.C.,* II, pp. 131–132.

121. Ibid., p. 133.

122. *Contrat social,* I, chap. 6, *O.C.,* III, p. 361.

123. Ibid., IV, chap. 2, *O.C.,* III, p. 439.

124. Ibid., IV, chap. 1, *O.C.,* III, p. 438. Compare n. 3, p. 1491.

125. *Dictionnaire de musique,* article "Unité de mélodie."

126. Ibid.

127. Ibid.

128. *Contrat social,* II, chap. 7, p. 384.

129. Ibid., p. 381.

130. Ibid.

131. *Rêveries,* fifth walk, *O.C.,* I, p. 1045.

132. *Dictionnaire de musique,* article "Air." This study owes a great deal to those of my colleagues and students at the University of Geneva who took part in a seminar devoted to Rousseau's writings on music in the winter of 1983–84. I would like to thank Samuel Baud-Bovy, Alain Grosrichard, and Jean-Jacques Eigeldinger for their valuable suggestions.

6. Fable and Mythology in the Seventeenth and Eighteenth Centuries

1. Revised, expanded, and transformed, Chompré's *Dictionnaire* became F. Noël's *Dictionnaire de la fable* (1801), which was used by the artists and poets of the nineteenth century. Noël's dictionary included myths from northern Europe, Asia, and other places. Although Greek and Roman materials remained predominant, they were no longer the only source of images.

2. This, of course, was not the afterlife of the Homeric poems but that of eighteenth-century mythological convention.

3. Vico proposed an incorrect etymology, according to which *mythos* was related to *mutus* (mute), which he said indicated that mythology arose in an age before speech and that the earliest articulate language was superimposed on another, earlier language composed of mute gestures and signs.

4. Among seventeenth- and eighteenth-century authors, see (in chronological order): G.-J. Vossius, *De gentili theologia* (Amsterdam, 1688). A. Van Dale, *Dissertationes de progressu idolatriae et superstitionum et de prophetia* (Amsterdam, 1696); *De oraculis veterum ethicorum* (Amsterdam, 1700). P. Jurieu, *Histoire critique des dogmes et des cultes, depuis Adam à Jésus-Christ* (Amsterdam, 1704). W. King, *A Discourse Concerning the Inventions of Men in the Worship of God,* 5th ed. (London, 1704). J. Toland, *Letters to Serena* (London, 1704). J. Trenchard, *The Natural History of Superstition* (London, 1709). B. Le Bovier de Fontenelle, *De l'origine des fables* (Paris, 1724). C. Rollin, *Traité des études* (Paris, 1726), 4 vols.; *Histoire ancienne* (Paris, 1730–1738), 13 vols. S. Shuckford, *The Sacred and the Profane History of the World Connected* (London, 1728), 2 vols. A. Ramsay, *The Travels of Cyrus, to which Is Annexed a Discourse upon Mythology of the Ancients* (London, 1728). T. Blackwell, *An Enquiry into the Life and Writings of Homer* (London, 1735). T. Broughton, *Biblioteca historico-sacra, or an Historical Library of the Principal Matters Relating to Religion Ancient and Modern, Pagan, Jewish, Christian and Mohammedan* (London, 1737–1739), 2 vols. A. Banier, *La Mythologie et les fables expliquées par l'histoire*

(Paris, 1738), 3 vols. N. Pluche, *Histoire du ciel* (Paris, 1739), 2 vols. G. Vico, *La Scienza nuova*, 3rd ed. (Geneva, 1787). D. Hume, *The Natural History of Religion* (London, 1757). A. Pernety, *Les Fables égyptiennes et grecques dévoilées* (Paris, 1758). P. Chompré, *Dictionnaire abrégé de la fable* (Paris, 1759). C. De Brosses, *Du culte des dieux fétiches* (1760). A. Court de Gébelin, *Le Monde primitif* (Paris, 1773–1783), 9 vols. R. Wood, *An Essay on the Original Genius and Writings of Homer* (London, 1775). J. Bryant, *A New System or an Analysis of Ancient Mythology* (London, 1775–1776). J.-S. Bailly, *Lettres sur l'origine des sciences* (Paris, 1777); *Lettres sur l'Atlantide de Platon* (Paris, 1779). J. G. Lindemann, *Geschichte der Meinungen älterer und neuerer Völker im Stande der Roheit und Kultur, von Gott, Religion und Priesterthum* (Stendal, 1784–1785), 2 books in 1 vol. C. G. Heyne, *Opuscula academica* (Göttingen, 1785–1812). C. A. Demoustier, *Lettres à Emilie sur la mythologie* (Paris, 1786–1798). R. P. Knight, *A Discourse on the Worship of Priapus* (London, 1786). J.-P. Rabaut de Saint-Etienne, *Lettres à M. Bailly sur Entstehung und Ausbildung der religiösen Idden* (Jena, 1794). C. E. Dupuis, *Origine de tous les cultes* (Paris, 1796), 12 vols. W. Jones, *The Works* (London, 1799), 6 vols. F. Noël, *Dictionnaire de la fable* (Paris, 1801), 2 vols. K. P. Moritz, *Götterlehre*, 3rd ed. (Berlin, 1804). J. A. Dulaure, *Des divinités génératrices, ou des cultes du phallus chez les anciens et les modernes* (Paris, 1805). F. Creuzer, *Symbolik und Mythologie der alten Völker, besonders der Griechen* (Leipzig-Darmstadt, 1810–1812). F. C. Baur, *Symbolik und Mytholgie, oder die Naturreligion des Altertums* (Stuttgart, 1824–1825), 3 vols. J. G. Herder, *Sämtliche Werke* (Berlin, 1877–1913), 33 vols. W. Blake, *Complete Poetry and Prose* (London, 1948). Jean Paul, *Vorschule der Aesthetic* (Munich, 1963). F. Hölderlin, *Sämtliche Werke* (Stuttgart, 1943–1961), 6 vols. F. Schlegel, *Kritische Schriften* (Munich, 1970).

Among modern studies of the history of mythology, the following are particularly noteworthy (in chronological order): F. Strich, *Die Mythologie in der deutschen Literatur von Klopstock bis Wagner* (Halle, 1910). Q. Gruppe, *Geschichte der klassischen Mythologie und Religionsgeschichte* (Leipzig, 1921)—important. R. Schwab, *La Renaissance orientale* (Paris, 1950). W. Rehm, *Götterstille und Göttertrauer* (Berlin, 1951); *Griechentum und Goethezeit* (Bern, 1952). F. E. Manuel, *The Eighteenth Century Confronts the Gods* (Cambridge, Mass., 1959)—important. J. De Vries, *Forschungsgeschichte der Mythologie* (Freiburg and Munich, 1961). R. Trousson, *Le Thème de Prométhée dans la littérature européenne* (Geneva, 1964). J. Baltrusaitis, *La Quête d'Isis* (Paris, 1967). Y. F.-A. Giraud, *La Fable de Daphné* (Geneva, 1968). P. Albouy, *Mythes et mythologies dans la littérature française* (Paris: A. Colin, 1969). M. Furhmann, ed., *Terror und Spiel. Probleme der Mythenrezeption* (Munich, 1971) (Poetik und Hermeneutik IV)—important. B. Feldman and R. D. Richardson, *The Rise of Modern Mythology* (Bloomington and London, 1972)—important—anthology of documents, commentaries, and bibliographies. K. Kerenyi, *Die Eröffnung des Zugangs zum Mythos. Ein Lesebuch* (Darmstadt, 1976)—collection of texts on myth from Vico to W. F. Otto. H. Blumenberg, *Arbeit am Mythos* (Frankfurt, 1979). M. Detienne, *L'Invention de la mythologie* (Paris, 1981).

EPILOGUE. "As I Detest Hades' Gates"

1. K. Goldstein, *La Structure de l'organisme*, trans. Burckhardt and Kuntz (Paris: Gallimard, 1951), pp. 266–285.

2. The reappearance of obsolete behavior is then conceived not as the resurgence of a latent or repressed tendency but as a return of the individual to a different level of integration.

3. ἐχθρὸς γάρ μοι κεῖνος ὁμῶς Ἀΐδαο πύλησιν, ὅσ χ᾿ ἕτερον μὲν κεύθῃ ἐνὶ ῾ρεσᾳν, ἄλλο δὲ εἴπῃ.

4. See R. B. Onians, *The Origins of European Thought about the Body, the Mind, the Soul, the World, Time and Fate* (Cambridge: Cambridge University Press, 1954), esp. pp. 13–44.

5. The English translation of the *Iliad* is by Richmond Lattimore.

6. Compare Proverbs 2:16–19.

7. Hysteria and neurosis are parodies of this restraint. Instead of flexible control of the exchange with others, these maladies involve a greedy *retention* of affect. Repression, which defines interior and exterior, becomes pathological when the individual chooses to avoid or lacks the capacity to engage in confrontation with the outside world. Freud and Breuer formulated the concept of "hysteria as retention" in their "classic" work of 1895.

8. This image, which seems general enough to have been used in all sorts of circumstances, occurs only in these two places in Homer.

9. The English translation of the *Odyssey* is by Robert Fitzgerald.

10. Erich Auerbach, *Mimesis,* trans. Willard Trask (Princeton, 1953), p. 6.

INDEX

Satire, 55–56, 57–58; in *Persian Letters*, 63, 65, 68; myths and, 177
Savagery, 4, 5, 6–7, 11, 14, 19, 22, 34–35, 104; noble savage concept, 14, 27; subcultures of, 30; in *L'Ingénu*, 104, 112, 114, 115; in *Emile*, 129. *See also* Barbarity; Paganism and myths
Schelling, Friedrich, 191, 192
Schlegel, Friedrich, 191
Science, 120
Self: protection, 40–42; estrangement from, 142–143; perversion, 145; explanation of, to others, 152–153; -inhibition, 204. *See also* Amour-propre (self-esteem)
Silence, 151
Smith, Adam, 4
Social Contract (Rousseau), 127, 130, 131, 164, 165, 166, 167
Society, 4–5, 7, 8, 11, 25–26; classless, 28; values, 30, 33; "good," 37; agrarian, 98; ills of, 119–123; elite, 120, language and, 151–152; musicalization of, 165
Solitude/isolation, 142–143, 148, 151, 154
Soul, 160–161, 165, 167, 202–203
Stranger, The (Camus), 110
Suffering and healing, 137–138, 139–150
Superstition, 18–19, 30
Surprise, in *Persian Letters*, 62, 63, 65–66, 68

Telephus myth, 137–140, 142, 144, 150, 156
Temperament (bodily humors theory), 57–58, 68
Theater, 124–127, 129, 158. *See also* Festivals

Theophrastus, 44, 45
Time, 195
Tranquillity, 8, 9, 15, 168
Tyranny and despotism: flattery and, 44–46; in *Persian Letters*, 71–72, 73–74, 75, 76, 77, 78–81, 82; in *Candide*, 85, 92–93, 94, 99; Oriental, 130–131; language and, 153

Unity, 162–166, 167–168
Utopia, 98–99

Valéry, Paul, 66, 221n17
Vanity, 43, 47, 48, 53, 56, 93
Village Soothsayer, The (Rousseau), 131, 154–155, 157, 160, 162, 163, 167
Violence and warfare, 13, 18, 104, 205; civility and, 51; in *Persian Letters*, 74, 77–78, 82; in *Candide*, 85, 89, 91, 92–93; in *L'Ingénu*, 103–104; healing and, 137–138, 139–140, 142, 144. *See also* War
Virtue, 39, 40, 41, 133, 178
Voltaire, François, 11, 63, 85, 91, 94–96, 99; style and philosophy, 89–90, 102–117; Rousseau and, 123, 126; myths and, 179–181. *See also* Candide; Ingénu, L'

War, 166, 176, 178. *See also* Violence and warfare
Wealth, 44, 45, 51
Weapons as healers, 137–138, 139–140, 147–148
Weil, Eric, 33